THE
LIGHTWORKER'S
 WAY

Also by Doreen Virtue, Ph.D.

THE LIGHTWORKER'S WAY

AWAKENING YOUR SPIRITUAL POWER TO KNOW AND HEAL

DOREEN VIRTUE, PH.D.

HAY HOUSE

Australia • Canada • Hong Kong
South Africa • United Kingdom • United States

First published and distributed in the United Kingdom in 2005 by Hay House UK Ltd, 292B Kensal Rd, London W10 5BE. Tel.: (44) 20 8962 1230; Fax: (44) 20 8962 1239. www.hayhouse.co.uk

Published and distributed in the United States of America in 1997 by Hay House, Inc., PO Box 5100, Carlsbad, CA 92018-5100. Tel.: (760) 431 7695 or (800) 654 5126; Fax: (760) 431 6948 or (800) 650 511. www.hayhouse.com

Published and distributed in Australia by Hay House Australia Ltd, 18/36 Ralph St, Alexandria NSW 2015. Tel.: 612 9669 4299; Fax: 612 9669 4144. www.hayhouse.com.au

Published and distributed in the Republic of South Africa by Hay House SA (Pty), Ltd, PO Box 990, Witkoppen 2068. Tel./Fax: 2711-467-8904. www.hayhouse.co.za

Distributed in Canada by Raincoast, 9050 Shaughnessy St, Vancouver, BC V6P 6E5. Tel.: (604) 323 7100; Fax: (604) 323 2600

The author of this book does not dispense medical advice or prescribe the use of any technique as a form of treatment for physical or medical problems without the advice of a physician, either directly or indirectly. The intent of the author is only to offer information of a general nature to help you in your quest for emotional and spiritual well-being. In the event you use any of the information in this book for yourself, which is your constitutional right, the author and the publisher assume no responsibility for your actions.

A catalogue record for this book is available from the British Library.

ISBN 1-4019-0558-7
ISBN 978-1-4019-0558-3

Edited by: Jill Kramer
Designed by: Jenny Richards

Printed and bound in Great Britain by Cromwell Press Ltd.

To my grandfathers,
Ben Reynolds and Fount Leroy Merrill,
whose visits to me from the afterlife
awakened the memory
of why I am here.

"All the prophets, seers, sages, and saviours in the world's history became what they became, and consequently had the powers they had, through an entirely natural process. They all recognized and came into the conscious realization of their oneness with the Infinite Life."

— Ralph Waldo Trine,
metaphysician, and author of
In Tune with the Infinite (1897)

C O N T E N T S

F O R E W O R D

by Louise L. Hay

In the Infinity of Life where we all are, all is perfect, whole, and complete. This is the truth of our being. We were born knowing this truth. Yet many of us have forgotten. Perhaps we were raised by parents who had learned to see life through fearful eyes. Fear can go back many generations. Our parents and grandparents and great-grandparents might have also lost this truth. When we are raised by fearful people, it is easy to lose touch with the essence of who we really are. I truly believe that we are Divine Magnificent Expressions of Life, with immense capabilities. We have talents and abilities within us that we have not even begun to tap.

The ability to do healing work is inherent in all of us. It is a normal and natural procedure. Some people speak of "laying on of hands" as though it is something abnormal and unusual. However, all of us, if we hurt some part of our body, will immediately place our hand over that place to make it feel better. Everyone does this because it is normal and natural. We need to look at all forms of healing in this way. If you feel "called" to do any form of healing work, or even psychic readings, then know that you have the essential ingredients to be proficient at it. I would like to encourage all would-be healers/psychics to follow their dreams and learn all they can about healing methods.

Our thoughts are so powerful that they create the circumstances of our lives. The way we think about ourselves, about others, and about life contributes enormously to the way we live. What we give out comes back to us, always. Therefore, if we want to live lives of harmony and well-being, then we must have harmonious, loving thoughts constantly in our mental atmosphere. We will never be able to help heal this planet if we criticize and condemn other people, places, and events. To be true healers, we must concentrate our mental energy on seeing the positive wherever reality shows us otherwise.

Whenever I hear of a gang member, criminal, crooked politician, drug baron, dictator, or anyone who is creating pain in this world, I bless them with Divine Love, for I know that within them is all the good that resides in all of us. They all have the ability to turn to this part of themselves in an instant. If I hear of a crisis or disaster, I immediately send love and healing energy to that place. On a daily basis, I visualize the world as harmonious and healed, with plenty of food, shelter, and clothing for all. I see everyone with meaningful work to do and an income that supports them. I visualize harmony in families and between nations. I use my mind to put as much positive energy as I can into the atmosphere. We all can contribute to the healing of the world through our collective consciousness.

If you feel that you are far too insignificant to do healing work, please remember that it is our true self and God that are the sources of our healing power. Confidence in ourselves has nothing to do with healing. We all rely on a higher power to help us. When we connect with this higher power, miracles can be accomplished. With *The Lightworker's Way,* Doreen Virtue has lovingly written a book that will inspire and empower all of us on the healing pathway.

— Louise L. Hay

Lightworkers are those who volunteered, before birth, to help the planet and its population heal from the effects of fear. Each lightworker is here for a sacred purpose. Very often, however, life on earth with its material focus creates a form of amnesia in lightworkers. They then forget their divine and perfect identities, and also their abilities to miraculously help the earth and all living creatures. When lightworkers forget their true identity and purpose, they feel lost and afraid.

You are a lightworker if you:

- feel called to heal others;
- want to resolve the world's social and environmental problems;
- believe that spiritual methods can heal any situation;
- have had mystical experiences, such as psychic premonitions or angelic encounters;
- have endured harsh life experiences that eroded the knowledge of your divine perfection;
- want to heal your own life as a first step in healing the world;
- feel compelled to write, teach, or counsel about your healing experiences; and
- know that you are here for a higher purpose, even if you are unsure what it is or how to fulfill it.

Everywhere on the planet right now, lightworkers are awakening to faint memories of why they came to earth. They hear an inner calling that can't be ignored. This call is a reminder that it is now time to stop toying with material dreams and get to work.

Many lightworkers are discovering innate spiritual gifts, such as psychic communication skills and spiritual healing abilities. These are the gifts that we volunteered to use to heal the earth and her population during the crucial decades surrounding the millennium. Prophecies predicted our coming, and now it is time for us to fulfill our divine purpose. The world depends upon us!

This is a book about my own journey of remembering my identity and abilities as a lightworker. Its purpose is to help you recall your own divine mission and your natural spiritual skills. For that reason, I've detailed the story of how I recaptured my gifts of psychic communication, manifestation, and spiritual healing. I have also described scientific studies and methods that will help you regain your spiritual vision and abilities. Many lightworkers are guided to write books and articles yet feel confused and intimidated by the publishing world. For that reason, I've included vital information about how to see your words get published.

In writing this guidebook for you, I have felt completely directed by Spirit. Although I have written about my upbringing in and interactions with various religions, especially Christian Science, this is not a religious book. I merely write about my experiences with religions that have intersected my path of spiritual growth and awareness. Although "spirituality" and "religion" often overlap, I do not believe that one is contingent upon the other. I've also included descriptions of my work on healing the scars of "religion abuse."

The completion of this book is part of my sacred mission as a lightworker. I am here, as you are, to illuminate the trail for the still-slumbering lightworkers who are just now beginning to awaken to their cause.

May peace be with you.

—Doreen Virtue, Ph.D.

ACKNOWLEDGMENTS

This book would not have been possible without the guiding help and inspiration of some angels who walk among us. First, I want to thank Jill Kramer, who suggested that I write this book. Jill is not only a superb editor, but also a wonderful friend and awakened lightworker. Next, I wish to thank Louise L. Hay, who is a role model for lightworkers everywhere. Louise has demonstrated that when you gratefully surrender everything to God, all of life's details are automatically taken care of. My gratitude also goes to Reid Tracy, Hay House vice president, who has been instrumentally supportive of my writing projects. In addition, Kristina Tracy has given so much of her personal time, energy, and enthusiasm to spreading God's love, and I feel honored to work with her. I am also thankful for the dedicated and loving work of Jeannie Liberati, who travels ceaselessly as a part of her lightworker role.

I also want to thank the other staff members who were supportive during this book's inception, including Ron and Heidi Tillinghast, Christy Salinas, Jenny Richards, Adrian Eddie Sandoval, Barbara Spivak, Margarete Nielsen, Polly Tracy, Gwen Washington, Lisa Kelm, Lynn Collins, and everyone else at Hay House.

My heart is also filled with gratitude for my teachers, including Jesus Christ, Phineas Quimby, Mary Baker Eddy, Ernest Holmes, Forrest Holly, Joan Hannan, William Hannan, Louise L. Hay, Wayne Dyer, John Randolph Price, Betty Eadie, Dannion Brinkley, and Rosemary Altea.

During the writing of this book, I received incredible guidance and research assistance from two lightworkers in my life, Pearl Reynolds and Ted Hannan. Thank you both for entering my dreams at just the right time with just the information I needed! A bouquet of "thank yous" to my wonderfully supportive family: Steven Farmer, Grant Schenk, Charles Schenk, Ken Hannan, and my angelic cat, Romeo.

I am also deeply grateful for the instrumental help given to me by the editor-in-chief of *Complete Woman* magazine, Bonnie Krueger, and associate editor, Martha Carlson, who made it possible for me to meet personally with and interview many of my life-changing teachers. I also wish to thank Beverly Hutchinson, Michele Gold, Nancy Griffin, and Dr. Jordan Weiss for their gifts of light. And eternal gratitude to my guardian angel, Frederique. Thank you, all! It is my deepest wish to take the gifts you have given me and pass them along to others.

SETTING THE SPIRIT FREE

The deceased father of my client Lauren was next to her right shoulder, begging for her forgiveness. Lauren could sense her father's presence, but she could neither see nor hear him. So I was using my faculties as a healer and medium to moderate their conversation.

"He says he can't excuse his abusive behavior toward you," I told Lauren. "However, he asks for your compassion in understanding how sorry he is and how much he loves you. 'Please, please forgive me,' he keeps repeating."

Lauren sat with her arms crossed, tears streaming down her eyes. In a halting voice, she expressed her desire to forgive her father for his cruel treatment. However, she feared that forgiveness might be misconstrued as condoning the abuse. Lauren understood that her longstanding resentment toward her father interfered with her deep desire to become a spiritual healer and author. She knew that she needed to release her pent-up anger in order to become an effective healer, but she wasn't sure she wanted to forgive her father. After all, he had caused her enormous anguish.

As Lauren grappled for words, a second spirit entered our session. He was tall, with a ruddy complexion and a disheveled beard. I could tell that the man had been physically strong during his lifetime. As I described his characteristics, Lauren identified the man as her paternal grandfather. His personality came through forcefully as he told Lauren through me, "*I'm* the one who needs your forgiveness. I was the one who hit your father so much that I turned him into an angry man just like me. It was my fault that he took all his anger out on you."

Lauren's grandfather explained that he frequently drank to drown his fears of losing the family business. This created a volatile mix of anger and physical abuse. Without trying to shirk responsibility for his actions, Lauren's grandfather asked us to understand his point of view and his role in creating Lauren's troubled childhood. He asked his granddaughter to forgive both of them so that they could all be released.

Upon hearing these words, Lauren sobbed into her tissue. Overwhelmed and unable to speak, Lauren vigorously nodded her head and lifted her right hand into the air to say, "Yes, I am willing to forgive you, Grandpa." Her grandfather put an etheric arm around her shoulder and gave her a final farewell squeeze. I saw a woman escort both her father and her grandfather to a plat-formlike area with a yellow glow, and then they disappeared.

After Lauren rested a few moments, I asked her to lie down on my sofa. Before our session had begun, her solar plexus chakra had been quite enlarged. Now, as I scanned and checked her chakras with my right hand, they pulsated with clean, bright energy. She sat up and smiled. As she wiped away the mascara from her cheeks, Lauren looked in a nearby mirror and remarked that a facial rash she'd had earlier was now gone.

Lauren later called me to report on the progress she'd made since our session. I was pleased to learn that she felt freed from many of the fears that had held her back from pursuing her healing aspirations. Her happy news didn't surprise me, however, since many of my clients report similar results. In fact, my own psychic and spiritual healing abilities are products of a journey of spiritual release and forgiveness similar to Lauren's. I recalled how frightened, like Lauren, I had been when I first walked the lightworker's way.

PART I

A
LIGHTWORKER'S
JOURNEY

Author's Note: All of the stories in this book are true. Only the names and identifying details about my clients have been changed to protect their privacy.

(To avoid the awkward "his or her/he or she" wording, I have used feminine pronouns throughout for consistency. However, I want to emphasize that this book is as much for men as it is for women.)

EARLY MIRACLES

"O Lord, your power is greater than
all powers. Under your leadership we cannot fear
anything. It is you who has given us prophetic power,
And has enabled us to foresee and
interpret everything."

— Dinka Prayer (Sudan) of the
African traditional religion

My earliest memory of the power of Spirit is when a miracle resolved a childhood crisis for me. My mother, raised in a metaphysical household herself, had taught me to use visualization, prayer, and affirmations since I was a small girl. On an autumn evening when I was very young, I witnessed the power of these spiritual practices.

As I was climbing into bed, I realized that my little red purse was missing. While walking home from school that day with friends, I'd stopped at a store's loading dock and had left my purse on the dock platform. It contained not only my milk money for the week, but several of my childhood treasures. In the midst of playing with my friends, I'd walked away from the loading dock without my purse.

I cried out to my mother. Losing that purse upset me as much as if I'd lost a favorite toy. I didn't care about the money inside the purse so much; I was mostly sad because I'd been so careless. It almost felt as if I'd abandoned a beloved toy, and I imagined it feeling alone under the cold night sky on the loading dock. I wanted to undo my mistake and to have the pretty little purse beside me.

My mother held my hands and firmly stated, "I want you to claim this truth repeatedly, Doreen: 'Nothing is lost in the mind of God.'" I trusted my mother without question and had complete faith in her assurances that these words would bring my purse back to me. I squeezed my eyes shut and repeated the phrase until I finally fell asleep from exhaustion. In the morning, my first thought was of the coin purse. I opened my eyes, fully expecting to see it. *And there it was, right beside my bed!* I was very excited, but not surprised. After all, my mother had promised that the prayer would work. Years later, I asked my mother if she'd actually found the purse and then placed it next to my bed. She swore that she'd had no part in the purse's mysterious reappearance. I believe her, because this prayer treatment has worked for me many times since.

Why shouldn't I believe in miracles and spiritual healing, after all? My very birth came on the heels of my mother's prayer request at a Religious Science prayer ministry. My parents were unhappy that after many years of marriage they were still childless. So Mom turned to prayer—not so much *asking* God for a baby—but *declaring* and *knowing* that a baby was on its way to her. Less than one month after submitting her prayer treatment request, my parents conceived me.

This affirmative approach to prayer, in which you state the desired outcome as a given, is based upon the New Testament declaration, "Whatsoever you ask in prayer, believe, and it shall be given." Pleading for our good to come to us is based upon fear. Since the Law of Cause and Effect creates whatever we truly believe in, those fears often manifest into form.

I remember having spiritual visions as a child. As a little girl, I saw angel lights in multihued greens and blues. As an adolescent and young adult, the angel lights appeared as large flashes of white, like a strobe. These days, I know an angel is near when I see small starlike white bursts of sparkling light.

My spiritual vision also allowed me to see spirits, although as a child I assumed I was seeing regular people. I'd tell my mother about the people I saw, and she convinced me that they were just reflections of images coming from our television set in the living room. Believing that my mother must be correct in her assertions, I turned off my ability to see spirits for many years.

I know now that I was seeing across the veil of death and that my mediumistic abilities began at a very early age. I believe that many, if not all, children are clairvoyant. Their invisible friends are spirit guides only visible to the unjaded eyes of children and some adults. I recently saw a man interviewed who, during his near-death experience, found that only children could see him while he was in spirit form. In a related 1995 study, William MacDonald of Ohio State University discovered that young people were statistically more likely to exhibit clairvoyant and telepathic abilities than were adults.[1]

We must be very cautious when talking with children about their visions, because we have the power to convince them that their visions are incorrect. These children will, as I did, shut down their spiritual sight in order to please their parents. However, if we infuse this gift with love, we will see that our children's and our own psychic abilities are as beautiful as any natural resource. As lightworkers, we are meant to use and enjoy these skills to the greatest extent possible.

Many of us lightworkers are beginning to remember the awesome power that we all naturally possess. Since we are made in the image and likeness of an all-powerful God, we have astounding abilities and power of which we may not even be aware. Lightworkers have the power, with their mental focus, to heal the planet completely.

My parents raised me to think that I was limitless, and as a young child I fully believed that anything was possible. I remember being on the schoolyard mentally commanding the wind to blow. I'd authoritatively say, "Wind, blow now!" and each time, I'd feel a strong gust of air rush through my hair and across my skin.

I have no idea what gave me the thought to command the wind to blow. Perhaps I was remembering the divine gift we all share that gives us the power to heal the earth. This is the gift that, once we fully reclaim and use it, allows us to heal ancient patterns of earthquakes, tornadoes, hurricanes, and flooding.

Scientific research on the links between human thoughts, emotions, and weather is currently confirming in laboratories what many lightworkers have suspected for a long time: our thoughts influence weather, cloud structure, water structure, water temperature, and air temperature.[2] Fear creates destructive patterns, and love heals them. We don't have to accept tragedies as natural or inevitable. They certainly aren't "acts of God," unless you are referring to God's Law of Cause and Effect, which turns our thoughts into realities. Fortunately, this Law allows lightworkers to manifest a tranquil earth by holding peaceful and loving thoughts in mind.

My mother took me to the Unity Church Sunday school in North Hollywood, California, until I was ten years old. I don't remember the teachers talking about metaphysics, religion, or the Bible much. Instead, we mostly colored and read regular children's books until we joined with the adult congregation in singing the hymns that marked the end of Sunday services. It's surprising that, against this ordinary backdrop of Sunday-school classes, one of my most profound life experiences occurred.

When I was eight years old, I was walking down the sidewalk toward my mother's car after Sunday school let out. It was a mildly warm day with clear skies and bright sunshine, and the whiteness of the sidewalk was particularly glaring as I walked along. Suddenly, an unseen force stopped me, and I was paralyzed as if frozen in time. In my next moment of conscious awareness, I was outside my body, looking at myself from approximately one foot away. I had no idea how I got outside my body, because it happened in a split second. I was shocked that my body could stand up on its own, without "me" inside it.

A male voice outside and above my right shoulder firmly said, "This is what you are here to teach, Doreen—this split between the mind and the body, just as you are experiencing it right now. You are here to teach people that the mind controls the body." Just as suddenly, I was back inside my body. Surprisingly, the experience did not frighten me; more than anything else, I was confused by what the voice had meant when it spoke of "the split between the mind and the body." It wasn't until many years later that I would put the pieces of my childhood out-of-body experience (OBE) together.

In his book, *Transformed by the Light*, Melvin Morse, M.D., discusses his study of adults and children who have had OBEs. Morse found that people who have an OBE or a near-death experience have subsequently higher rates of verifiable psychic activities, as compared with control groups.[3] I believe that, like all children, I was born psychic. I also believe that my childhood OBE greatly opened up these natural channels of awareness.

At the time it happened, I had never before heard of an OBE. Although my family raised me in a spiritually minded household, we never discussed psychic phenomena. It was outside our realm of knowledge and interest.

Some people, after hearing of my childhood experience, have asked me to recommend books or classes on how to have an OBE. I tell them that my OBE happened spontaneously and that I didn't will it. Nor *would* I have willed it, even if I'd known at the time that leaving the body was possible. Although I've seen books about how to have an OBE, I've never wanted to read one. Still, each of us has to follow our own guidance if we feel attuned to any OBE books or classes. I think we must always follow our intuition about our own path.

However, I'm not sure that forcing oneself to have an OBE would be helpful. In some of my meditations, I have had very real journeys to the afterlife. I have clearly seen crystal buildings and brightly hued etheric landscapes. Yet, I was never consciously *trying* to have an OBE. The fact that my consciousness was out of the earthplane was a secondary fact, not a primary goal.

I didn't notice many changes in my life immediately following my childhood OBE. I didn't tell anyone about my experience until many years later. I didn't want to discuss it because, although the event had been extraordinary and otherworldly, it had also felt natural and a bit predestined. Today, I believe that I prescripted the event with my guides before my incarnation as a way to remind me of my life purpose. The OBE was startling but didn't have a feeling of being unexpected in the way that many of my other mystical experiences have seemed.

In the next chapter, I'll tell you a little more about my early influences.

FAMILY INFLUENCES

"Every soul is immortal—for whatever
is in perpetual motion is immortal. Every man's
soul has by the law of his birth been a spectator of eternal
truth, or it would never have passed into this our
mortal frame, yet still it is no easy matter
for all to be reminded of their past
by their present existence."

— Plato

When I was a child, Dad worked as a technical illustrator and graphic art supervisor at Space Electronics Corporation, a NASA-related space program. Our family's income was comfortable, yet my father was unhappy working in the corporate world.

Then when I was seven years old, Space Electronics merged with another company and became Space General Corporation. The firm moved to the distant Southern California suburb of El Monte. To avoid a long commute, my father chose to work at home as a consultant. This gave him the opportunity to do other work more to his liking, such as writing magazine articles about model airplanes, his childhood passion. He also did freelance editing for a small publisher near our home.

One day, he decided to quit his consulting and freelance jobs. Dad and two of his friends started a mail-order model airplane blueprint plans business. Eventually, the other fellows turned the operation over to Dad, and this led him to write a series of model-airplane books. My parents turned the original mail-order business into "Hannan's Runway," a mail-order house specializing in aviation books. They still run the business from their home.

Although years later the business would thrive, initially our family income dropped sharply. Dad began working in his home office around the clock. He was at home all day, every day, yet I rarely saw him. He spent most of his time writing articles and books and designing model-airplane plans. On weekends, he attended model-airplane meets, both to relieve stress and to display his models' flying capabilities to prospective customers. Whenever Mom would complain that Dad's entire life revolved around model airplanes, he'd reply, "Well, at least I'm not out chasing the *other* kind of models!"

When he wasn't working, Dad gave me lots of attention to make up for our lost time together. He constantly assigned me creative writing projects, which I would gladly dive into—both to please my father and because I enjoyed challenges. He'd also engage me in friendly debates about rhetorical concepts to sharpen my logical mind and to practice the skill of batting philosophical ideas back and forth.

Dad's a mild-mannered man, a thin vegetarian with his own brand of spirituality. Never one for formal religion, Dad prefers to espouse and practice the virtues of kindness and generosity. Whenever we went somewhere together, Dad consistently drilled politeness into me. He'd always hold open doors for strangers and didn't care whether they thanked him. Dad also taught me that everything occurs for a reason and that there are no such things as coincidences. He said that if you hold a thought about something, you draw it into your life. He once taught me about the "law of flow" by saying, "We are all like tubes. Things flow into our lives, and we must let them flow out of our lives or we will become plugged up. That's why I'm always circulating the various books and articles that I get, giving things away as fast as they come in. Yet, I've always got more coming to me than I do going out."

Dad must have inherited his generosity and spiritual nature from his parents. My natural grandfather, Ted Hannan, was a high-level Amway distributor who achieved his elevated position by demonstrating abundance to prospective marketers and customers. Ted had silver dollars sandwiched between two business cards with holes in them so you could see the money. His cards read, "Do you want more of these? Call Ted Hannan." Ted's idea of fun was to pay the toll for several cars behind him on the bridge near his Washington State home. He'd say, "All day long, I imagine how surprised those drivers must have been when they got to the toll booth and were told that someone had paid their fare!"

My dad's mother, Pearl, also influenced his spiritual nature. When I'd visit her home, we'd play with her fortune-telling sticks. Similar to tarot cards, each stick had an engraved number. You'd ask a question, then pull out a stick and read in an accompanying book what that number meant. The book and sticks fascinated me, especially since the answers in the book seemed deeply meaningful and relevant to each question I'd ask.

Grandma Pearl was a physically and emotionally beautiful woman. She was a voracious reader, often finishing two or three books a week. She also loved sweets, especially chocolate, yet she never showed any signs of weight problems. She first met my grandfather Ted while working as a dime store clerk. He came in and asked what he could buy as a gift for the prettiest girl he'd ever seen—her.

Unfortunately, their marriage ended in divorce, and both of them remarried. Yet, Ted continued annually to send Pearl red roses on her birthday. I doubt that either of their spouses knew of this practice. Meanwhile, Pearl married Ben, whom I affectionately called "Pop-pop." Ben was the man whom I thought of as my grandfather when I was growing up. The two lived near us in the San Fernando Valley for many years. Then, Ben retired and they moved to Bishop in Central California so he could fish in nearby lakes. Once or twice a year, Grandma Pearl and Pop-pop would drive from Bishop to see us, and it was always a joy-filled treat.

My mother's family was also deeply spiritual. My Grandma Ada had been a member of the New Thought religion, Christian Science, for many years, as had my maternal great-grandmother. Ada's first marriage to my natural grandfather, Fount Leroy Merrill, had been tumultuous, mostly because he was an extreme-ly heavy drinker. The two would argue constantly, sometimes to the point where my mother's stomach would ache with nausea. Fount Leroy died of illness related to his alcoholism before I was born. No one talked much about him, and for years I assumed that Grandma Ada's second husband, Lloyd Montgomery, was my real grandpa.

Both my parents had endured hardships as children because of their parents' arguments, which often involved alcohol. As a result, when my parents met and married, they made a solemn pact never to argue in front of us children. They were also teeto-talers during most of their adult lives. To this day, I can't recall hearing a single argument between my parents. I know they must have disagreed over the years, but all I can assume is that they peacefully worked out any differences during the long walks they took (and still take) together.

In November of 1968, when I was ten years old, we moved to Escondido in northern San Diego County. I was terribly unhap-py with the move. In North Hollywood, I had many friends at school and in the neighborhood. Life had seemed magical, as if I were on a roll. Yet, my parents worried about Los Angeles County's increasing crime rate, smog, and traffic. So my mother found a new tract of homes in Escondido.

She took us to see the model home, and its colorful Mediterranean decorations enchanted me. One bedroom had a wicker Indian elephant adorned with tiny cut mirrors. I remember thinking, This is my bedroom! I love this elephant and the other Indian decorations! However, when we finally moved into our home, I was shocked to discover that my new bedroom and the entire house were completely empty! I'd just assumed that the wicker elephant and the other decorations came with the home.

So here I was in a new town, in a new home, not knowing anyone. Even worse, my proficiency examinations upon entering the San Diego school district had shown that I was performing above grade level. So they skipped me from the fourth grade into the sixth grade. Instead of feeling elated by this scholastic advancement, I felt embarrassed to be the youngest person in my classes. At this new school, I deeply missed the feelings of acceptance and popularity I'd experienced in North Hollywood. Several girls made fun of the clothes I wore, saying my dresses and hairstyle were outdated. How could a county line make so much difference in what was considered fashionable? I wondered.

I now realize that my own self-consciousness led the other children to avoid me. Every morning, I'd bury myself under my blankets, fervently praying that when I opened my eyes I'd be back in North Hollywood. Yet every morning, I'd still be in Escondido. I believe this was my first sense of doubt about prayers' effectiveness.

We initially attended the Unity Church in Escondido after the move. My mother spent much of her time practicing her violin and soon joined the Palomar Community College orchestra. Mom got to know a woman named Lois Crawford who sat next to her in the orchestra. Lois was a Christian Scientist, and she invited my mother to join her at an upcoming church workshop. Mom gladly accepted, and found herself feeling very inspired by the Christian Science speaker.

The very same evening of the workshop, my Grandma Ada, Grandpa Lloyd, great-grandmother, and great-aunt and uncle were hit broadside while driving their Volkswagen van. The van flipped over, leaving everyone hanging from their seatbelts.

Grandpa Lloyd and my Great-Aunt Ruby suffered serious injuries.

My mother told me, "The truths I learned just in that short hour at the lecture were real comforts to me, and I'm sure they helped in the healing." Lloyd and Ruby rapidly recovered, which my Mom credits to the Christian Science faith.

This demonstration of healing inspired my mother to join the local Christian Science church. She pulled my younger brother Kenny and I aside and explained that we were going to attend a new church. She told us that she expected us to go to Sunday school, no excuses. I don't know why she was so firm about the matter. Maybe we had been acting up since the move because of our unhappiness. Regardless, I was soon enrolled in Sunday school at the Escondido First Church of Christ, Scientist.

I liked those classes right away. They were an oasis where I felt completely accepted. My teachers were fascinating, and each week they'd tell us stories of how our minds affected our reality. For example, I heard the story of a woman who had lost her husband to war. When he died, time stood still for this woman, and she ceased aging. She just sat in her rocking chair day after day, waiting for her husband who was never to return. As she grew older, the woman's hair and skin remained identical to the day when her life froze in time. We also heard about people healing from injuries and diseases because they aligned their thoughts with prayer. The classes reminded me of the things my mother had taught me when I was very small.

One of my Sunday school teachers, Forrest Holly, was an amazing man who made quite an impression on me. Apparently Forrest impressed many people, because in 1996, a network television movie and a book called *What Love Sees* highlighted his life story.[1]

Forrest was physically blind in both eyes, yet he was "sighted" in many ways. Far from disabled, Forrest was a successful building contractor who used balsa sticks as a Braille outline of his architectural plans. He designed the beautiful and expansive home in which he and his family lived on an Escondido bluff. Forrest even wrote a weekly column called, "Ask the Builder" for the local paper. His wife, Jean, was also blind, as was "Hap," one of their four children. I learned from Forrest that the only limitations we have are self-imposed. Other than that, no one and nothing stands in our way.

One day, Forrest used a 3-D Viewmaster to make a metaphysical point to our Sunday school class. He passed around the Viewmaster and discussed how our mind takes two flat images and creates it into a three-dimensional effect. Forrest explained that this was an example of how perception creates the impression that matter is real, when in fact, it is an illusion of the mind. One student looked at a particularly beautiful photograph of a majestic snow-covered mountain. He gasped in awe at the picture, quickly handed the Viewmaster to another student, and exclaimed, "Look at this!"

Forrest stopped the boy and said, "Why are we so often anxious to give away a personally beautiful experience, instead of first taking a moment to fully enjoy it ourselves?" He explained the importance of accepting goodness completely, and to avoid the impulse to only lightly bump against beauty before sending it along. "Absorb the beauty fully for yourself, and *then* share it with others," he emphasized.

My mother also enjoyed the Christian Science church, perhaps because it was the religion in which she'd been raised. She soon enrolled in classes to become a licensed Christian Science practitioner. After receiving her license, her clientele quickly grew until she finally required an office outside our home. Still, Mom's clients would call us at home, and it seemed that the healing practice completely absorbed her.

Mom used spiritual treatment on my brother and me whenever we'd have cuts or bruises. I remember that, many times, our scrapes would practically vanish in front of our eyes. Between witnessing these miracle healings on myself, my brother, my mother's clients, and the other churchgoers, I began to feel in sync with God again. I forgave Him for my being in Escondido, and I started to regain a forgotten sense of peace with my life.

Once in Sunday school, we learned of a burglar who had come home from an evening of "working" to discover that someone had burglarized his own apartment. "Because he had a consciousness of dishonesty, he allowed and created dishonesty to happen in his own life," our teacher explained to us. The story ended well, though: the burglar realized that his life of crime had created the mental conditions leading to his own apartment's burglary. When he found that he'd been a victim of his own form of crime, he decided to go straight.

My impressionable young mind thirsted for such stories, for they underscored my increasing knowledge that our minds create every experience. The evening after hearing about the reformed burglar, I had a vivid dream in which I was an adult living in my own apartment. I dreamed that a man forced his way in through my front door and threatened to harm and rob me. Instead of submitting to his demands, I screamed, "No!" at him loudly. Then I shouted at him, "God is good!" Upon hearing these words, the intruder froze and then wordlessly exited my apartment.

I woke up from the dream feeling empowered. I knew that although my experience had been a dream, its implications were very real. I realized that I could set my own limits on what I would and wouldn't accept from life and from others.

This newfound inner strength served me well in some areas of my life, but unfortunately, I still struggled with my social life at school. One reason I felt disconnected from other children was that our family's spiritual practices were kept somewhat secret. There was a covert agreement in my family not to discuss our experiences of miracle healings lest other people think we were kooky. Besides, I'd already had at least one instance of rejection when a classmate asked where I went to church. When

I replied, "Christian Science," she said, "Oh, you're those people who don't believe in doctors!" There was disdain and sarcasm in her voice, and I didn't like it. From then on, I kept my spiritual beliefs and practices a secret from all but my closest friends.

Two of my more intimate buddies, Anita and Silvia, came with me to Sunday school a few times and seemed to enjoy it. Anita had a wonderful healing from chronic acne that had defied her pharmacist father's best medication attempts. Through spiritual treatment in which a practitioner prayed for her and gave her Bible passages to read daily, Anita's skin glowed with clear beauty. Although she didn't talk about God or spirituality much, I felt that Anita's life shifted as a result of her experience with the miraculous. She seemed happier and more at ease with herself, and this joy complemented her beautiful new complexion.

Besides Anita and Silvia, though, no one at school knew of the miracles that had practically become a matter of course in our family. Meanwhile, I attended Wednesday night testimonial meetings with my mother and learned how other people applied spiritual mind treatment to their lives. I remember hearing about healings from cancer, broken bones, and mishaps such as choking and near-collisions.

For those unfamiliar with Christian Science, I'll give you a little background about its origins. (Please let me emphasize that I'm not writing about Christian Science to advocate the religion, but merely to explain my background. Since Christian Science played such an intense role in my life, I am including this material so you will better understand my early influences.)

Briefly, Christian Science is a religion of the "New Thought" movement, which owes much of its origins to the teachings of Jesus Christ as interpreted by the spiritual healer Phineas Quimby (1802–1866). One of Quimby's patients was Mary Baker Eddy, who in 1879 founded Christian Science. Years later, a patient of Mrs. Eddy's, Emma Curtis Hopkins, taught classes on Quimby's philosophies, and some of Hopkins' students became the founders of other New Thought religions. For example, Ernest Holmes started Religious Science in 1927; Charles and Myrtle Fillmore began the Unity church in 1889; and Nona Brooks, along with Fannie James and Althea Small, founded Divine Science in 1898.

Quimby, often called the "Father of New Thought," came from humble beginnings as a poor and uneducated man with a voracious curiosity about science and spirituality. Quimby's attendance at a seminar given by Franz Mesmer, the father of modern hypnotism, sparked his decision to hypnotize people in order to heal them. Quimby discovered that he could clairvoyantly find the patient's underlying thoughts that caused his diseases. Then, he would talk with the patient about these erroneous beliefs until the patient's symptoms subsided. Quimby's healing practice was so successful that he had little time to publish his philosophy, except for a few articles.

In one of these rare articles, Quimby wrote:

> Every disease is the invention of man, and has no identity in Wisdom, but to those that believe, it is a truth. It may seem strange to those in health that our beliefs affect us. The fact is, there is nothing of us but belief. It is the whole capital and stock in trade of man. It is all that can be changed, and embraces everything man has made or ever will make. People never seem to have thought of the fact that they are responsible to themselves for their belief. To analyze their belief is to know themselves, which is the greatest study of man. There is one thing that man is ignorant of. It is this: that he is a sufferer from his own belief, not knowingly, but by his own consent. [2]

Quimby staunchly believed that medicines and herbs were only effective because of the patient's faith in his or her doctor. He blamed the medical community for "sentencing" patients to death and disease by conferring diagnoses that patients accepted as their sealed fate.

Mary Baker Eddy, as both a student and patient of Quimby, blended his philosophies with her own insights about the origin of God, man, and disease. Both Quimby and Mrs. Eddy emphasize the mental causes and cures of human suffering. However, they differed in other ways. For example, Quimby believed that erroneous thoughts create imbalances in the body's fluids and temperatures, which ultimately results in illness. Mrs. Eddy asserted that erroneous thinking creates the *illusion* of illness, and that fluids, temperatures, and other bodily functions are as illusory as the so-called illness. Quimby emphasized mind treatment that focused upon the patient's thoughts. In contrast, Mrs. Eddy declared that the human "mortal mind" was unreal. She said that only a total focus upon the one Mind of God could return men to their reality of perfect health.[3]

Today, New Thought churches subscribe to the use of prayer and affirmative statements in their healing treatments. Words in and of themselves have no power. However, they can be used to align the healer's and the client's thoughts with God and Christ energy. Words heal because they help us to raise our thoughts from fear to love.

Christian Scientists use an affirmation called "The Scientific Statement of Being" in their healing treatments. They say this statement repeatedly, until the mind releases false beliefs that cause death, disease, and limitations:

> *"There is no life, truth, intelligence, nor substance in matter. All is infinite Mind and its infinite manifestation, for God is All-in-all. Spirit is immortal Truth; matter is mortal error. Spirit is the real and eternal; matter is the unreal and temporal. Spirit is God and man is His image and likeness. Therefore, man is not material; he is spiritual."*[4]

Affirmative words help us focus upon what is real and eternal, and help us escape the grips of a fearful mindset. Once we let go of fear and focus upon the unchanging reality of all life—harmony, health, and happiness—the outward situation reflects our loving expectations. As affirmative words heal our thoughts, the Law of Cause and Effect reveals a healed world as an effect of our thoughts.

MIND AND MATTER

*"Law rules throughout existence, a Law which is not
intelligent, but Intelligence."*

— Ralph Waldo Emerson (1803–1882)
American author and philosopher

I entered high school feeling pulled in two directions. On the
one hand, I felt safe and happy at Sunday school and at home.
I was glad to have my friend Anita in my life, and we spent many
happy hours playing with Breyer model horses. We also played
with our pet animals, which included cats, rabbits, lizards, and
even rats.

I'd gotten the rats for a school science project in which I
wanted to study the effects of crowded conditions upon aggres-
sion. During the project, I put my rats into progressively smaller
cages and then counted the number of aggressive acts, such as
clawing and biting. Of course, the rats got meaner and nastier
each time I downsized their living space. Soon enough, the
experiment was over, and I had my hypothesized results. I moved
the rats to a more spacious living environment and realized that
I'd grown attached to them. So Anita, my brother, and I decided
to keep them as pets. They were clean black-and-white furry animals whose whiskers shook back and forth as they munched
appreciatively upon vegetables, fruits, and peanut butter-and-
jelly sandwiches. Anita and I would take our rats everywhere,
even to church.

One day we were playing with the rats out in the yard when our attention was momentarily diverted. The rats scurried away, and Anita and I searched everywhere for them. Then I remembered the spiritual treatment my mother had taught me when I'd lost my coin purse. Anita and I solemnly held hands as I repeated the phrase, "Nothing is lost in the mind of God." We reminded ourselves that although *we* couldn't see the rats, God knew where they were. So, in truth, they weren't really lost at all.

The peace of spiritual treatment lifts the heavy cloak of fear inhibiting harmony. The spiritual textbook *A Course in Miracles* says: "Miracles are natural. When they do not occur, something has gone wrong."[1] I believe that the "something" that prevents miracles from freely occurring is our uptight attitudes and fear. When you affirm, "This situation is already healed, right now," the words' soothing effects lift fear long enough for miracles to occur naturally.

When I declared that our rats weren't lost in God's mind, I received a strong mental impression. It said, "Think like a rat would think, and you will find them." Something told me to focus upon the redwood borders lining our home's driveway. "If I were a rat, I'd walk along the protectiveness of these redwood borders," I told Anita. We traced the borders a few feet and found our beloved pet rats cowering under two pine bushes.

Spiritual healing is very effective upon animals, partly because humans' thoughts and emotions affect pets' physical health.[2] In fact, you can tell a lot about a family's emotional health by looking at the physical health of their children and pets. I'd learned, from listening to testimonials and from my mother's healing practice, that babies, children, and animals absorb household stress like sponges. When couples repeatedly argue, their home fills with a toxic stress that creates health problems for their children and animals.

Fortunately, children and animals also respond rapidly when their households return to peace and sanity. My own household must have experienced some stress soon after we adopted a new kitten named Alfalfa. The little cat seemed healthy enough, although he did seem mellower than most kittens. I remember Alfalfa being shy but sweet. Then something horrible happened, and he became deathly ill. I still don't know whether he ate some poison, he absorbed some stress from our family, or his predestiny was to show the power of love to our family. I just know that when Alfalfa was an adolescent kitten, he died very suddenly.

I remember my mother cradling his limp, lifeless body in her arms as she sat cross-legged on the linoleum kitchen floor. I was crying loudly, begging my mother to do something. "Bring him back, bring him back!" I practically shouted at her. Poor Alfalfa hadn't even begun to experience life, and I couldn't stand the thought of being away from his purring affections. My grief was overwhelming, yet I had faith that my mother could save him.

"Do not be afraid; only believe, and she will be made well," Jesus said to a crowd who watched as he raised a young girl from the dead.[3] As a small child, I had this sort of intense faith in my mother's ability to save my precious little kitten. My mother closed her eyes, and her familiar smile of heavenly love come across her face. She said some commanding words to the cat, such as "There is no death" and "All is love." Suddenly, I saw movement in the nest of fur. I thought I must be imagining it, yet I also had full faith that my mother's prayers would bring Alfalfa back to me.

Sitting about two yards from my mother and Alfalfa, I felt dazed as I watched my kitten come back to life. Where moments before, he'd been limp and lifeless, now he looked like a being thawed from an icy coldness. My mother's expression looked radiant, yet I could see my own surprise reflected in her eyes. She looked dazed, too. I believe that she went into a trance that took her out of normal consciousness. To this day, although she is a lucid and brightly alert person, she only remembers fragments of Alfalfa's healing.

This miracle taught me the importance of letting go of our own conscious awareness of the healing objective. We can't force a healing to occur; we can only forcefully hold the knowingness of divine truth within our hearts and mind. Then, we must let go of attachment to the outcome and allow God's Law of Love to effect its natural course. Studies of spiritual healing emphasize that successful outcomes are related to the healer's ability to hold positive expectations without deliberately trying too hard to influence the outcome.[4]

A major block that prevents healing is seeing death, disease, or injury as real conditions needing "undoing." Healing comes from acknowledging *only* what is real and eternal, not from acknowledging what is temporal. Research from quantum physics provides evidence that our expectations and observations will determine whether we see and experience health or sickness.[5]

Let's say you wanted to be a healing conduit for a friend's illness. You would not start with a premise that the illness was a real condition and then try to eradicate it. Healing attempts based upon the thought of "Go away, disease!" are inherently rooted in the incorrect premise that there is a problem requiring a solution. You are thus giving energy and mental power to that which doesn't exist, so you will experience the illness as having a life and a mind of its own. It doesn't. No disease does.

The whole point behind spiritual healing is to remember that there are no problems, there is no death, and there are no diseases, illnesses, or injuries. There is nothing to heal, fix, or change because everything that is real is already perfect. When we consciously experience this as the truth, even for just an instant, love heals our minds from fear. Our material experiences then change to reflect our healed mindset.

All matter responds to our thoughts, not just so-called living flesh and organs. The impact of mind upon matter has been studied by Princeton researchers Robert Jahn and Brenda Dunne, who had volunteers sit in front of a machine that randomly flipped coins. The volunteers were asked to concentrate on mentally influencing the coins to land a certain way, such as "heads up." Most volunteers were able to influence the coins' landing in a statistically significant way. The researchers later replicated their findings in a similar experiment involving a large automatic pinball machine containing 9,000 marbles. This time, volunteers concentrated on having the marbles land in the pinball's outer bins. As before, the results were both successful and statistically significant.[5]

The results of Jahn and Dunne's studies should not surprise us, however. Why couldn't we control matter with our thoughts? After all, everything in the material world is an outpicturing of our mortal thoughts and beliefs. This is an important point for us lightworkers to remember, as our most vital contributions to the planet are done on a mental and spiritual plane. If a lightworker is frustrated because of feeling unable to "contribute" to the world through bodily efforts, those thoughts of frustration thwart her healing abilities. Similarly, if a lightworker frets over this or that world problem, the fretting adds fuel to the mass world consciousness of fear.

The stuff that bodies consist of in no way differs from any other form of matter. In that respect, all matter responds to prayer and corrected thinking. I learned this at an early age, when my mother and I were driving home from a grocery shopping trip. Suddenly, our Ford Pinto conked out, leaving us stranded by the roadside with melting groceries in the back seat. My mother tried turning the ignition, but the engine wouldn't respond.

Immediately, my mother began saying The Scientific Statement of Being aloud, affirmatively declaring that the entire situation was already healed. I joined my mother in prayer. After five or ten minutes, my mother turned the ignition, and the Pinto purred into action as if nothing had ever been wrong. And of course, nothing *had* been wrong, except the erroneous thoughts that initially created the situation. I have witnessed similar healings of cars, computers, and other machinery throughout my adult life.

Although spiritual truths and healings resonated naturally with me, I seemed to have difficulty applying this knowledge to my own self-image. Our family's move and my skipping a grade had badly shaken my self-esteem. It would be many years before my spiritual growth would bring harmony back to my life.

Anita and I began our sophomore year after spending a magical summer together. We'd leased horses and had filled our summer afternoons riding gymkhana, jumping, and even barrel racing in a few local horse shows. Our maturing bodies had also grown and changed during the summer. Anita had become a tall, willowy blonde, and boys were definitely giving her a lot of attention—a lot more than they were giving me, I grudgingly admitted to myself. In fact, Anita was becoming extremely popular with both sexes at our high school. I feared I was losing her and that I'd soon be without my best friend.

As a Christian Scientist, I followed several lifestyle dictates that marked me as different from my classmates. The religion asked us to avoid mood-altering chemicals such as caffeine, alcohol, and cigarettes, which interfere with divine communication and could put another "god" before God.

Christian Science also asked us to avoid the media, and classes that taught that disease, sickness, or death was real. Since our thoughts lead to illness, if we avoid medical television programs and the like, we are more apt to stay physically healthy. People, pets, and little children who become ill with diseases that were unbeknownst to them have absorbed thoughts about illness from the mass consciousness of humanity. So, if we keep our minds freed from medical theories about diseases, we not only keep ourselves healthy, but we also positively affect the entire world.

Whenever a commercial or show about illness comes on, I always switch the channel or leave the room. I also say The Scientific Statement of Being to myself to release any unhealthy thoughts that may have entered my mind. I believe this is one reason why I am rarely ill.

Schools excuse Christian Scientists, by law, from taking classes about health. Not wanting to be different from the other kids, at first I insisted on taking the high school's required health-and-safety class. During the first day of class, our teacher discussed the topic of accidents and lectured about how to avoid injuries at home and in the car. His words contradicted my beliefs that there are no accidents, only results of right-minded or wrong-minded thinking. So, at the end of the class period, when the teacher asked us to write an essay defining what an accident was, I had to write what I truly believed: "An accident is a lie and an illusion, caused by errors in one's thinking."

For some reason, the teacher didn't take offense or think my test answer was a smart-aleck joke. Instead, he pulled me aside and recommended that I sign the Christian Science class exemption paperwork and transfer into an elective class. From then on, instead of taking classes about health or life science like the other kids at school, I took extra art classes. I loved my painting, drawing, and lettering classes. However, skipping science class felt like another chink in my social self-esteem, another example of my being different from my classmates.

Meanwhile, Anita began hanging out with the popular kids at school. They dressed in the latest fashions, drove expensive sports cars, and treated the rest of us students with indifference. Since Anita's family income was sizably larger than mine, she could afford stylish clothing. My family was dependent upon my father's income from his home-based business of writing model-airplane books and articles, and from my mother's healing practice. My parents' values also differed from those of Anita's mother and father. Therefore, I couldn't elicit much sympathy when I told my folks that I wanted to dress like the popular kids at school. It wasn't practical to spend money on trends, they told me. Better to invest in longer-lasting classic styles.

So while Anita hung out with the cool kids, I spent more time with kids who were bookworms like me. Suddenly, there was a social divide between Anita and myself, and I didn't like it at all. It brought up all the old feelings of rejection that I'd fought to overcome.

Anita told me one day that she'd begun smoking pot with her new friends, and she gave me an ultimatum. "I don't want to hang out with you anymore unless you smoke pot," she said with unrecognizable sternness. Today, I know that marijuana had stolen away the Anita I knew and loved. But at the time of her ultimatum, I only felt shock and stinging anger toward my friend.

I purposely avoided Anita for the following days, feeling betrayed and sad that she was using marijuana. I hung out with my bookworm friends, but I soon found myself missing Anita's more upbeat and exciting companionship. By then, Anita had formed fast friendships with two girls who lived near Orange Glen High School. One girl, Tammy, was tall, tanned, and beautiful like Anita. The other girl, Amy, was a down-to-earth tomboy who lived on a small ranch and owned a show horse. Every afternoon, the three of them got stoned and went horseback riding. I, on the other hand, hung out with the horses in the pages of my Marguerite Henry and Wesley Dennis books. I longed for the experiences Anita was enjoying, and the earthiness of riding real horses and living life on the edge.

I bumped into Anita walking home one day, and she excitedly described the many "kegger" (beer keg) parties she and her new friends attended. She explained that all the kids would gather in the orange groves near Amy's ranch on San Pasqual Road. One boy's older brother would make "keg runs" and bring beer to the grove in his van. Then everyone would drink, listen to loud music, and laugh together. Anita asked, while looking at me out of the corner of her eye, "Do you want to come to the kegger party we're having this weekend?"

The lure of friendship and good times with Anita sorely

tempted me. But I worried aloud how I'd ever get permission from my parents to stay out so late. And with our religion's prohibition against alcohol—I'd never even held an alcoholic drink, let alone drunk any—I didn't know how I'd handle such a volatile situation. Anita shrugged off my concerns by saying, "No problem! Tammy's mother is really cool, and she lets us stay out all night. Just tell your parents you're spending the night at her house."

Anita was right in that my mother readily agreed to my staying overnight with Tammy. I justified to myself that I was telling my mother the truth, since I really was staying with Tammy. I just hadn't mentioned to Mom the other messy details like, "Oh, by the way, Mom, I'll be going to a kegger party in a nearby orange grove. But never you mind about that."

My mom drove me to Tammy's house Saturday afternoon. The first thing I noticed was that the household stereo played Grand Funk Railroad full-blast, and Tammy's mother seemed oblivious to it. She just casually cooked a pot of spaghetti in the kitchen, while Tammy openly smoked Virginia Slim cigarettes, picked out which pierced earrings to wear to the party, and cursed in front of her mother. I was both shocked and impressed. Cursing, pierced earrings, rock-and-roll, and cigarettes were all prohibited in my house. I'd never heard of a parent tolerating them. In fact, I'd never even considered them desirable before that moment when Tammy made them all seem so cool.

Tammy looked at me and said, "Oh no, that shirt is all wrong." She opened her closet and handed me a Pendleton red-and-white plaid shirt, which I slipped on and tucked into my jeans. Now I looked like Anita, Amy, and Tammy, as the four of us walked the quarter mile to the party site.

I was in for more surprises when I saw three of the cutest boys from school casually drinking beer while sitting on a large rock in the orange grove. I'd never had the nerve even to say "Hi" to these boys before. Now, I was clinking beer cups with them and laughing about our high school teachers. The whole evening was fantasy-like, and before I knew it, I'd consumed several beers. I didn't realize how high I'd gotten until I stood up and found that my legs wouldn't cooperate. The rest of the evening was a blur of laughter, Amy's silliness, and the cute boys from school hanging out with us.

Over the following months, I adopted the habit of smoking cigarettes. Tammy, Amy, and Anita smoked openly when we were at coffee shops, hamburger stands, or malls. I, however, was terrified that some church member might see me smoking, since cigarettes were definitely off-limits. Before I'd light up, I'd look in all directions to make sure I didn't see any familiar faces from my congregation.

Every chance I got, I attended kegger parties with Anita and rode horses with Amy. One rainy afternoon we all sat in the shelter of the dry, musty barn. Amy pulled out a loosely rolled marijuana joint from her back pocket and lit it. She took a deep puff and passed it around. When it got to me, I took it and looked at it. The other girls were aware of my inexperience with marijuana and showed me how to "take a drag." They told me to hold the smoke deeply in my lungs, but when I tried, I coughed painfully. The girls kept telling me how stoned they felt, but that first time that I tried pot, I didn't feel a thing.

Smoking pot with Amy, Anita, Tammy, and the other kids meant I was now fully initiated as a cool kid at school. My bookworm friends began avoiding me, my grades dropped, and my personality and interests markedly shifted. I quit the expensive violin lessons my Mom had paid for and began playing guitar. When I wasn't with my friends, I was alone in my room imitating the guitar riffs from my Led Zeppelin and Robin Trower records. My musical ear was good enough that I soon played most of Jimmy Page's songs.

I asked my parents to buy me a Fender Telecaster electric guitar. My father agreed under the condition that I'd first bring home a report card with straight *A*s. That was incentive enough, and I put all my thoughts and efforts into schoolwork. I got all *A*s and one *B*+ that semester, and Dad bought me a maple-necked Telecaster and a Fender Twin-Reverb amplifier. I joined a rock-and-roll band with several members of the Emmanuel Faiths' born-again Christian church, and we played at parties and school dances.

Although I suddenly had more friends than my schedule allowed for, I didn't much enjoy it. I saw how kids at school, who had mocked me for being a geeky bookworm several months earlier, now wanted to be my best friends. The popularity felt fake and insincere, so I continued to limit my socializing to Anita, Amy, and Tammy, and of course my new "friend," marijuana.

My band members must have learned of my marijuana use, because one day, they confronted me in kangaroo-court style. "You've got to start coming to our church, or you're out of the band," they said. I didn't even have to think about the matter. I simply packed my Telecaster into its case and left without another word.

I was still actively going to Christian Science Sunday school, yet my hangovers from Saturday night parties definitely interfered with any depth of thought. Sometimes, Anita and I would go to church stoned, which for some reason we believed was a hilarious thing to do. When it was time for me to go on my annual summer trip to the Christian Science youth camp in Colorado, I packed several marijuana joints into my camping gear.

At the Colorado youth church facility, we'd mix outdoor activities such as rock climbing, horseback riding, and river rafting with inspirational seminars. Many famous Christian Scientists such as Jean Stapleton of "All in the Family," Ginger Rogers, and Alan Young of "Mister Ed" fame, gave lectures during my summers at camp. That particular summer, however, I isolated myself from the other kids and snuck off into the dense Colorado woods to smoke pot.

I came back into my cabin after one smoking episode and noticed that someone had shifted my belongings around. Suddenly, the hair stood up on the back of my neck because I knew what the scene I was looking at meant. I had been drug-searched, and they'd found my stuff! I knew I was in trouble, and my stomach churned as I waited for the inevitable punishment. After all, any youth camp would frown upon drug usage. But worse, this was a Christian Science youth camp, and *nobody* was allowed to use drugs in any form.

The punishment was swift and merciful. A female camp counselor sternly drove me in a staff golf cart to the camp administrative office. There, I sat in a barren room while the counselor called my parents from an adjoining office. Mom and Dad had to pay for an airline ticket for my immediate departure back home to California.

I felt deeply ashamed when I saw my parents' reddened, moist eyes as I got off the airplane. My father was angry, but he was at a loss for words. My mother just stared straight ahead wordlessly on the way home. I suppose she was praying, but I just felt guiltier and guiltier with each silent mile we drove.

My friends Anita and Amy thought my being kicked out of church camp was cool, and they laughed hysterically at the story. The closer I bonded with my friends, the further I got from God and my parents. I was hooked on marijuana and also hooked on my friends' approval and companionship.

Besides the little bit of money I made as a guitarist, I also had started an airbrushing business in which I'd hand-paint clouds and exotic birds on T-shirts and sell them at my high school. These products were so popular that the high school store soon began carrying them for sale. I loved the beauty of creating wearable nature scenes for my friends and teachers. Often I'd be stoned on pot as my airbrush painted rainbows and seagulls on my cotton canvases.

My mother, meanwhile, was becoming ever more active in

the Christian Science church. Her practice was filled with clients, and she'd become a second reader (the equivalent of an assistant minister) at our local church. Mom also volunteered at the Escondido reading room, and she was considered a church pillar. I was still involved at church, too, although I could tell that many people had heard of my "bust" at church camp. I felt shunned and judged by a few members of the adult and youth congregation. Yet, I took responsibility for my social outcast status, so instead of blaming them, I just avoided them back.

I didn't realize it at the time, but my mother and several other church members were fervently praying that I would stop using marijuana and tobacco. After being kicked out of camp, my mom and I had shared an intimate discussion about my drug use. I'd felt comfortable enough to tell her my thoughts and feelings about marijuana, saying that I didn't see anything harmful about it. She didn't lecture me, but simply listened.

Mom was very smart to handle the situation with prayers instead of punishment. One day, I woke up and had absolutely no desire for marijuana. When my friends passed around a joint after school, I didn't even want it. It was so black-and-white: one day, my appetite for marijuana was all-consuming. But the next day, something within me shifted, and I had absolutely no desire for marijuana at all. Prayer had healed me, all without my knowledge or consent.

In his book *Healing Words*, Larry Dossey, M.D., describes scientific studies of prayers' effectiveness.[6] Many studies show prayer has a statistically significant healing effect, regardless of whether the patient knows about the prayers.[7] Several studies show that prayed-for plants and microbes grow faster than those that aren't prayed for.[8] This body of research illustrates that spiritual healing is more than a placebo effect of the patient's positive expectations.

My own sudden and dramatic healing from marijuana dependency—although I didn't want a healing, didn't think I needed healing, and had no foreknowledge of others' prayers for me—had proven prayers' effectiveness to me. This was a powerful lesson for me that would later greatly influence my career as a psychotherapist treating addictions.

My use of marijuana had clouded my thought processes, and it was about three days before my mind cleared. I was happy and awestruck about instantly and painlessly losing all desire for marijuana, alcohol, and tobacco and did not miss them one bit. The healing had happened naturally, like walking out of one room into another.

With my mind lifted from the influences of drugs, I willingly recommitted to my spiritual studies at Sunday school. My healing had heightened my interest in the links between the mind and body, and I lapped up every word I could read or hear about metaphysics. I felt a bliss that I'd never experienced before, a high much greater than any drug-induced state.

A VISIT FROM THE OTHER SIDE

*"Ah, the spirits of my ancestors have looked down
from heaven, watching over and helping me."*

— *Nihon Shoki 3,*
spiritual text of Shinto (Japan)

B etween my time as a partier, my very public lead guitar-playing in local bands, and my thriving airbrush business, I had achieved my goal of social popularity. Yet, it was a hollow victory because I knew that the other kids only liked me for what I did and not for who I was inside. The popularity gave me no satisfaction at all. I only enjoyed the company of people who had been my friends before I'd become an artist and guitarist.

Most of those true friends, it turned out, were at church and at home. My family had stood by me even when I'd been impossible to live with during my marijuana-induced mood swings. My church family, with the exception of a few people, had shown me unconditional love. Those who had stuck by me loved me because I am—just like you—a holy child of God. I deserved their love—just as you do—just for being God's child.

The conditional love I received at school paled in comparison. Looking back, I now realize that most of my school friends did not know how to show love. Many of them came from tumultuous households. And mainly, when drugs blunt your thoughts and feelings, your awareness of love's presence is also dulled. So, although well-meaning friends surrounded me, I felt like that cliché: lonely in a crowd.

When I was 17, my paternal grandmother, Pearl, and my step-grandfather, "Pop-pop" Ben, drove from Bishop to spend several days with us at our Escondido home. I remember excitedly awaiting their arrival, intently listening for the sound of their station wagon pulling into our driveway. We had a wonderful visit. I felt especially close to both my grandparents as I watched them pull out of the driveway when it was time for them to return home.

Several hours after they'd left, the phone rang. I watched as my Dad held the telephone receiver, and his body shuddered. "Ben and my mom were in a car accident," he said with urgency. "A drunk driver crossed over and hit them head-on. Mom's in the hospital, and . . . Ben's dead."

We all protested the news with tears and cries of "No, no!" I ran into my darkened bedroom and grabbed my acoustic guitar, hugging it for comfort. I strummed some chords, and the music helped me feel peace in my heart. I could hear my parents and brother crying in the living room, and I felt guilty that I didn't share their grief. Yes, I loved my Pop-pop as much as anyone. Yes, I would greatly miss his presence. But in the depths of my soul, I didn't feel sadness at his death. My only despair was related to the fact that I didn't feel any grief.

Just then, a glowing light beyond the foot of my bed caught my attention. I looked over and there, clear as day, was my Pop-pop Ben. He looked exactly as he had when I'd last seen him, wearing a plaid shirt and comfortable pants, only he was smaller and slightly transparent. The colors of his clothes were muted from the bluish-white light that seemed to emanate from within him. He clearly expressed to me through some sort of telepathic means: "You are right to feel this way, Doreen. I am fine, and everything is okay." Then his image dissolved, and he was gone. I was left with the certainty that my peacefulness was appropriate.

When I later told my parents about Ben's appearance, they

shared with me that Ben's brother—who lived very far from our home in Escondido—also saw Ben shortly after his death. Had Ben visited all of us, unbeknownst to the other family members? Perhaps the intense grief of my parents and brother prevented them from noticing his presence, or maybe their strong feelings actually blocked his arrival. I don't know, but I *do* know that while grief is a perfectly normal emotion that can serve a useful healing function, it also can block our awareness of life-after-death.

My sobriety, Ben's death, and mixed feelings about my relationships at school confused me. I felt much older than my 17 years, yet uncertain about my life's direction. Somehow, I came to possess a self-help book that would rescue me from my feelings of self-recrimination. *You Are Not the Target* by Laura Huxley[1] was like healing balm on my wounded adolescent ego. Huxley's words convinced me that I wasn't a victim and that I could take control of my thoughts and feelings. I read the book repeatedly until its pages were dog-eared. I decided to someday make a similar contribution by writing a self-help book when I got older.

Writing had always been a passion of mine, beginning with my elementary school essays and continuing through my stint as a cub reporter on my junior high school's newspaper. My father, the author of over a dozen books and a monthly magazine column about model airplanes, had always encouraged me to write. He also spent a few years working as an editor for a small publishing company near Los Angeles that specialized in writing about airplanes. During this time, the president of the company discovered an unknown writer who had written articles about conversations he'd had with a bird. The company president convinced the writer to turn these articles into an inspirational book, and my Dad edited the resulting manuscript.

As a child, I remember riding in the back seat of my father's Volkswagen bug. As children often do, I complained about the length of the trip. To entertain me and hush my incessant "When are we gonna get there?" questions, Dad reached over the seat and handed me a ream of rice paper-thin typewritten sheets. It was the book that he was editing, and I read those original galleys about the bird's philosophy of life with great interest.

Somewhere along the publishing process, the author decided to take his manuscript to a bigger publishing house. My Dad's boss reluctantly but peacefully allowed the writer to take his book elsewhere. The book, which I've agreed not to name here out of respect for my father's wishes, became an international bestseller.

Naturally, my father and his boss were disappointed that their hard work had benefited another publisher's coffers. Still, they were happy to have been instruments of a book that ultimately would help many people. Then, one day, the author appeared on a talk show promoting his book, making some hurtful remarks about Dad's publishing house. That was it! My Dad's boss decided to sue the author for breach of contract. A huge lawsuit resulted, and my father spent days with lawyers in deposition. Dad cautioned my brother and me not to answer strangers' questions on the telephone or at the door. The whole incident taught me how one book could considerably influence many lives in many ways.

As a high school senior, my sobriety and renewed enthusiasm for writing considerably elevated my grade-point average. The change in my grades was so dramatic that my history teacher suspected I was cheating on my homework assignments. Right before graduation, the teacher assigned a class project to write a report about a historical figure whom we admired.

I chose to write about Charles Lindbergh, and as I still do today, I dove into researching my subject. After many trips to the library, I felt sufficiently inspired and educated about Lindbergh to tackle my report. The words flew effortlessly out of my fingers as I typed. Imagine my shock and disappointment when my teacher returned the report to me a week later with a big *F* scrawled across its top. When I asked the teacher why, he said that the report was so well done that I'd obviously plagiarized it.

I stammered my protests that my report was my original work, but the teacher wouldn't listen. The grade of *F* on my history report threatened to block me from graduating from high school. It took my father going to the high school and talking with the teacher before we convinced him of my report's originality. Just in time for my graduation, the teacher changed my final grade to an *A+*, and at the high school commencement ceremony, he repeatedly apologized for misjudging me.

After high school graduation, I entered freshman classes at Palomar Community College in San Marcos, California, with a double major in music and journalism. I learned musical theory and scales, studied jazz guitar, and wrote interviews and essays for the college magazine. Then one day I heard about an editorial job opening at a small weekly newspaper called *The San Marcos Outlook*. I applied for the position, although I had barely started learning the "who, what, why, where, and how" basics of journalism.

The newspaper publisher, William Carroll, asked me why I wanted the job. I explained my dream of being a professional writer and talked about my college journalism classes. After the interview, I prayed that he would hire me. Two days later, I got the job, dropped out of college, and went to work as the full-time editor of *The San Marcos Outlook*.

My job entailed wearing many hats, including proofreading, layout, reporting, and editing. For a small weekly newspaper, the pressure was enormous and nonstop. The job consumed most of my hours during the week, and my evenings were spent covering city council and planning commission meetings.

I was dating a fellow named Larry, who at age 20 was one year older than myself. We met at a party after I'd read an article about a supposedly foolproof way to meet guys by making eye contact with them for six seconds. At the party, I joked with my

friend Laurie about this method, and we decided to test its effectiveness. We selected as our target a tall lanky fellow we'd never
seen before. I caught his eye while Laurie and I counted 1001,
1002, for what seemed like the longest six seconds on record. The
method *did* work, and the man approached me. However, his
intensity frightened me, and I made an excuse to get away from
him. But the more I evaded the man, the more determined he was
to meet me. I felt like prey.

Ten minutes of cat-and-mouse chasing throughout the house
ended in the kitchen with a large crowd of partygoers. I walked
up to a harmless-looking man whom I'd never before met and
impulsively put my arm around him. He glanced at me sideways
as I explained, "I need you to pretend that you're my boyfriend.
There's a guy after me." That man who "rescued me" was Larry,
and we became a steady couple.

Larry was accustomed to my demanding work schedule at
the newspaper. He'd often stay at the apartment I rented near the
newspaper office, waiting for me to arrive home from covering a
news event. Larry and I had a delightfully romantic relationship,
although our spiritual backgrounds were very different, and I
rarely shared that side of my life with him. My hours and
thoughts, consumed by work and time with Larry, pulled my consciousness away from the spiritual path. I hadn't attended church
or opened a spiritual text in months. So it's not surprising how
willingly I joined Larry in smoking a joint one evening.

Although I hadn't smoked marijuana in years, I was rapidly
drawn back into the lifestyle. I don't know why my mother's
prayers for spiritual healing didn't have a lasting effect upon my
appetite for the drug. All I can think is that free will—my decision to abuse marijuana—usurped the spiritual power of prayer. I
believe that we all have free will to do whatever we want with our
lives, even when our decision is self-destructive. Even so, every
time I wander off the spiritual path, some unseen force always
intervenes to pull me back.

One night following a marijuana and drinking binge, I sat alone in my darkened living room, trying to lull myself to sleep in a rocking chair. I saw a vivid mental picture of a large silver trash can. The can's cylinder grew upwards until it finally arched back down to the ground in the shape of a child's Slinky spring toy. A strong feeling accompanied this vision that essentially said to me, "You are throwing your life and talents in the trash can by using marijuana. Stop this immediately."

The vision shook me, and I quit marijuana, alcohol, and tobacco, and only kept using birth control pills because Larry and I had become intimate. When I once ran low on pills, my demanding work schedule made it difficult for me to find time to refill my prescription. On the day I ran out of them, I promised myself that the next morning I'd get more. I did, but during that one day of skipping the Pill in 1977 when I was 19 years old, I became pregnant with Larry's child.

I didn't know what to do! Although the 1960s and '70s had markedly changed the social and sexual climate, unwed mothers still carried a stigma. I'd already decided against getting an abortion, and Larry's mother had convinced him that marriage was a mistake because of our youth and financial insecurity.

Larry's family pressured me to enter an unwed mothers' home run by their Catholic church. I reluctantly agreed to meet with the Catholic adoption agency, although I'd already fallen in love with the baby I carried in my womb. So every time the adoption counselors would come to my apartment door, I'd pretend not to be home. I avoided them to the point where they quit pursuing me. Eventually, I announced my decision to keep my baby. I was completely sure of this decision, but I was unprepared for how embarrassed I would feel about my unwed pregnancy status. When my pregnancy began to show, I quit my newspaper job out of shame and took a job making sandwiches at a local deli.

Getting birth control and prenatal care instigated the few times in my life when I saw a physician. During my obstetrical examination, the doctor commented on my excellent health, and somehow the subject of my Christian Science background came up. "Oh yes, Christian Science," the doctor remarked. "I have a neighbor who is a Christian Scientist. I believe there is some credence to the fact that the emotions can play a part in the body's health."

I was happy that my doctor accepted what most people then considered a wacky idea—that the mind and body have links to one another. I had been raised to believe that not only did the mind control everything, but that only the mind existed. The body was an unreal illusion, projected by the ego. I never expected to hear a doctor proclaim that our thoughts affected our health. As a child, I remember wanting to make a difference in the world by showing the validity of the mind-body link scientifically. It never occurred to me that someday science would come to accept as factual the metaphysical principles with which I'd been raised.

Once during my pregnancy, a substitute physician conducted my examination. I complained to the doctor that my baby frequently kicked me very hard. I wondered aloud if the stress of my sandwich-shop job contributed to my baby acting this way. The doctor smiled at the thought and then laughed out loud. "Stress!" he guffawed, and then he rapidly changed the subject. I took his reaction to mean that he didn't believe stress could affect one's health. Most people didn't, until very recently.

I frequently get asked why Christian Scientists don't go to doctors. These questioners often bring up the occasional media reports about a child dying because his Christian Science parents refused medical intervention. Many have erroneously concluded that Christian Scientists are extremists who recklessly sacrifice their children's welfare. I'm often asked the rhetorical question, "Didn't God make doctors and medicine?'

It's not that Christian Scientists are against doctors or don't believe in them. It's just that Christian Science teaches that God is the only power. No one can dispute that medicines work; however, their power comes purely from human belief. Therefore, it's our option to eliminate medicine as an unnecessary middleman, and rely purely on faith.

As Mary Baker Eddy wrote in *Science and Health with Key to the Scriptures*:

> Material medicine substitutes drugs for the power of God—even the might of Mind—to heal the body. When the sick recover by the use of drugs, it is the law of a general belief, culminating in individual faith, which heals; and according to this faith will the effect be. Christian Science deals wholly with the mental cause in judging and destroying disease. Christian Science exterminates the drug, and rests on Mind alone as the curative Principle, acknowledging that the divine Mind has all power.[2]

Scientific research verifies that medicine's curative powers hinge upon the positive expectations of prescribing doctors and their patients. A dramatic example is that many drugs, including vitamin E and the tranquilizer, meprobamate, are only effective when administered by doctors who strongly believe in their effectiveness. When doctors who doubt these drugs' efficacy administer *identical drugs*, they don't work. Apparently, the doctors' attitudes are conveyed to the patient, thus influencing the patients' faith or lack of faith in the drug. [3]

Prayer's efficacy also appears to come from the Law of Cause and Effect that says that "what you expect and believe is what you experience." When prayer doesn't seem to yield desired results, it is usually because the recipient is unable to release fear long enough to restore health and harmony. Death or destruction are their overriding thoughts, and these thoughts manifest into reality through the Law of Cause and Effect. Also, if a patient *chooses* death or debilitating illness, then the Law of Free Will manifests these desires into realities.

When a person's fears block prayers' effectiveness, common decency say that they should seek a physician. Christian Science does not endorse those parents who allow their children to suffer physically instead of contacting a doctor. The feeling is that such parents are not spiritually aware enough to hold a thought of complete truth, and so they cannot create a mental climate for healing to occur. Common sense and self-honesty about one's abilities to hold truthful thoughts determine whether to take material action concerning one's health.

TRUSTING SPIRIT

"The body is the temple of God;
in every body, God is installed whether the owner
of the body recognizes it or not. It is God that inspires you
to good acts, that warns you against the bad. Listen to that
voice. Obey that voice, and you will not
come to any harm."

— Sathya Sai Baba,
renowned Indian spiritual teacher[1]

My son, Charles Wesley Schenk II, named for Larry's late father, was born on June 7, 1978. I was in heaven as I cradled my baby boy. Three months later, Larry and I were married. Two years after that, I gave birth to our second child, Grant William Schenk, named for William, my father. Grant looked and acted just like a little cherub.

Years earlier, while driving on rural roads in San Marcos, I had seen two little boys playing. They looked adorable in their baggy little jeans, and right then I asked God if I could have two sons of my own. As always, God came through, although I hadn't expected to have children while I was still so young myself.

I'd stopped smoking marijuana after my vision; however, Larry's consumption of the weed increased. His moods grew sullen, and he complained continually. I believed his marijuana consumption contributed to most of our financial and marital problems, and several times he yielded to my pleas to quit the habit. However, when he'd quit smoking pot, his moods would sink into a smoldering, low-level anger. During one detoxification when his mood was especially abusive, I even begged him to smoke pot again just to give me relief. Other times, Larry would return to his habit behind my back.

Despite his drug usage, we attempted to maintain a traditional family household. Larry worked at electrical supply stores while I stayed home with Chuck and Grant. I loved sewing their clothes and watching "Sesame Street" and "Mister Rogers" with them. We'd play games and sing songs together.

Money was extremely tight. For a while, we couldn't even afford a bed, and I had spent my first pregnancy uncomfortably sleeping on blankets on the carpeted floor. My grandfather, Ted Hannan, the Amway "diamond level distributor," and my parents frequently gave me small gifts of cash that helped us get by.

Soon after grandfather Ted passed away, I began receiving financial support in miraculous ways. One day I was walking down Grand Avenue in Escondido when, for some reason, I went into a bedroom furniture store. It was the store's grand opening, and they were having a drawing for a free king-sized bed. I wrote my name on an entry blank, and two days later, I learned that I'd won the bed and a complete bedding set! The new bed was delivered to our apartment soon after Chuck's birth, and I was grateful to no longer have to sleep on the floor. Another time, when our utilities were about to be shut off for nonpayment, I received a check for $1,000 from a contest I'd forgotten I'd entered. To this day, I can feel Grandpa Ted's angelic energy supporting my brother Ken's and my own finances. In my mind, I see Ted smiling with delight each time he helps Ken and me heal our thoughts of lack or limitation.

Ted's miraculous gifts helped my little family's income somewhat, but we still struggled to pay our bills. Larry often argued with his bosses and frequently quit his jobs. I was unhappy a great deal of the time, feeling trapped in a hostile, financial-

ly insecure lifestyle that felt foreign to me. Larry and I had completely different ways of resolving our many differences. I'd
come from a small family of introverts who quietly discussed
problems, or who ignored matters in the hopes that they would go
away. Larry, in contrast, had been the youngest in a large family,
and he'd learned to be extremely vocal to get his needs met. To
Larry, it was normal to scream and bang cupboard doors in anger.
I just cringed in fear at his loud expressions.

My respite came in the form of endless bowls of chocolate ice
cream. When Larry was at work or asleep, I'd sneak an ice cream
carton from the freezer and consume its contents without making
a sound. Its velvety creaminess and sweet chocolate taste seemed
to elevate my mood and thoughts to another dimension where
everything was happy and harmonious. It wasn't until years later
that I'd understand I was binging upon mood-altering psychoactive chemicals in chocolate ice cream to soothe my depression.

The ice cream binges put many pounds on my body, and soon
Larry complained that I was fat and ugly. "You're lucky you have
me, because no other man would want you," he'd say. The more
he needled me, the more I'd turn to food for comfort. Eventually,
I ballooned to 50 pounds above my normal weight. His insults
then became even more personal and cruel. He told me that I was
stupid, incompetent, and worthless. Like a defenseless creature
who didn't know how to fight back, I let Larry's opinions per-
meate my self-image. I'd had no experience or even knowledge
about abusive behavior. So, it didn't occur to me that I had the
right to tell him to stop, or else. I was too afraid of the loud blast
of anger that spewed forth from his mouth whenever he blamed
me for something.

Today, I realize that my husband was psychologically abusing me. Like many abuse survivors, my "learned helplessness"
paralyzed me. When anyone abuses creatures, they eventually
give up their self-worth, believing that only their abuser has
rights. My husband's loud and belligerent voice and self-assured

demeanor led me to believe that his opinions were more valid than my own. So, if he told me I was inadequate, it must be so. This sort of learned helplessness often correlates to debilitating depression in abused animals and humans.

My mother and Grandmother Ada saw that my marriage was falling apart. The two wondered aloud what to do, and I imagine that they prayed for a solution, because my life soon took another radical and miraculous turn.

One afternoon when I was changing Grant's clothes, I saw a mental image of myself. It was like seeing a black-and-white movie in which I both saw myself, and in which I was in the middle of the action. In the vision, I saw myself in a different type of life where I was fit, attractive, and happy. I was an accomplished published author and a professional healer, helping people through my teachings.

I shut my eyes tightly to block out the vision. It wasn't a welcome sight, but instead something that added to my painful futility. It seemed masochistic to entertain thoughts about such a good life. But for the following days, these visions continued. They were always the same, but they often had extra details and dimensions. I saw myself appearing on national talk shows and living in a beautiful seaside home.

The visions would stop whenever I'd eat ice cream, so I started eating more. It was my way of ignoring the divine guidance that I neither trusted nor believed. Eating ice cream was my equivalent of sticking my fingers in my ears and saying to God, "I can't hear you!" Yet, I could hear Him at some level, and the visions reawakened a long-forgotten part of myself.

I'd always been creative in art, music, and writing. Yet, except for sewing my children's clothing, I'd ignored my creative side for many years. Larry's words had also convinced me that I was stupid. Although I'd mostly been a straight *A* student who had skipped fifth grade, I wondered if the times I'd smoked pot could have destroyed my brain cells. Instead of seeing Larry's opinions as abusive and incorrect, I bought into them.

The visions motivated me to dabble in creative outlets such as gardening and painting, and I found these pursuits invigorating. I'd meditate while gardening, and the visions of my life as a writer turned from black-and-white to full-color images. The thought of writing books that helped people as much as Laura Huxley's book had helped me was truly exciting. Still, I wondered, How could I, a fat, uneducated housewife, even begin to become a published author? If I were stupid, as my husband claimed I was, what could I possibly write that would help anyone? I looked up to published writers so much that I practically saw them as a separate and superior race of beings. Publication seemed the domain of an elite few, with an exclusive rank closed to the public.

Well, it's true that angels often come into your life in the form of books, which you tend to pick up at the perfect moment. The book *Positive Imaging,* by Norman Vincent Peale, was my saving angel.[2] Dr. Peale wrote about the power of affirmations and visualization to effect positive changes in your thoughts. I learned that your expectations create your reality. "Hmm, I've been expecting failure and money problems," I concluded, as I read *Positive Imaging* further.

I recalled how my mother had taught me to use affirmations and visualization. When, as a teenager, I became concerned about my weight, she'd taught me to visualize myself as trim and toned. I'd been especially concerned about being overweight in my stomach region. Mom worked with me to hold a mental image of myself with a flattened stomach. To this day, although I've been unhappy with the shape of other areas of my body, I've always had a flat stomach.

There was no question in my mind regarding the awesome power of visualization and affirmations. But I worried that my self-confidence level had dropped to such a low level that I was beyond the help of these metaphysical tools. However, Dr. Peale's writings urged me to give affirmations another try. He quoted Jesus's comforting words that we only need faith "the size of a mustard seed" to move mountains in our lives.

Since I couldn't afford a prerecorded affirmation tape, I decided to make my own. So I wrote down some positive statements from my visions such as "I am a published author," "I have a fit, attractive body," "I attract loving people into my life," and "I help many people with my work." I voiced each statement in the here-and-now positive wording that Dr. Peale's book had suggested. He'd written that it was important to claim our good as already given to us and to give thanks that this was so.

I read these statements into a cassette tape recorder and then listened to this tape twice a day for almost two months. I didn't tell anyone what I was up to, feeling that if my husband or friends even slightly criticized my actions, that I'd quit listening to the affirmations prematurely. At first, my self-esteem was so low that I couldn't stand hearing my own voice. I had little regard for myself, even disdain. I'd wince at hearing my affirmations, wondering whether the whole thing was a waste of time or a setup for painful disappointment. Still, I kept remembering Dr. Peale's and my mother's promises about the power of affirmations.

Within a month of listening to affirmations that I was a successful author, I began to feel motivated to write. I pulled my old manual typewriter from the hall closet and placed it on the kitchen table. Then when the boys were taking a nap, I carefully rolled a sheet of white paper into the typewriter, making certain that it was positioned straight up and down.

My first attempts at writing were magazine articles that I sent out to various national and local publications. I tried writing a couple of essays and some nonfiction articles about marriage and family life. I hadn't investigated the publishing process enough to know that it's customary to first send a "query letter" to editors, asking whether they are interested in seeing your article. The editor then replies with a telephone call or a letter sent in the self-addressed stamped envelope the author includes in the query letter. I hadn't queried, I hadn't included a self-addressed stamped envelope, and I consequently sabotaged any chance of publication.

I decided to return to Palomar Community College as a part-time student. In my visions, I was a professional healer. I couldn't tell what sort of healer, but since I wanted to write self-help books, I chose the psychological realm. So I signed up for three classes: Psychology 101, Aerobics, and Income Tax Preparation. The psychology class was so I could test the waters to see if I liked the topic or not. The aerobics class was to help me lose weight. The income tax class seemed practical to me. I thought, I can use this knowledge when filing my own taxes and maybe do some part-time work at tax time.

The classes were just the sort of therapy my wounded self-esteem needed! In the income tax course, I discovered a part of myself that loved mathematics. I'd never regarded myself as good with numbers, and viewed math as the territory of right-brained males. Yet, I thrived in this class, and when I received an *A,* I knew that my brain cells and intelligence were still intact.

The aerobics class whittled away my extra pounds, and I started to feel better about the way I looked. I dressed up a bit and even applied makeup before leaving the house. Larry became suspicious, accusing me of trying to attract another man. Then he'd warn me not to even try by threatening, "If you leave me, I'm going to get custody of Chuck and Grant." Sometimes he'd tell me, "No other man but me could ever want you, since you have two children, and guys don't like women who have kids." His stinging words were beginning to have less of an impact on me, though, since I felt stronger and more confident.

I made new friends, female and male, at school. I especially enjoyed the people in my psychology class. My professor, Barbara Erickson-Williams, was a bubbly psychiatric nurse with a talent for telling wonderful stories that made our lessons come alive. She started many of her sentences by saying, "As psychologists, you will discover that..." as if we already had Ph.D.'s. Her words tickled my imagination, and I loved feeling as if I were already a psychologist. I enrolled full-time in college, working around Larry's job schedule so that one of us was always at home with our sons. My studies and grades soared, and I continued to exercise and lose weight. My confidence reached an all-time high, but it seemed that my newfound independence grated upon Larry. He accused me of plotting an extramarital affair and began stalking me during my shopping excursions. Several times as I entered a store, a clerk would ask, "Is your name Doreen?" When I'd say yes, the clerk would hand me the telephone and say, "Your husband's on the phone for you."

"What took you so long to get to the store?" he'd demand to know, saying that I had taken five or ten more minutes than he'd calculated was necessary. Once, as I arrived at my friend Silvia's home for a visit, Larry was on the telephone waiting for me. Again, he accused me of taking too much time to arrive. "Did you stop off at some man's home?!" he angrily asked.

Before, Larry had complained that I was too fat and stupid. Now that I had a slender figure and a high grade-point average, his complaints changed directions. Daily, he'd tell me that he just *knew* I was cheating on him. Larry ignored my reassurances of fidelity, so eventually I simply tuned him out. I realized how far apart we'd drifted when both of us forgot our wedding anniversary one year. We didn't even notice this oversight until a week later!

The back of our marriage broke one night when Larry woke up from an afternoon nap and asked me to make him some coffee. I guess I didn't hear his request, because about 30 minutes later, he began screaming at the top of his lungs, "Why didn't you make the coffee like I told you?!" I looked at his twisted angry face and felt nothing. I felt no anger, contempt, or love—only numbness.

We tried marriage counseling briefly, but it seemed hopeless. At the time, I was detached from spiritual practices, so it never occurred to me that prayer or spiritual healing could have healed our relationship. I was seeing our marriage from a purely human perspective, and it looked very grim from that level.

We decided to separate, so I looked for sources of income. Every job for which I applied paid minimum wage, and I didn't think I could support myself and the boys with so little income. So Larry and I agreed that I would move in with my parents. However, Mom and Dad were unable to have the boys stay in their home. We all agreed that I would initially move into my parents' home alone, then find a job, get my own place, and move the boys into my new home.

The day of our separation was the most painful in my life. Everyone was crying over the situation. Although the new arrangement was awful, we felt that there was no alternative. I kept telling myself, "Better for the boys to come from a divorced home than to live in a home with so much anger and arguing."

But I hadn't planned for what would next occur. I telephoned the boys to talk with them and heard a recording that the number had been disconnected. Larry and my sons were gone, and I had no idea where they were! I was frantic, but I felt trapped by my limited resources that didn't even allow me to hire a private detective.

On my own, I tracked Larry's whereabouts, finally discovering that he'd moved to a remote town in Colorado near his brother's home. I flew out to reunite with my sons. By then, I'd begun working as an insurance company secretary to support myself and pay my college tuition. I wanted the boys with me as Larry and I had agreed, but he refused to allow them to come with me. Since our separation, Larry had become even more bitter toward me. He'd built such a negative image of me in his mind that he now believed that he was protecting the boys by retaining custody.

When I returned to California, I hired a lawyer and began a child custody battle. The boys were too young to be involved in the custody trial, so the bulk of the decision rested upon the judge. My lawyer and Larry's lawyer slung horrible insults back and forth, each trying to paint the other's client as an unfit parent. This created a good guy/bad guy dichotomy. My lawyer and I did our best to make Larry out to be the bad guy, while Larry and his lawyer did the same to me.

The day of the court decision, I fully expected to win. After all, I was the boys' mother, and a good mother at that. When the judge decreed in Larry's favor, citing the fact that the children had already spent months with their father and he didn't want to change their status quo, I thought I would pass out in shock.

I'd never before heard of a mother losing custody. It seemed that only abusive or criminal women could ever have their children taken away. Yet, the unthinkable had occurred, and now I'd only see the boys during weekend visitations. Deeply saddened and incredibly ashamed of my noncustodial status, I moved to a new town and didn't tell anyone that I even had children. It just hurt too much to answer questions such as, "Why don't your children live with you?"

Not until two years later would I learn that more than two million American women were in my same noncustodial position. Most of these women lost custody under circumstances similar to my own. Contrary to stereotypes, only a fraction of mothers lose custody due to "unfit" mothering.

I entered another petition for child custody and hired a lawyer who was the head of the Bar Association and a part-time judge in San Diego County. My new lawyer told the judge how Larry wouldn't allow me to see the boys during my designated visitations. The judge lectured Larry about the importance of children maintaining regular contact with both parents. I promised the judge that if he would grant me custody, I would make sure the boys saw their father regularly. Three days before Christmas, I won custody, and Chuck and Grant came to live with me.

During this time, I dated a man named Dwight Virtue whom I'd met in college. Dwight, who was also a psychology major, had an amazing photographic memory. In fact, I was first attracted to him because he always scored the highest grades in class. He claimed to only study for the tests one hour before the exam.

Dwight was a Buddhist and the tall, husky son of a French-Canadian father and a Japanese mother. He'd been an air traffic controller in the Marines, and he told me of his dreams to become a controller for the Federal Aviation Administration (FAA). At the time, it seemed a faraway dream to him. Then, history intervened.

In the summer of 1981, members of the Professional Air Traffic Controllers Organization (PATCO), staged a mass walk-out. Air traffic controllers across the country picketed and demanded changes in their job conditions. The flight system of the entire country shut down, and President Reagan demanded that they return to work immediately or be fired. The controllers thought Reagan was bluffing and continued their strike. Two days later, Reagan made good on his threat, and most of America's air traffic controllers were instantly unemployed.

The FAA scrambled to hire replacements and immediately recruited anyone with military air traffic control experience. Dwight was among the first wave of trainees sent to the FAA school in Oklahoma City before ultimately being placed as a full-time air traffic controller. We didn't want to be apart, so Dwight and I were married. He accepted his final assignment as a high-level controller for Los Angeles's en route center in the high desert of Southern California. We began our life as a little family in a modest tract home in Lancaster, and I transferred my studies to Antelope Valley College.

I continued working as a secretary while taking classes, but I was growing increasingly dissatisfied with clerical work. I was ready to get my feet wet doing counseling. But who would hire me without a college degree? The answer came as an intuitional nudge that told me to volunteer at a mental health center. Volunteer work would give me much-needed experience on my résumé and could even result in my being hired!

THE CareUnit

*"Mind speaking truth through the lips, or thinking
truth consciously, can bring all the satisfaction to the world
which the world is seeking. Nothing material can
strengthen people, but the Omnipotent Truth can
strengthen them with all the power of Truth."*

— Emma Curtis Hopkins,
author of *Scientific Christian Mental Practice*

I was so nervous the day I started calling mental health centers, asking if they needed volunteer assistance. Many said, "No, thank you." Finally, a kindly man named Andy Palmer at an alcoholism treatment hospital called "The CareUnit" asked me to come in for an interview.

Andy asked if I'd had any experience with "the 12 steps," and I had to admit that I didn't. I'd never even heard of them! Although I was a complete greenhorn with respect to alcoholism, Andy must have realized that I had good intentions. Either that, or the same Spirit that gave me the idea to volunteer influenced Andy's decision. Regardless, he said I could volunteer at the detox unit for four hours a week and that he would supervise me. I was elated!

My first day of volunteering at the Palmdale Hospital CareUnit was a real eye-opener for me. I sat next to a pajama-clad man named Dave who was half-asleep in his bed in the semi-private detox room. We talked about his life, his family, and his reasons for being in the hospital. We seemed to connect on a deeply spiritual level, and I prided myself on the fact that I was really doing some good. Imagine my surprise when, the next time I saw Dave, he didn't recognize me or remember a single thing we'd discussed! His drug-induced stupor had wiped out his memory of the detox process. Most of my dealings with detoxifying patients ran in a similar fashion.

I was rapidly initiated into the world of alcoholism and drug addiction. I learned the hard way that addicts will say *anything* to procure their drugs. Once, a man swore to me that his grandfather had just died and that he had to be allowed out of the hospital to attend the funeral. He embellished his story with tears and sentimental details about dear old Gramps. When I shared his story with the head nurse, she rolled her eyes and promptly made a phone call to the man's family to confirm the death. Gramps had died all right—ten years earlier.

Within two months, I was volunteering two hours a day. Most of my duties involved doing intake interviews. That meant sitting with newly admitted patients and asking them questions about their family and addiction history based upon a "psycho-social questionnaire." One page of the questionnaire asked about their history of arrests. Almost every patient had an arrest history, some for very serious crimes. Eventually, instead of asking if a patient had ever been arrested, I'd ask, "How often have you been arrested and for what reasons?"

Once, I was alone in a counseling room conducting an intake interview with a man who seemed extremely edgy. When I got to the questions about arrests, he told me he'd been in prison for murder. I didn't ask him for details, but simply rushed through the remaining questions so I could get away from him. I asked him a question, and instead of answering, he stared straight into my eyes. He finally said, "You know what? You look just like my old girlfriend. The one who just left me!" That was enough for me to hear, and I hurriedly made excuses to leave. I rounded up a male psychiatric nurse, and he completed the questionnaire with the patient.

After volunteering for four months, I asked the CareUnit program management to hire me as a paid employee. They agreed, and I quit my secretarial job and began full-time work as a counselor. I had just received my associate of arts degree and was beginning night school for my bachelor's degree in psychology at Chapman University.

There are no coincidences, my father had always told me. I didn't know it at the time, but my Grandmother Pearl's brother Bill had died in the same Palmdale Hospital where I worked. While crossing a street near the hospital, he'd been hit by a car and brought to the emergency room, where he never recovered. Had I been brought to the same hospital to work out some family karma or to fulfill some unfinished business for Bill's spirit? I still don't know. The fact that two family members ended up at the same small hospital *many* miles from where we all lived amazes me.

I still had a burning desire to write self-help books, but I couldn't find a topic about which to write. At the time, I didn't think anyone would be interested in reading about alcoholism or drug addiction, as this was before Melodie Beattie and John Bradshaw wrote about family dysfunction and co-dependency. I kept wondering, "What topic would I like to read about that doesn't already have books published about it?"

My answer came like a thunderbolt that I know was divinely directed because it was such a complete vision. I saw that I would write a self-help book for parents enduring child custody battles. There was no such book at the time, although I sure could have used it years earlier. There was only one problem—my deep shame about my former noncustodial status. To write such a book authoritatively, I'd have to break my own confidentiality and discuss my experiences. I'd kept my secret for so long that it had grown into a hideous and distorted monster. I'd convinced myself that if any of my friends knew about my past noncustodial days, they would judge and reject me.

Finally, my deep desire to contribute a much-needed book won over my ego's fears. I purchased a manual called *How to Write a Book Proposal* by Michael Larsen[1], and decided to create a proposal for my self-help book. At first, I procrastinated writing. I wanted to be published so much that the pressure within me was almost painful. A part of me feared that I might die before publication. My quest wasn't so much for fame or fortune, but to make a difference in the world. I kept telling friends, "It doesn't matter whether my books are only found on Salvation Army bookshelves. At least there will be some evidence that I lived."

I'd made publication so important, such a crucial goal, that I deeply feared failure. If I kept my dream as an eternally future possibility, then I didn't have to face actually pursuing it and possibly failing. So every time I'd sit to type my book proposal, I'd think of something around the house that needed doing, such as the dishes, the vacuuming, or even cleaning the lint out from under the refrigerator. I became a compulsive cleaner to avoid the pain of possible rejection.

When I shared my frustrations with one of my psychology teachers, Ricki Gherardi, I hoped that she would sympathize with me. Instead, she kindly motivated me by saying, "You want to know the secret to getting your book written? Just write it." Her words rang in my ears as the truth that I needed to hear. I purchased a large calendar and created a writing schedule for myself. Each evening, after the boys went to sleep, I followed that schedule without question or compromise. When Dwight and our friends went to movies, restaurants, or parties, I said no if my schedule called for a night of writing.

My book proposal for *The Custody Crisis* was finally done, and I had an overview, chapter-by-chapter outline, and two sample chapters neatly typed. I photocopied the book proposal and sent it with a cover letter to four self-help book publishers I'd chosen from the *Writer's Market* book.[2]

Within a month, all four publishers rejected the proposal. I tried rationalizing, but I honestly felt as if *I'd* been rejected. I put my original book proposal in a desk drawer and sighed to myself, "I knew I wasn't meant to be a writer."

About a month later, however, I got a letter from Pepperdine University. They asked me to speak at their International Conference on Family Studies about child custody battles' effect upon parents' emotions and mental health. I'd forgotten that, two months earlier, I'd submitted to Pepperdine's "call for papers" request! The fact that Pepperdine was interested in the topic of my proposed book reignited my determination to get published.

This time, I figured I'd let the law of averages work in my favor. So I photocopied and sent book proposals to 40 publishers simultaneously. In my cover letter, I also mentioned my upcoming speech about child custody at the Pepperdine conference. I still remember the look of curiosity on the post office clerk's face as I walked in with 40 padded envelopes.

The next day at work, I told my supervising psychologist about my publication aspirations. He immediately retorted, "You'll never get published until you get your Ph.D.," as if it were a cut-and-dried fact. But I didn't let his words deter me. Besides, my proposals were already in the mail. I vowed to keep my goals to myself from then on—or, at least far from the ears of skeptics.

I went about my work while awaiting word from the publishers. By then, the CareUnit was having me conduct initial interviews with prospective patients. I would sit with people who, because of personal convictions, employer threats, or family pressures, were considered entering our treatment facility for a 30-day stay. Naturally, they were hesitant to commit to a month's treatment, worrying about insurance reimbursement, losing a month's worth of pay, being away from family, and most of all, being deprived of their drug of choice.

My job was to answer their questions and, if appropriate, encourage them to enter our program. Once, I was unable to convince an elderly man to check in for treatment, although his doctor and family warned him that his alcoholism was killing him. The following week, paramedics rushed the man to the emergency room of Palmdale General Hospital for complications related to alcohol overconsumption. The doctors tried to save him, but he died.

When I heard the news the next day, I was shocked and angry with myself for failing to convince this man to get treatment. I vowed to make something good come out of the tragedy. A few hours later, a man and his wife came to talk about the possibility of the husband entering the CareUnit. I decided to use what I'd learned in Norman Vincent Peale's book to extract my desired outcome.

As the man and his wife talked to me, I stared at him and willfully visualized him saying to me, "Yes, I will check into the CareUnit now." I mentally replayed this image repeatedly until I fully believed that he would check in. When, a few minutes later, the man said virtually the same words I'd imaged, I was a little startled. I then shared with him the story of the man who'd died of untreated alcoholism the previous night. He smiled and said that he was even more happy about his decision to seek treatment.

Yet, was it really his decision? A feeling of guilt washed over me as I realized I had probably influenced him with my visualization. In Christian Science testimonial meetings, I'd learned that they call such use of mind power "malpractice." We must be very sure of the purity of our motives for using mental power. While my desire not to see another alcoholic needlessly die was altruistic, I had combined it with willfulness in trying to manipulate another person's behavior. We can't know whether this man would have checked into the CareUnit despite my visualizations. However, I learned an important lesson that day: the end does not justify the means. Any goal that comes from the ego brings with it pain, even if the goal is honorable.

A favorite part of my job was spending time talking with the patients. A man once told me with solemn sincerity and great detail about the near-death experience he'd had. I listened attentively, yet didn't know what to make of his story. I'd heard of a book called *Life After Life* by Dr. Raymond Moody[3], and had even read an excerpt that had appeared in *The Reader's Digest.* The man asked, "Do you believe me?" I told him, "Yes," and relayed the story of my post-death encounter with my Grandpa Ben. Still, the man's near-death experience didn't seem relevant to my everyday life, so I simply forgot it.

I placed most of my attention on collecting information about a pattern I saw among the CareUnit patients. I'd noticed that the addicts whose drug of choice was cocaine had a markedly different personality than those who used marijuana, which was also different compared with those who used heroin, and so on. Even those who used a mixture of drugs, or who had no drug preferences, exhibited unique personality characteristics. I began writing down these observations in a file and logged other data about clients, such as their family history of addictions, their occupations, and their relationship patterns. Sometimes, I'd mentally play games with myself when talking to new patients. To myself, I'd guess their drug of choice before they could tell me, based upon their personality and occupation. I found that my guesses were nearly always correct. When I'd miss, I would pore over the indicators that had misled me.

I tried hard to understand my clients' motivations for drug use. After all, I'd had both intensely pleasant and also horrible experiences with marijuana and alcohol. And a part of me was raw and unhealed from the abuse I'd received from Larry's marijuana-induced mood swings. Sometimes I'd feel that marijuana was a personal dragon that I wanted to slay so that others wouldn't suffer the same sort of pain. Still, I knew that angry judgments wouldn't heal anyone from their addiction. Instead, I tried to get inside the head of my clients and see the world through their eyes. In this way, I hoped to speak in words that were meaningful to them.

I had a bit of difficulty empathizing with heroin addicts at first. The thought of sticking a needle in one's arm seemed horrifying to me. So I tried to focus on my client's emotions, instead of my judgments and fears about needles. Whenever a client would say the word *heroin,* I would mentally substitute an image of chocolate cake or ice cream. I couldn't relate to the thought of being drawn to heroin, but I could *definitely* empathize with being helplessly compelled to eat chocolate.

The role of counseling is a delicate balancing act. You are the teacher, but you are not superior to the student. In fact, the teacher who is open-minded constantly learns from his or her students. A counselor must remain objectively detached from the patient's emotions. Yet, the counselor's detachment cannot be so extreme as to prevent the student from receiving the counselor's love, which ultimately is the healing agent. And intuitive counseling, which is what I was doing whenever I'd "get inside a client's head," requires the counselor to have a dual awareness of her client's and her own thoughts and feelings.

At some level, I have to admit that I was judging some of my clients as weak. Yet, I was deluding myself by not facing the fact that my own pattern of compulsive overeating was just as much an addiction as their drug habits. Every evening, I'd walk out of the hospital unit feeling that I'd failed to fully help my clients that day. I'd always say to myself, "If only I knew more about psychology, then I could cure my clients' addictions." This unrealistic belief that I was responsible for rescuing my clients from their addictions led me to feel empty inside. I tried to fill this emptiness with external things, such as chocolate ice cream and cake, or with meaningless shopping excursions.

It struck me one day while I was wallowing in compulsive overeating that my clients were trying to better their lives. The thought, "At least they are getting help for their addictions!" went through my mind like a thunderbolt. After that, I had no choice but to get help for my own addiction.

My psychology teacher, Dan Matzke, worked at the CareUnit

with me. One of his class assignments had been for us students to attend and write about a 12-step meeting. Twelve-step meetings originally began when two alcoholic men used prayer and a set of thoughts and behaviors to abstain from drinking. Many people think that these steps were divinely inspired since, more than any other form of treatment, they have successfully helped people heal from addictions. The first 12-step group was Alcoholics Anonymous, and the same steps have been used successfully to treat drug addictions (Narcotics Anonymous, Cocaine Anonymous, and Marijuana Anonymous); psychological maladjustments (Emotions Anonymous); relationship problems related to loving an addict or alcoholic (Al-Anon); compulsive spending, gambling, or promiscuity (Debtors Anonymous, Gamblers Anonymous, and Sexual Addicts Anonymous); and eating disorders (Overeaters Anonymous).

Since my professor knew that part of my job at the CareUnit involved accompanying patients to Alcoholics Anonymous and Narcotics Anonymous meetings, he told me to choose another 12-step group for my class assignment. I arbitrarily picked Overeaters Anonymous (O.A.). I went to the group in an intellectual frame of mind, merely intending to observe the group as a detached student and not as a participant. When everyone attending the O.A. group introduced themselves as, "Hi, I'm so-and-so, and I'm a compulsive overeater," I simply said, "Hi, I'm Doreen, and I'm an observer." They smiled, nodded knowingly, and said, "Hi, Doreen." That night, I listened to the women and men in the group share their stories. Since I was in a judgmental and defensive mind frame, I callously decided that everyone in the room but me was nuts.

But the day I honestly admitted to myself that I was eating addictively, no different from my clients who used drugs in that fashion, I decided to give O.A. another try. This time, I listened to the group members with new ears, and everything they said started to make perfect sense to me. When they said that openly discussing one's food disorder had a therapeutic, humbling effect, I summoned the courage to publicly talk about my compulsive eating.

What a humbling experience! I recognized two of the O.A. group members as wives of my current CareUnit patients (it is common for compulsive overeaters to be married to alcoholics). I feared that if these women learned of my eating disorder, they would judge me, and my reputation at the CareUnit would be ruined. Nothing could have been further from the truth, I happily learned. Talking openly about my addiction to chocolate was an important step in helping me to recover from compulsive overeating.

I devoted my time and energy to my eating-disorder recovery—checking in with my "sponsor" (a person who has had long-term recovery and who serves as a mentor to newly recovering people) before every meal; reading every book I could find on the topic; and attending O.A. meetings. I also volunteered at the CareUnit's outpatient eating-disorder program. I felt an affinity to the women in that program who were struggling to let go of their food obsessions and asked my boss if I could transfer to the eating-disorders program. However, budget constraints didn't allow the small program to have another counselor on staff.

Still, my brief time volunteering on the eating-disorders unit sparked my desire to work full-time with compulsive overeaters, bulimics, and anorexics. Having identified this goal, I grew restless. A burning impatience deep inside my gut screamed at me: "Write books!" "Counsel the eating disordered!" "Break free from constraints and limitations!"

"But how?" I'd wonder late at night, when the stillness would leave me face-to-face with myself. "*How?*"

THE DIVINE PLAN

"By converging to unity, all things may be accomplished.
By the virtue which is without self-interest, even
the supernatural may be subdued."

— *Chuang Tzu 12,*
Taoist spiritual text

The pressure within me grew worse each time I set foot within the CareUnit. Although I was grateful for the knowledge I'd gained there, I knew it was time for me to leave and begin work in my chosen field of eating-disorders counseling. Even more, my gut ached with a longing to write books. Now that I had let go of my old overeating and binge-shopping compulsions, I had no way to deaden the pain of my unfulfilled dreams. I decided the only solution, the only way to seek relief from the incessant inner longing, was to work on making my dreams become a reality.

I decided to put my knowledge of visualization into practice. It had been nearly six weeks since I'd sent out 40 book proposals for *The Custody Crisis*. A few rejections had trickled in, and occasionally I'd lose faith that I would ever be published. Still, my desire for publication was incessant, so I turned to visualization half out of desperation. Just as I'd learned from my mom's instructions and from Norman Vincent Peale's book, I closed my eyes and imagined my dream being a present reality. I pictured my name on the spine of a published book, sitting on the shelf at the local B. Dalton Bookseller's store. For some reason, every time I'd conjure up this mental image, I'd see the rooster logo for Bantam Books above my name.

Deciding that this image was a sign, I collected all my old Bantam paperback books and cut out the rooster logo from them. I taped these roosters on my bathroom mirrors, my car dashboard, and the bulletin boards at my home and CareUnit offices. Then, I'd daily visualize seeing my name and the Bantam rooster on my book's spine as it sat on the B. Dalton bookshelf. As Dr. Peale had advised, I thanked God that this image was already a reality.

When a Bantam editor called a week later to say that he was interested in my book proposal, it somewhat stunned me. "This visualization really does work!" I told myself as I struggled to sound lucid while speaking with the editor. He explained that each proposed book had to pass approval of a committee of sales representatives, marketers, and senior editors. If my book made it through the committee, he'd call me back to negotiate an offer. Wow! I thought as I hung up the receiver. Thank you, God!

Visualization is based upon the Law of Cause and Effect, and whatever you see and believe forms a mold for your outer reality. In my meditations, I really saw and believed my book being published by Bantam. If you hold on to your faith and dreams, anything you see will eventually become a physical reality. However, if your faith wavers or your dreams constantly flit from one image to another, your reality will reflect this fear and confusion. And this is what happened to me.

The suddenness of my visualization's manifestation caught me off-guard. I started to think, I don't believe this! and this negation contaminated all the good work I had done. At some level, I didn't feel deserving of my dream. I would find out why many years later.

After that call from the Bantam editor, it seemed as if a floodgate opened. Every day I'd get rejection letters. I'd heard of authors posting rejection letters on their office walls like wallpaper. But each rejection letter seemed to contain a negative energy that repelled me. So I destroyed each one and then removed the refuse from my home right away. I made myself hold positive thoughts of my publication.

I soon discovered that rejections came as letters, while telephone calls delivered acceptances. Three more publishers called, each offering to buy my book on the spot. Since I was waiting to hear back from Bantam, I didn't want to commit to any other publisher, especially since they were much smaller than Bantam. Yet, I worried that I'd lose my "bird-in-the-hand" offers if I waited for Bantam too long. I asked the three publishers if I could have a little time to think about their offers, and they agreed. What would I do? Deep down, I doubted that Bantam would publish me. When two more weeks went by with no word from Bantam, I mustered the courage to call the editor for a status report. He told me that he was just writing me a letter explaining that my proposal was too similar to books already published by them.

This experience taught me the importance of keeping my focus upon the inner world. Manifesting requires allowing your beliefs about reality to flow *from* your inner mind's eye and *to* the outer world. As you are manifesting, pay no attention to the seeming obstacles that may pop up or else you will reverse the manifesting direction and flow. In other words, you will use pictures from the outer world to influence the pictures in your mind's inner eye.

My doubts about Bantam publishing me had influenced the outcome, just as my original affirmative thoughts had attracted the Bantam editor's initial interest. In meditation, I heard these explanatory words:

> *"Our thoughts are messengers and magnets. Guard them carefully and only choose thoughts of love and success. In this way, you ensure that you attract only love and success."*

Of course! I wasn't a victim of a hapless, cruel world that plays favorites with some people's lives. I had deliberately chosen my route with my thoughts. Instead of allowing myself to become depressed over Bantam's rejection—and messing up the three remaining offers I had with the other publishers—I visualized myself as happily negotiating a wonderful book contract. I talked with all three editors and ultimately went with the largest of them. The editor asked if I would change the book's title to *My Kids Don't Live with Me Anymore.* When I agreed, a deal was struck.

I was elated, but also very aware of the huge responsibility I had just taken on. I had to write 250 pages within 6 months. Even more, much of the writing would involve openly divulging some of my more painful memories. Nevertheless, I set up a specific writing schedule for myself.

About this time, I was halfway through taking night-school classes to complete my master's degree in counseling psychology. I had become fast friends with several classmates, including a woman named Judy Wisehart. Judy had a metaphysical background similar to my own, yet she'd also done independent study on Eastern meditation, hypnosis, and neurolinguistic programming (NLP). Her husband, Robert, had taken classes at the University of California at Santa Cruz on esoteric religions and philosophies. He'd also been a pupil of one of NLP's originators.

Robert was a natural-born teacher who always wore white, which complemented his pale gray hair and beard. I invited Robert and Judy to my house and asked if they would give private instruction to me, my husband Dwight, and a few of our close friends. They agreed, so one weekend a month, we held classes in my living room.

In Robert's classes, I learned about and experienced past-life regressions and various hypnotic and meditative practices. I had been curious about hypnosis ever since seeing a stage hypnotist perform at a high school assembly. Once when attending a show at the Del Mar Fair (in Del Mar, California) with my parents, a hypnotist asked for audience participants. When I asked my mother if I could volunteer, she explained that Christian Scientists did not participate in hypnosis. My father agreed with my mother and added that if one was ever hypnotized, he or she would forever be gullible to others' suggestions.

I never thought again about hypnosis until my conversations with Robert and Judy resparked my long-forgotten interest in the subject. I still wanted to learn about and experience hypnosis so I could draw my own conclusions. I ultimately found hypnosis to be both relaxing and stimulating. Far from leaving me a vulnerable sop, hypnosis helped me focus my mind sharply upon my goals. I enjoyed each of Robert and Judy's classes immensely and decided to share what I'd learned with the CareUnit patients.

My CareUnit psychological supervisor agreed to let me conduct group relaxation and hypnosis sessions with the patients. Each afternoon, interested patients would gather in the "Day Room" lounge and lay upon fold-out mats. Sometimes I'd be startled by the sight of hardened former criminals and tough-looking addicts lying like children on kindergarten-style mats. I'd begin each session with an explanation of hypnosis and progressive relaxation. Occasionally, a patient would defiantly say, "There's no way you're going to put me under!" I found that patients who made such remarks were usually the first to go under during the group process.

The patients and my co-workers deemed the group hypnosis experiences successful, and this further boosted my self-confidence. I decided it was time to leave the nest and fly on my own. One of my college classmates, Melinda, told me of an opening for a program director job at an adolescent alcohol and drug addiction outpatient facility where she worked. I applied for and got the job, and although I still wasn't working with eating disorders as I'd dreamed about, the new job felt like a step in the right direction. I loved working with the teenagers, and the work helped me heal from the wounds I still carried from my alcohol and marijuana abuse.

The size of the teenage program rapidly doubled, and word spread in the community about the program's clinical and business success. A local psychiatrist asked to meet me to discuss the work I was doing. When our discussion turned to my possibly opening an outpatient eating-disorder center for him, I was both thrilled and frightened. Again, my visualization was manifesting into form. And, as before, when the Bantam editor had called, I was unsure that I was prepared to accept the dream as a reality.

I decided to learn from my past mistake with the Bantam editor, however, so I kept my thoughts and actions steadily fixed on my vision of treating eating-disordered clients. Although my decision to leave the adolescent program was not well received by my boss, co-workers, and clients, I knew I had to seize the opportunity. One of my colleagues whom I highly respected even cautioned me against going to work for the psychiatrist. "He's got a horrible reputation for mistreating people," my friend said knowingly. Still, I had to trust my gut feelings that signaled me to make the move.

I now know that the most reliable advice we can ever receive comes from our intuitions and gut feelings. People often ask me how to know if a feeling is truly "intuitive." They tell me about incidents where they've listened to their inner voice, only to find out later that they'd made a mistake. There are big differences between the true inner guide and the voice of the ego. First, inner-guide instructions are loving and positive, while the ego's advice is based in fear, contempt, and beliefs in scarcity. The inner guide occasionally tells us to take sudden action, but it never uses fear tactics or belittling words. Second, the inner guide's voice usually leaves you with a feeling of certainty, and you just *know* that you must follow your intuition.

If you don't heed your inner voice, it will patiently repeat the advice until you are ready to hear it. The ego's guidance, in contrast, urges you to make impulsive decisions in its quest for temporary adrenaline rushes. The ego changes its "mind" constantly, and if you follow it, your life will be chaotic and crisis-filled. Some people like this sort of roller coaster lifestyle, mostly because if you constantly have a fire to put out, you don't have to think about fulfilling your life purpose.

Of course, we each have a purpose or mission in life. It is the reason we incarnated on this planet. As lightworkers, we volunteered to come during the crucial earth times before and after the year 2000 to spread our loving energies and to dissipate destructive mass consciousness. Most of us came for the specific purpose of using our knowledge of healing to teach, write, counsel, heal, or enlighten others on Earth.

We each created a basic life plan for ourselves before incarnation. However, we made this life plan while we were fully in our "true self" state of mind. After incarnation, we got trapped in thoughts about materiality, and our ego mind developed. Yet, every lightworker with whom I've spoken always tells me how they know, deep down, that they are here on Earth for a higher purpose. When this purpose remains dormant, a horribly painful pressure bubbles in one's solar plexus, near the stomach. There's a terrible feeling that you are forgetting to do something—which you are, if you are not working on fulfilling your life purpose.

I hadn't even realized how long I had carried this sort of pressure around in my own solar plexus until the day that my published book arrived in the mail. I held the freshly printed copy of *My Kids Don't Live with Me Anymore* as gingerly as a newborn baby. Seeing my name on a book felt surreal, and I felt detached from the book as if it had a life of its own, apart from me. I knew that I wasn't its creator. Spirit was. Yet, realizing that I had participated in something that would help many people felt like a huge relief, both physically and emotionally. The fear I'd held on to—that I would die or otherwise be prevented from fulfilling this mission—rushed out of my body and has never returned.

That fear, I learned while counseling people and through meditative contemplation, is both paralyzing and rampant among lightworkers. One of the greatest fears that we lightworkers suffer from, perhaps the only fear, is that we won't fulfill the purpose for which we came to Earth. This fear, ironically, binds us to the point where we forget what our purpose is. This is important for lightworkers to understand, because so many of us feel that we are the only ones who suffer from fear and confusion.

The circumstances behind the life purpose creation were later explained to me in my meditations:

> *"Before your birth, you and a spiritual council of guides created a life plan tailored to meet your material, spiritual, and karmic needs. This Divine plan has three elements: a purpose, personal growth lessons, and relationships with other people to support the overall plan.*
>
> *"Your purpose is a task you are to do through your career, volunteer work, or a special project that uses your natural talents and interests to benefit humanity. Your plan's second element entails well-timed life events that teach you about love and help you to shed self-defeating personality traits. The third element involves pre-birth arrangements you made with certain people who will serve as catalysts for your purpose and personal growth. These people may function as your family members, co-workers, friends, or acquaintances. Your interactions with these people simultaneously help them to fulfill their own plans.*
>
> *"You predestined your plan as a rough outline of what your life would look like, including your purpose, significant life lessons, and relationships with particular people. Because the plan is only a rough outline, you must choose the finer details of your plan as you go through life. You are free to ignore the plan completely, but the emotional and societal consequences of this choice can be devastating."*

In our previous incarnations, many of us didn't fulfill our purposes. During our post-death life reviews, we felt ashamed that fears and material desires thwarted our plan. This lifetime, we swear to ourselves before birth, we won't forget our purpose. The trouble is, we design the Divine plan in a "true self" state of peaceful mindfulness. When we experience ego-based fear during our human lifetime, we can't remember why we came here. If we do remember, fears keep us from ever starting our plan.

Those who procrastinate or forget their plans, as I had, feel a deep, low-level anxiety. They unconsciously know another painful life review awaits them if they let themselves down again. They feel depressed, as if they're forgetting to do something important—which they are. Many lightworkers have faint ideas or gut feelings about the life they are supposed to be living. Yet they feel undeserving or unqualified to follow their intuitive urges. They may try to muffle the volume of their intuition by pouring food, alcohol, or addictive behaviors on their gut feelings. However, there's not enough substance in the world to dim the inner urges to take steps toward fulfilling the plan. The only choice available to lightworkers is to stop giving air time to our egos, and to allow our healed true self to shine forth. *The planet is depending upon us!*

So much changed for me after my book was published. If you sense that your divine plan involves writing a book, let me encourage you to put energy into that endeavor. The first thing I noticed, beyond the huge release of anxiety, was that my childhood clairvoyance began to return. When this initially happened, though, I didn't know what to make of it.

I began seeing what was going to occur about 30 seconds ahead of time. Whenever I drove, for example, I intuitively knew what the drivers ahead of me were going to do. I'd first see a driver turning left in my mind's eye. Then, half a minute later, he'd turn left.

When I was with the clients at my new eating-disorders clinic, I could see pictures of what they were about to describe to me before they'd voice the words. I'd see very clear visual images of the foods they had overeaten. For instance, if a client had gone on an ice cream-eating binge, I'd see a big double-scoop cone or a similar symbol next to her before she'd tell me about the binge.

This clairvoyance allowed me to listen to clients without taking many notes. My clients consistently complimented me on my ability to "remember" all the details about their lives. Yet, I wasn't *remembering* their circumstances. I was just tuning in and mentally reviewing movie clips of their lives. I could actually *see* what was bothering them, and this insight allowed my clients and me to get to core issues rapidly.

Many of my clients had histories of child abuse, particularly sexual abuse. At times, I intuitively knew the emotional struggles of abuse so well that I could practically describe how my client felt without her saying a word. More than once, I wondered, How do I know what it feels like to be a child-abuse survivor? Did I repress a memory of abuse from my own childhood? Yet, I could clearly recall every year of my life. Instead of repression, I was experiencing clairsentience or "clear feeling."

I didn't tell anyone about my psychic awareness, partly because I wasn't sure what to make of it myself. Only once did I share an instance of prescience with anyone, and that was accidental. I told my friend Melinda of an odd dream I'd had the previous night in which I saw a store full of cheese that was poisonous. The day after I told her about my dream, national headlines announced a big recall of a certain cheese contaminated with poisonous bacteria. Melinda thought that my dream's psychic nature had been exceptional. But instead of being happy about the incident, I turned away from looking at it.

After all, so often as a child I had learned not to discuss psychic or spiritual phenomena. My family's code was never to discuss miracle healings publicly. With a few exceptions, whenever I had told anyone about our Christian Science practice, they had ridiculed me. And when I had told my mother about the people I was "seeing" (whom I now know to be deceased), she had assured me that it was my imagination or a reflection from the television set. I didn't feel safe to discuss my prescience with anyone. I barely wanted to admit it to myself.

Instead, I focused on my clinical research about eating disorders. When I had worked at the CareUnit, I had noted a correlation between my clients' personality traits and their drugs of choice. The same clear pattern was emerging before me in my eating-disordered clients. Those who binged upon bread were quite different in temperament than those who binged upon ice cream, and so on. I began researching this phenomenon and found that each "binge food"—such as chocolate, dairy products, baked goods, and nuts—contained mood- and energy-altering properties. My clients intuitively chose the exact food that would alleviate their specific emotional issue.

For example, I found that the chemical and textural properties of many dairy products have antidepressant effects. Not coincidentally, my clients who suffered from depression craved dairy products. Further, the specific type of dairy product, say, ice cream with nuts, had even more detailed correlations with my clients' specific emotional traits. This is because ice cream with nuts has chemicals that not only boost a depressed mood but which also trigger the pleasure center of the brain.

I began to ask my clients at the beginning of our sessions what their food cravings were as a way to guide our therapy to the target issues. Several years later, I wrote about this system of food-craving analysis in a book called *Constant Craving: What Your Food Cravings Mean and How to Overcome Them.*

My clinic's patient population began to boom, and I was quickly overwhelmed with more patients than I had time to treat. Diana Whitfield, a friend of mine who had worked with me at the CareUnit, came to help me at the clinic. Still, so many people at our clinic were healing from food obsessions that word-of-mouth generated more clients than we both could handle.

During this time, I got a sudden intuitive directive. Most of the time, our intuition guides us in tiny successive increments. Occasionally, however, we receive inner instruction as one whole and complete idea. I got this type of intuitive message one day, and I knew that it was time for me to write another book. I also knew that it would be called *The Yo-Yo Diet Syndrome*, about emotional causes and cures for weight fluctuations, and that it would be a very successful book. All this information just popped into my mind one day. I was so certain of its inevitability that I talked about my book, *The Yo-Yo Diet Syndrome,* at speeches and in a couple of newspaper articles in which I was interviewed.

Manifestation requires faith. Usually, we have more faith that our fears will turn into reality than we have faith in our happy dreams becoming real. The only reason that manifestation feels difficult is that sometimes we feel that we must strain to make our dreams come true. With *The Yo-Yo Diet Syndrome*, however, my vision for the book came complete with full faith. I didn't wrestle with any doubts or fears. I just knew that it would occur, and now I realize that the unfailing Law of Cause and Effect propelled it into existence.

Going completely on my gut instincts, I decided to secure a literary agent to negotiate a book contract for *The Yo-Yo Diet Syndrome*. Something told me to look in the "Acknowledgment" section of a weight-loss book in my library, and I found that the authors thanked a particular agent. I looked up the agent's telephone number and address in a book in the library's reference section called *Literary Marketplace*.[1] Next, I called the agency and asked the receptionist for their submission information. The woman sharply told me, "Oh, we never accept new clients unless they are referred by an existing client."

I contemplated what to do next, and decided to call my uncle Lee Reynolds for advice. Perhaps, since he was a Hollywood screenwriter, Uncle Lee would know someone at the agency who could recommend me as a client. He told me that, yes, he was very tightly associated with the agency. However, he persuaded me to send a query letter first. "The receptionist's job is to screen people." Uncle Lee added, "Don't let her scare you from your dream."

With this, I drafted a one-page letter. Before mailing it, I ceremoniously circled my hand above the envelope and said a prayer. One week later, the agent called and asked to see my book proposal. So I wrote nonstop until I was satisfied that I'd written the best possible proposal. As I mailed the manuscript to the agent, I surrounded it with prayers again.

Two days later, the agent called. Would I please come to Beverly Hills and join her for lunch? I did, and afterward I had coffee with Uncle Lee to celebrate my successfully signing with the literary agency.

My agent sold the book by auction, and one publisher who bid for *The Yo-Yo Diet Syndrome* was Bantam Books. I still had the little rooster on my bathroom mirror and hadn't abandoned the vision of my name on a book spine under the Bantam rooster. However, Bantam's bid wasn't high enough, and Harper & Row paid a very large advance to win the contract.

I happily began writing my new book. Writing has always been one of my favorite pastimes. To feel that you are making a difference in the world, and to get paid to do something you love, is a miracle. I had also discovered, when writing my first book, how cathartic it is to write about your painful moments. In fact, existential therapists such as Viktor Frankl believe that happiness and mental health are contingent upon our ability to find meaning in our lives.[2] We do this when we turn a tragedy into something purposeful, such as teaching others our hard-won lessons. When I wrote about my struggles with food and weight in *The Yo-Yo Diet Syndrome*, I had the same sort of existential release.

With my book advance, my psychotherapy income, and my husband's salary, we were very financially secure. We moved to a new custom home in Quartz Hill, ten miles outside Lancaster.

Yet, although our material life was set, I felt stressed due to my hectic schedule divided between long days at the clinic, time with family, attending night school, and completing my new book. Additionally, the publicity demands for my first book had been nonstop since its publication. Already, I'd appeared on several national television and radio shows, and calls for new talk-show appearances came in daily.

While unpacking boxes at our new home, a crumpled piece of paper fell at my feet. I smoothed the sheet and recognized it as an assignment given in a sociology class several years before. During a lecture about goal-setting, our professor had asked each class member to write ten specific five-year goals. At the time, I didn't see how I could possibly achieve any of them. Yet, I had accomplished each one: child custody regained; a book published; my college degrees completed; a brand-new home; a new Mercedes; a private psychotherapy practice; frequent Hawaiian vacations; body weight in a certain range; television appearances on "Donahue" and other talk shows; and a specific amount of money in savings. My professor's theory of the necessity of writing goals on paper had been correct.

An uneasiness at the thought that I had everything I wanted washed over me. You should feel on top of the world, I scolded myself. But I honestly didn't. Something was wrong, and I needed to discover what. I hastily arranged for a family vacation to Maui, where I could be away from ringing telephones and clinical pressures. I needed to spend time among the fragrant flowers and think about my life.

"A NEW DOOR WILL OPEN"

"The Self within the heart is like a boundary
which divides the world from That. Wherefore he
who has crossed that boundary, and has realized the Self;
if he is blind, ceases to be blind; if he is wounded,
ceases to be wounded; if he is afflicted,
ceases to be afflicted."

— *Chandogya Upanishad,*
Hindu spiritual text

When we arrived in Oahu, we boarded a small "island hopper" jetliner bound for Maui. The long flight from the mainland had drained me. Since the Maui flight had no prearranged seating, I plopped down in a first-row seat. The boys and Dwight decided to sit in the back of the aircraft for the short flight.

A tanned, white-haired man sat next to me and we chatted briefly about the islands. As is customary for airplane seatmates, we also discussed our occupations. I told him about my psychotherapy practice and book writing, and we discovered that his daughter and I attended the same college. Then I asked what he did for a living.

Hesitantly, he said, "Well, I do seminars of a sort." This sparked my interest, as I frequently conducted seminars myself.

"What sort of seminars?" I asked.

Again, he seemed reluctant to answer. Finally, he looked at me and asked, "Have you ever heard of the Crystal Cathedral?"

"Of course," I replied. "You mean Robert Schuller's?"

"Yes. I am Robert Schuller," he said without a hint of pride or arrogance.

I felt awkward that I hadn't recognized his famous face with its distinctive nose and eyes. Yet, during my book tour, I'd met many movie and television stars. When they are off-camera, without makeup and with their charisma turned down several notches, famous people don't often resemble their on-screen selves.

For the next 20 minutes of the flight, I opened up to Dr. Schuller about my confusion over my life's direction. I told him that, at age 30, I had accomplished every goal I'd set for myself. Now I had no new goals, and felt empty and fearful about facing a future without knowing where I was going. He told me about his own life crossroads and how he'd resolved his difficult moments through faith and prayer.

Without sermonizing, Dr. Schuller gently encouraged me to trust in life's process. "A new door will soon open for you, Doreen," he reassured me. "Meanwhile, don't worry that you don't know what is next for yourself. When the door opens, you will *know* it is the right one for you." When the plane landed, Dr. Schuller and I hugged, and I felt renewed hope. God had arranged for the perfect seatmate at the perfect time for me.

I decided to take Dr. Schuller's advice and have faith that a door would open before me.

I concluded that the best way to find my door was to stop setting goals, and instead see what life would bring me. After all, this was my second experience in achieving all my goals (the first time was when I'd achieved popularity in school). Both times, I had expected that my achievements would create happiness equivalent to the heavens opening up and angels singing. In reality, my achievements had felt disappointingly ordinary. I had reacted to those disappointments by "upping the ante" of my new goals, thinking, Well, being on "Donahue" wasn't it. Maybe if

I'm on "Oprah," *that* will make the difference. So I'd set a new goal, achieve it, and find that no matter how high a peak I climbed, it didn't create lasting satisfaction.

My new goal, after meeting Dr. Schuller, was happiness. I knew happiness was possible, since I'd experienced it. But this time, I wanted it to last.

Soon after returning home from Maui, my agent sold my third book, and this time, Bantam Books was the successful bidder. I believe that my decision to surrender all my goals to God had something to do with my Bantam visualization finally manifesting into form.

Usually, the author gets a first glimpse of the finished book when the publisher sends some complimentary copies. With this book, however, I first saw the book during a shopping excursion. My son Chuck needed some new shoes, and we'd gone over to the mall one evening. As we walked by a B. Dalton Bookseller, we stopped to see whether they carried my books. I caught my breath as a glistening brown book spine caught my attention. There, in front of me, was a tangible copy of the mental visualization I'd held for so long. A beaming fire engine-red Bantam rooster stood above my name on the spine, on the shelf at B. Dalton, just as I had imaged for nearly four years.

Visualizations can instantly outpicture into reality if our minds accept this as a possibility. We do this all the time, such as when we make a grocery store list and then get the items from the list. We never question, "Will I be able to get the cream of mushroom soup on my list?" Instead, we accept that it will happen.

However, when we feel afraid or undeserving of an image coming true, we often try to force the dream into reality. Our visualizations become tense and pressure-filled, as if we're trying to squeeze matter out of the ethers. This is how I had been operating on my Bantam rooster logo visualizations, and my tension was blocking the goal's fruition. It was as if I'd written a request to God, but then refused to give it to Him. But when I surrendered the vision completely, it could come about.

"There is no order of difficulty in miracles," says *A Course in Miracles.*[1] This means that one miracle is no harder to manifest than another, unless we believe it to be so. Our judgments of, "Oh, this goal is too high for me to achieve," or "I couldn't possibly attain that," create the tension that bars us from manifesting our inner visions.

I started to see the delicate balancing act of goal manifestation. On the one hand, we all have a strong drive to create and to serve a meaningful life purpose. Since we were created in the image and likeness of an eternally creative Creator, this makes perfect sense. However, our health and happiness depend upon our keeping our heart centered on Spirit and not on the material world.

Simultaneously, I noticed that my eating-disordered and addicted clients' compulsions masked deep fears and depression about their own unfulfilled life purposes. Many of my clients knew what they wanted to be doing with their lives. However, false beliefs such as "I don't have enough time, money, intelligence, good looks, connections, education, or talent to make my dream a reality," kept them from even trying. Still, their inner voice nagged them to fulfill their purposes. But instead of listening to that voice, my clients tried to silence it by pouring food, alcohol, or other compulsive behaviors on top of the gut feelings.

I found that whenever a client would abstain from compulsions, she would begin to remember her life purpose. Her inner voice would urge her to take certain steps toward fulfilling this goal. If she would then take these steps, her cravings for her compulsion would heal. However, some clients—terrified or intimidated by their inner voice's urging—would run back to their compulsions to cover their higher selves' voice.

My clinical work and book publicity tours often involved traveling to different areas of the country to conduct hospital staff in-services and to give lectures. Along the way, I accepted a job as an administrator at an all-women's psychiatric hospital in

Woodside, near San Francisco.

Dwight and I had recently ended our seven-year marriage, for so many reasons that it would be too difficult to briefly summarize them. I only want to say that my divorce was extremely painful. Whenever my clients tell me they are thinking of getting a divorce, I caution them to explore their reasons for wanting to end their marriage. Too often, we look to externals—such as getting married or getting divorced—to fill the emptiness within us. Nothing external can quench our inner longings for love. Only heavenly love, from within, fills the void.

As a newly single mother, the boys and I felt a sense of adventure as we moved to the Bay Area. We found a lovely home near an elementary school. Daily, I'd commute to the hospital on the Dumbarton Bridge across the bay.

The hospital where I worked specialized in treating female abuse survivors who suffered from eating disorders and other addictions. With its Susan Rios-like setting of lavish gardens and white wicker furniture with cabbage rose cushions, the hospital was a popular retreat for San Francisco women. We rarely had empty beds and usually had a waiting list of potential patients.

My sons and I were home when the San Francisco earthquake of 1989 hit. As a California native, I'd endured many earthquakes and had a nonchalant attitude toward them. But this earthquake was in an entirely different category! I watched with horror as the tile entryway and walls of my house buckled and bent like a wrist watchband. I held on to Grant tightly and heard Chuck screaming in his bedroom. I felt helpless not being able to reach him. I couldn't do anything except hold on to Grant and pray that the earthquake would soon be over. With other natural disasters, you can run away or seek shelter. But when the very earth beneath you shudders, there is no way to escape.

Several months later, I appeared in a national infomercial related to *The Yo-Yo Diet Syndrome*, which we filmed in Nashville. The infomercial's film director became my friend, and he introduced me to the marketing director of a Nashville psychiatric hospital. The woman and I hit it off, and she was excited about the success of my California psychiatric hospital. Her hospital administrators offered to open a similar all-women's psychiatric unit in Nashville. Still reeling from the earthquake, the boys didn't object when I suggested another move.

For the next two years, I stayed busy overseeing a hospital unit I'd named "WomanKind," and my work entailed administration, marketing, and patient treatment. Every afternoon, I drove to Nashville's Music Row to host a daily radio talk show at WSIX. Evenings usually found me giving speeches to local civic organizations.

My therapeutic work in Nashville focused upon patients who were child-abuse survivors. The cultural differences between California and the South, in which incest seemed more prevalent, unsettled me. Many patients also suffered from negative self-images that seemingly sprang from regional stereotypes about women. I wrote newspaper articles, gave speeches, and did radio broadcasts urging Southern women to give up their be-every-thing-to-everyone ambitions. I'm sure my Yankee viewpoints hackled a few Southern feathers. Still, I was concerned about women who were driven by guilt and low self-esteem.

At the end of two years, I returned to California and decided to write more books and magazine articles. One of my overriding interests then was love relationships. My dating experiences since my divorce had been trying and challenging. I deeply wanted a long-term, committed relationship, but not at the high cost of being with an incompatible partner. Breakups and divorce are so painful, and I didn't want to rush into a new relationship. Yet, I also longed for companionship.

My parents' own marriage had taught me that real love—deeply romantic, tinged with best-friendship, and founded upon trust and fidelity—was possible. I had also experienced clinical successes with many of my patients' counseling sessions. I'd seen many instances of how wonderful love could be, and I wanted that experience for myself.

Almost on a lark, I decided to experiment with metaphysical principles to see if I could manifest the relationship for which I was searching. I set out to manifest Mr. Right in the same way I'd manifested successes in my career. So I wrote a two-page list of all the characteristics important to me in a mate and in a relationship. I left out any details that didn't matter to me and only concentrated on traits that I felt were crucial.

Then, I closed my eyes and gently affirmed that if he truly was my dream man, the person on my list would also love me exactly as I was. I also stated that he was looking for me right then with as much fervor as I longed for him. Then I released the situation, in full faith, to the universe, and put my list in a file drawer.

Within a few days, I received gut feelings to go to certain places and call specific people out of my ordinary routines. Sometimes I'd ignore these intuitions, but they would eventually hound me until I'd comply. All these gut-directed activities eventually culminated in my walking into a French restaurant near my home where I bumped into a man in the entryway. When I first saw Michael, I felt time slow down and saw the room around me spin into a blur. He invited me to sit with him and have a glass of mineral water, and we talked as if we were interviewing one another. At the end of our time together that evening, I knew that Michael was the man on my list. We became inseparable after our first meeting.

Subsequently, I began writing books and articles about love relationships. One of the magazines for which I penned articles, *Complete Woman,* made me a contributing editor. I also began appearing on talk shows as the "Love Doctor," giving advice about relationships. A literary agent in New York City who handles top relationship authors encouraged me to keep going with this genre. Shortly after completing some books about relationships, however, I knew that my heart was not in it. I wanted to write solely about spiritual principles of healing the mind, body, and emotions.

I decided to write a book about the reams of research and case studies I'd accumulated on eating disorders' link to child abuse. So I stopped doing clinical work and compiled the data into a book proposal called *Losing Your Pounds of Pain*. I needed the time off, and it was one of my better decisions. The contrasts between my deepest spiritual beliefs and the psychological treatment philosophies that I'd learned to use in my clinical work had bothered me lately. I needed to reconcile the two before returning to counseling work.

My spiritual beliefs are that we can create whatever we desire. In fact, whatever we concentrate upon always outpictures in the physical plane. This is the basic Law of Cause and Effect. It was also why I was conflicted. Psychology asked me to violate this law by having my clients concentrate upon their problems. Therapists and other healers are trained to ask their clients what is wrong, then analyze these problems. Such a focus initially makes problems grow, however.

I often witnessed instances in which my own clients and those of my peers would describe, for instance, a relationship problem. The therapist would spend hours with the client working on this problem. Nine times out of ten, the relationship would immediately worsen in response to this focus. The therapist would reassure the client that this worsening meant she was "out of denial" over the problem and was finally seeing the relationship clearly.

"That's not what I was raised to believe!" I realized one day. I was taught to focus on the truth of a situation and to declare always that we are all perfect, whole, and complete and that only love is real. This focus allowed harmony to grow and replace the so-called problem. Yet, how would my clients react if I suddenly began telling them that they were perfect? What would they say if I reassured them that they were wholly loved, lovable, and loving? I worried that they would run, screaming, out of my office—similar to the jibes and rejection I'd suffered as a child. I was afraid to come out of the spiritual closet, so I dropped out instead.

THE PRESENCE

"Life is something spiritual.
The form may be destroyed; but the spirit remains
and is living, for it is the subjective life."

— Paracelsus (1493–1541),
alchemist and physician[1]

I was at my parents' mountaintop home near Paradise, California, when Reid Tracy, the vice president of Hay House publishers, invited me to lunch to discuss the book proposal I'd sent him. When my mother heard this news, we both shrieked with delight, as we're huge fans of Louise Hay (the founder and publisher of Hay House) and her work.

The following week, I sat in a restaurant booth with Reid, and Dan Olmos, Hay House's editorial director. I instantly felt at ease with both men. When Reid said that the wording of my book proposal sounded like words that Louise would use, I knew I'd found the right publishing house. We discussed our metaphysical backgrounds and struck an agreement that Hay House would publish *Losing Your Pounds of Pain*. I was delighted.

Soon after beginning work on the book, I called Dan to ask him a question. The Hay House receptionist sounded flustered when I asked for him, and I heard my call being transferred to a different extension. Expecting to hear Dan pick up the phone, I was confused when I heard a woman's voice instead. "They must have transferred me to the wrong extension," I said. "I was calling Dan Olmos."

There was silence on the other line. Then the woman asked, "Didn't anyone tell you?"

"Tell me what?"

"Dan Olmos passed away. I'm your new editor." Jill Kramer explained that Dan had died after a lengthy illness, on the very first day she'd begun working at Hay House. Jill and Dan had been friends for years, and Jill believed that Dan "let himself leave the planet" when he was assured that someone he knew and trusted would be taking over his position. As editorial director, Jill would later prove to be a remarkable friend to me and my books. However, while I was writing *Losing Your Pounds of Pain*, I found that Dan wasn't quite ready to pass along the blue editorial pencil.

I'd never given much thought to life after death, which seems remarkable considering my grandfather Ben's after-death visit to me. Yet, while writing the book, Dan's presence was palpable physically and mentally. Each time I would pull the book up on my computer screen, I could feel an air-pressure change just above my left-hand shoulder. And, just as you can sense the presence of someone in the room, even to the point of knowing who it is, I could clearly feel Dan next to me.

Even more, I could hear Dan's words in my mind. Dan gave much of the philosophy in the book to me, and he dictated beautiful messages about the role forgiveness plays in healing our pain. They were messages I had never before heard or thought of. I knew from my clinical work that most abuse survivors blamed themselves for parts of their experiences. I also knew that honesty about this self-blame was crucial to recovering from the emotional pain of abuse.

However, I had never heard of the importance of forgiveness during my years attending church or university classes. Yet, Dan told me that self-forgiveness was the key to healing the wounds of child abuse. Most abuse survivors are unwilling to forgive their abusers; but by forgiving themselves, they are able to heal since there is only one mind in truth. He told me to write an affirmation that would heal abuse survivors: *"I forgive, accept, and trust myself."* These were the beautiful messages Dan gave the readers of *Losing Your Pounds of Pain*. From reading the letters I receive, it's clear to me that Dan's message has positively affected many people's lives.

I didn't tell many people about my heavenly editor because I still wasn't sure what I thought about life after death myself. It's odd how we can compartmentalize our logic, isn't it? On the one hand, I knew that Ben really had visited me after his death. There had never been one sliver of doubt in my mind! And I also knew that Dan was guiding my writing. But I also didn't make the leap in logic that, ergo, there was life after death.

Growing up, I often heard my mother, Sunday school teachers, and church members say, "Death is an illusion," and "There is no death." I had always assumed that this meant that we could extend the human body's life indefinitely through prayer. Now I realize that they meant that the soul never dies and is eternal. Our bodies may wither, but *we*—that is, the true person inside the body—lives forever.

After the publication of *Losing Your Pounds of Pain*, its success pleasantly surprised all of us. I suppose, however, we should have expected it. After all, our heavenly help extends from start to completion on any divinely inspired project. God doesn't just give us a good idea and then leave us on our own to finish it. He gives us the complete package.

I appeared on several talk shows, including "Oprah," while promoting the book. The talk-show hosts and audiences always gravitated toward one part of the book in which I'd briefly described my research on the emotional meanings of our food cravings. Each food we crave corresponds with a specific feeling we want to soothe or mask with food. My book had included a small sample of specific food cravings and their corresponding meanings. Consistently, this is what the talk-show hosts wanted to discuss.

The same thing had happened during my speeches and talk-show appearances for *The Yo-Yo Diet Syndrome* years earlier. Each time I'd mention to audience members that I could "interpret" the meaning behind their food cravings, they would clamor for more information. I described these occurrences to Reid and Jill at Hay House, and together we decided that a book devoted solely to this topic was in order.

Meanwhile, Bonnie Krueger, editor-in-chief of *Complete Woman* magazine, asked if I would interview an author of a book with which she'd fallen in love. "It's called *Embraced by the Light*.[2] I've bought dozens of copies and I'm giving them to everyone I know," Bonnie explained. "Would you please find and interview the book's author, Betty Eadie?"

Although I'd noticed *Embraced by the Light* on the *New York Times* bestseller list, I didn't know much about it. Betty Eadie's publicist set up an appointment for me to interview her at the Whole Life Expo in Los Angeles. Michael accompanied me to take photographs for the magazine, and my son, Grant, decided to come along as well.

We were set to interview Betty following her Friday night lecture, so we sat in the audience and listened to her talk. I had read her book and press material in preparation for the interview. But while listening to her, I felt that Betty spoke on an even higher level than the writing in her book. She described the inner light within each of us, and how we can brighten its glow by our awareness of love's ever-presence. Her speaking style enthralled me, as she combined power with gentleness, and strength with feminine beauty. She was a model of peacefulness, I thought as I watched her speak. Dressed in a beautiful white, Indian-style flowing dress, she glowed with the same light about which she spoke.

Her words resonated some long-neglected areas in my psyche. Like a machine rusted from disuse, I felt a part of my consciousness sleepily respond to Betty's talk. This part of me, which had been fully awake during my younger days, had hibernated for many years. As I sat in Betty's lecture, dressed in an uptight navy blue suit and white polyester blouse, I suddenly felt alien in my own skin.

I felt even more awkward when I interviewed Betty after her lecture. She was kind and generous with her time. Still, I could sense a distance between us as she responded to my tension. I later replayed the tape of our interview three times as I wrote the article for *Complete Woman.* Each time, I'd hear new meanings in Betty's words.

I realized I'd lost a great deal of my spiritual awareness somewhere along the way. I hadn't attended any church or spiritual functions, and hadn't prayed, meditated, or read any metaphysical books or articles in ages. My beliefs hadn't shifted; I just wasn't conscious of them. Instead, I'd say, "I'll turn back to metaphysics if I ever become ill." Since my health remained perfect, I didn't focus upon spirituality because it just didn't seem currently relevant to my life. Besides, I was very busy writing *Constant Craving* and didn't want to take time for anything else.

My writing and attention were sharply diverted late that November, however, when my mother called with some distressing news. My paternal grandmother, Pearl, was quite ill and wasn't expected to live much longer. My parents were driving the following day, Thanksgiving, to Cousin Betty's home near Sacramento. There they would spend the night and then drive to be with Grandma Pearl.

The news shook me, but I knew my worrying wouldn't contribute to Grandma's health. So I kept my focus centered on writing my book. Two days later, my mother called again to say Grandma's condition had worsened. On top of that, someone had stolen my parents' car during the night while they were at Betty's home. Police were looking for the vehicle but didn't hold much hope of ever recovering it. In the meantime, my parents would drive a rental car to Grandma Pearl's bedside.

I broke into tears, crying so hard that I couldn't speak into the phone to my mother.

I handed the receiver to Michael, and he explained that I was overcome and would call her later. When I regained my composure, I realized my feelings were connected to sadness for my father. Dad had always feared that his car would be stolen. I remembered how on family driving vacations he'd get up in the middle of the night and peek out the curtains to make sure the car was still outside. Now his worst fear had manifested. I grieved terribly that my father, who is such a good man, would be on the brink of simultaneously losing his mother *and* getting his car stolen.

For the first time in ages, I began to pray. I prayed for my Grandmother's peace and for my parents' car to be recovered. I repeatedly affirmed what my mother had so long ago taught me: "Nothing is lost in the mind of God." I affirmed this until I knew that God saw where the car was right then.

I also prayed for the car thieves to come to light. I honestly don't believe that there are any evil people in the world, since God is all-in-all. I just believe that there are frightened people acting in evil ways. Many spiritual texts affirm that the human ego is the only devil walking around the world. Everyone can awaken from their ego-based fears and mend their ways, and I prayed that the car thieves would become conscious of their actions.

My Grandma Ada was also praying, as were many other friends and relatives. Betty Eadie had told me about the power of joining prayers with other people. She said that one prayer sends a beam of light to heaven. When several people's prayers are united for the same cause, it is like intertwining beams together forming a huge rope of light.

Five days after I'd learned of my parents' car theft, my brother, Ken, called me. "I don't think Grandma Pearl's going to live very much longer," he said.

Ken is extremely tuned-in to the invisible universe. One of his more remarkable psychic episodes came one week before the Challenger space shuttle disaster. Ken had a sudden and clear vision in which he saw the space shuttle exploding in what he assumed was a crash landing. Immediately concerned, Ken contacted an engineer friend of his who had worked on the space shuttle's design. He shared his vision with the engineer and asked, "Could something like this ever happen?" The engineer replied, "Absolutely not!" and Ken put the vision out of his mind. When the news of the space shuttle's explosion hit the airwaves a week later, it horrified Ken, and the engineer was shocked. Both men sadly pondered whether Ken's prescience could have somehow averted the disaster.

Growing up, I had repeatedly heard the phrase, "There is only one mind." Psychic experiences remind us of our connection with this one mind. Researchers across the globe are also tracking scientific evidence of the one mind's existence. For example, studies show that when someone thinks about you, your body exhibits physiological impulse changes correlated with whether that person is thinking calm or excited thoughts about you.[3] Other studies found that, *prior* to viewing a slide of either a calm scene or an exciting scene, subjects' brain waves and heart rates exhibited signs of calmness or excitement. In other words, the subjects' bodies registered appropriate emotional reactions to each picture before it was actually shown.[4]

Additional studies show that meditators' brain waves synchronize to identically match the brain waves of other people in the room, especially when the others are also meditating. A meditating person's brain waves also match identically with a person whom the meditator is thinking about, and with whom there is an emotional bond, even when great distances separate the meditator from the other person.[5]

My brother's link inside the one mind had alerted him to Grandma Pearl's impending death, and he urgently scrambled to book a flight to her Oregon bedside. He asked me to join him. But before Ken even had time to purchase tickets, he got another vision that it was too late. After making two phone calls to relatives in Oregon, Ken confirmed that Grandma Pearl had just passed away. She'd held on just long enough for my father and my Uncle Lee to reach her bedside before her transition.

Everyone is inherently psychic, and this is mostly evident in little children who talk about seeing angels and invisible friends. In families where they discourage psychic vision, the children shut off their spiritual sight. Our family encouraged one aspect of psychic skills: the ability to tune-in to loved ones. In fact, my mother frequently calls me or my brother when she intuitively knows we are experiencing a challenge. I had used this ability as a psychotherapist and with my own children. My brother, Ken, had psychically tuned-in to Grandma Pearl and accurately intuited the time of her death.

I never second-guessed Ken's psychic insights or thought them strange. This was partly because I'd grown up with them as an ordinary part of life, and partly because I rarely gave thought to my own intuitions. Although my Betty Eadie interview had momentarily pricked my attention, my focus of the past several months had fixated upon the surface material world. As a freelance writer, I put my daily energies into query letters, negotiating freelance deals, and turning in my assignments before deadlines. I also drank wine nightly to help me sleep, and then boosted my energy in the morning with coffee.

The day after Grandma Pearl's passing, police recovered my parents' car. The police said that stolen automobiles in their district were rarely found, and they were amazed to recover the car. In fact, the car even had a new addition: a shiny air freshener hung from the rearview mirror. Obviously, the car thieves had been conscientious about not smelling up the auto's interior with their cigarette smoking! I believe that Grandma Pearl—freed from bodily limitations so she could help her beloved son—plus our collective rope of prayers, resulted in the miraculous recovery of my parents' automobile.

About one week after Grandma's passing, a voice outside my head clearly spoke to me. I had not heard this sort of disconnected voice since my out-of-body experience nearly 30 years earlier. Just as when I was eight years old, I heard a strong male voice coming from outside myself. The voice said these exact words to me: "Quit drinking and get into Course in Miracles."

The sentence wasn't a request, but a very firm command, spoken without anger or accusation. I winced at hearing these words, knowing deep down that my lifestyle, including nightly wine drinking, wasn't benefiting me physically or emotionally. But the last part of the sentence, "...and get into Course in Miracles," puzzled me. I had heard of "the Course," but was unsure exactly what it meant. Was it a series of classes held at special schools? I wondered where they held these courses and how I could find out more.

Without mentioning why I was inquiring, I questioned my mother about *A Course in Miracles*. She welcomed my inquiry, and revealed to me her own intense interest in the subject. My mother also reminded me that, years earlier when I was a first-year psychology student, she had told me about the *Course*. She reminded me that when she'd told me about "a book that Jesus Christ channeled as an antidote to the pain the world is suffering from," I had told her the author must have been suffering from schizophrenia. Actually, I was the one who was suffering at the time, suffering from the naive and narrow-minded psychoanalyzing for which Psych 101 students are famous.

She faxed me some pages from an interview with Marianne Williamson, a well-known author who lectures on *A Course in Miracles*. After reading the material, I still wasn't ready to quit drinking and become a *Course* student. But I was sufficiently intrigued to investigate the topic further.

I asked Bonnie Krueger, *Complete Woman* magazine's editor,

if she would assign me to interview Marianne Williamson. She agreed, and after several phone calls to Marianne's office and publicist, I had an appointment to interview her over the telephone. I also arranged a magazine photography session on a Friday evening at the Huntington Beach Church of Religious Science where she was giving a lecture.

I was more than a little nervous before telephoning Marianne for our interview. I felt enormous respect for her, admiring her public candor about her spiritual beliefs. In contrast, I still barely admitted my deeply held faith to myself, let alone to my friends or book readers. When I thought about Marianne's work, I wondered, Could I also speak and write openly about my spiritual faith? Could I teach principles about spiritual healing without risking my reputation and income? She reignited my desire to use my spiritual knowledge to make a difference in the world.

Marianne was enormously gracious during our interview. As I listened to her discuss *A Course in Miracles* principles, I thought, This sounds just like the principles I learned as a child from my mother and Sunday school teachers! A few days later, the photographer; Kristina Reece, the publicity director of Hay House; and I met Marianne Williamson at the Huntington Beach church. I felt an immediate and enormous connection with Marianne, and she hugged me in a warm, familiar way. I also felt an affinity with the atmosphere of that particular church and would later regularly attend its services.

The next evening, when I sat at the computer to write Marianne's article, I felt an air-pressure shift around me. It felt similar to when I'd sensed Dan Olmos's spiritual presence while writing *Losing Your Pounds of Pain*. However, this pressure felt like more than one single soul. Dan's presence seemed to fill the approximate physical space of one person. In contrast, this presence spread horizontally across the entire top half of the room, as if a giant thick cloud had rolled into my office. I felt the presence crouching in anticipation, patiently waiting for me to begin writing. I sensed that I was in the company of something highly evolved and extremely intelligent—an ascended master, avatar, entity group, or Holy Spirit—who had come to help me write my Marianne Williamson article.

The presence seemed to direct my writing by manipulating pressure changes around my upper body. If I were writing in a preferred direction, the presence would surround my chest like a warm and loving embrace. If my writing turned awkward or contrived, though, it would push down on my shoulders as if holding me beneath deep water. Strangely enough, I didn't question or feel frightened by this spiritual intervention. Perhaps its strong loving essence helped me to immediately accept it as both real and positive.

It was nearly 10:30 at night when I'd nearly completed my article. I always type "30-30-30" at the end of my articles. This is a customary journalism signal that tells editors that the piece is finished. As I typed the first "30" on my article that night, however, the computer suddenly froze. I pressed the "Enter" and space bar keys, but the cursor wouldn't budge. I sensed the presence's intervention upon my computer and mentally asked it to explain its message. Immediately, I saw a paragraph become blackened with the computer's highlighting function.

Mentally, I asked, "Do you want me to change this paragraph?" and I received an affirmative sense. As I reread the paragraph, I found that its words were ambiguous and could have led the reader to some erroneous conclusions about the *Course*. So, I tightened the phrasing and reworded a few sentences. I asked, "Is this okay?" and suddenly felt the office air pressure return to normal. The presence was gone, which seemed to mean, "Our work together is now over." As I typed "30-30-30" across the bottom of the article, I thought, Amazing!

That night, for the first evening in a long time, I went to bed without my customary glass of wine. I wanted nothing to numb my thoughts and emotions in response to the miraculous events

I'd just experienced! As I fell into bed, I had a vivid lucid dream where I was the sole passenger in an enormous bus driving through a valley near a beach. The colors of the sky, landscapes, and ocean were so intensely bright that they were practically of the Day-Glo variety. This was unlike any dream I had experienced in my adult lifetime. It was so real, so colorful, and I still wonder what actually occurred. All I know was that the experience was connected to the presence that had earlier helped me to write my article.

I woke up the next morning feeling confused. My values were definitely shifting into a more spiritual focus, but I wasn't yet ready to make big changes in my lifestyle. In the days that followed, I disregarded the advice of the spiritual voice that had told me to "quit drinking and get into *Course in Miracles.*" I continued drinking wine, and put any additional thoughts about the *Course* out of my mind.

CHAPTER TEN

A REAWAKENING

"The Way out into the light often looks dark,
The way that goes ahead often looks as if it went back."

— *Tao Te Ching,* spiritual text

I managed to finish *Constant Craving*, so I sent the manuscript to Jill Kramer at Hay House. Jill called me a week later to say the book wasn't quite what she'd wanted. She was right. I'd written a very cold and mechanistic book about the scientific studies on food cravings. There was little metaphysics in the book, and even less warmth or emotion. Jill asked me to rewrite and resubmit the manuscript.

I was so tired and felt beaten up by life. I'd poured months of research and writing work into the book and was emotionally exhausted by my family tragedies. Now, I faced a complete rewrite of my manuscript, a rewrite that I knew was absolutely necessary for me to produce the kind of book that I was capable of producing.

As I sat at the computer screen and pulled up a copy of the book's text, I felt a familiar pressure change around my head, shoulders, and chest. The presence that had helped me with my Marianne Williamson article was back! I welcomed the assistance. Soon my fingers began typing as if they had a life of their own, and they poured out ideas onto the computer screen. I was writing about spiritual principles that were not of my own thoughts or making. These were original ideas to me, filled with truths about the metaphysical bases of food cravings, gut feelings, and the fear of trusting our inner voice.

I was aware of not being fully conscious during the writing process. As if I were half-asleep, the writing had a life of its own. My only awareness was that uniquely truthful ideas were pouring into my mind and then out through my fingertips onto the computer keyboard. I also realized that, while writing, I lost all track of time. I would think I was writing for 20 minutes, only to discover afterward that 4 or 5 hours had passed.

I, or rather "we," rewrote *Constant Craving* and resubmitted it to Jill within two weeks. Her telephone call a few days later confirmed that something miraculous had occurred during the rewriting process. "I am amazed by how quickly you have managed to change this entire book," she said. "This manuscript is now exactly as I had originally envisioned, and I am going to put it into production!"

I didn't explain what had occurred to Jill, or to anyone other than my mother. I still feared that anyone outside my family who discovered my spiritual beliefs and mystical experiences would reject me. I was covering up who I truly was and what I deeply believed, not allowing anyone in the world to know about my otherworldly experiences or beliefs. I kept telling myself, "I'm not yet ready to write about spiritual healing. I'll write a book on that topic someday, but not now."

Once or twice a month, television talk-show producers would ask me to appear as a "Love Doctor," since I'd written books on the subject of romance and relationships. A couple of weeks after Jill accepted *Constant Craving*, two national East Coast talk shows requested my appearance in time for their Valentine's Day shows. Although I didn't believe being a Love Doctor was part of my life purpose, I also feared turning down media opportunities. At the time, I thought I needed to appear on television to boost my writing career, so I agreed to appear on both programs.

The first program, "The 700 Club," is a national talk show produced and televised by the Christian Broadcasting Network and hosted by Pat Robertson. They slated me to fly to their Virginia Beach studios and appear live on Valentine's Day. From there, I would fly to New York City to appear on the now-defunct Charles Perez show.

I spent the night of February 13 sleeping in a beautiful hotel within the Christian Broadcasting Network compound, which is a self-sufficient city containing a restaurant, hotel, stores, offices, and the television studio. I was a little nervous about appearing on the talk show because of my nontraditional Christian background. I also was aware that Pat Robertson was a politically influential figure, and also extremely controversial.

That evening, I read the hotel room copy of his autobiography, *Shout It from the Housetops*[1], and found that I actually could relate to his personal story. Robertson had been a hard-drinking, unhappy misfit before a preacher friend inspired him to find God. Robertson's friend talked about Jesus and God nonstop to whomever he met, often to Robertson's embarrassment. However, his friend's example inspired Robertson later to shout his own message from the housetops. Despite my reservations, I found myself admiring Robertson's courage to come out of his "spiritual closet," when I was struggling to do the same.

Backstage the next morning, in the 700 Club studios "green room," the talk-show producers, guests, crew, two co-hosts, and I stood in a circle holding hands. We each said a brief prayer aloud before the show began. I marveled at the difference between this show's green room and those of the talk shows on which I normally appeared. I had never before been in a group prayer at a talk-show studio. I liked it and started to feel more at ease.

I was televised live for nearly an hour, discussing romantic tips for Valentine's Day and giving suggestions to a newly dating couple who were on the show with me. I wanted to talk about spirituality but felt afraid since I'd never before talked about God on television. At the end of the show, I ended with a vague but unmistakable statement, "And we all know where the true source of love comes from." The show's co-host took the cue from my words and wrapped up the show by saying to the audience, "Yes, the true source of love is God." I looked at her and gulped, wishing I'd had the courage to say that simple but powerful truth.

Afterward, all the guests and crew went to lunch at the restaurant behind the studio. We chatted happily, and I felt very comfortable—that is, until someone at the table started asking each talk-show guest where he or she went to church. As it neared my turn to speak, I thought about how I'd answer. I infrequently attended a Methodist church but more regularly went to a Religious Science church. I knew that I would be safe to limit my answer to the Methodist church; however, to do so would feel inauthentic. I decided to tell the truth, even though I realized my answer would garner negative reactions. *I* knew I was a Christian, but I also knew that Religious Science was viewed as non-Christian, even though its founder had based the church on Jesus Christ's healing principles.

When they got to me, at first I gave a vague reply. "Oh, I go to a church in Huntington Beach, California." A man at the table said he was from Southern California and asked me exactly which church I attended. Here goes, I thought, and felt my face flush as I said, "The Church of Religious Science." Someone asked me, "You mean Scientology?" I said no and then gave a brief summary of my upbringing in Christian Science, Unity, and now Religious Science. I felt a sharp change in the atmosphere as my dining companions began mumbling nervous excuses to leave the table. With awkward abruptness, lunch was finished.

One of the talk-show producers, a woman named Ivory, silently escorted me to my hotel room to gather my belongings so a staff member could take me to the airport in time for my flight. As we entered my room, Ivory said, "Do you mind if I ask you a question?" I shook my head, and she asked, "Do you have a personal relationship with Jesus Christ?"

My face turned warm with intense feelings. I felt a sense of déjà vu, as if I were reliving being expelled from the Christian Science youth camp, and my band members' ultimatum to join their Emanuel Faith church. Again, I felt cast in the role of the bad girl unworthy of being in the company of the righteous.

I stammered to Ivory that I felt my relationship with Jesus was fine. I also mentioned that I regularly read the Bible. She turned to me and asked me to say again what religion I had been raised in. When I replied, "Christian Science," Ivory remarked she'd never heard of it and would have to do some research on it.

Then she asked something that at first stunned me in its implication. "Aren't you afraid that God is mad at you?"

I looked at her directly and said, "I don't believe in an angry God."

What could she say at that point? We exchanged quick good-byes, and a "700 Club" crew member drove me to the airport. When he dropped me off at the airport, he said, "I hope you have a nice life." His words confirmed what I already knew: I had just been excommunicated from the Christian Broadcasting Network for attending the "wrong" church.

I tried to put the whole scene out of my mind, but inside I struggled to regain a sense of peace. The producer's questions had unearthed some of my most deeply buried feelings of confusion over religion and spirituality. Coming on the heels of my own questions about how to put my spiritual beliefs into practice, Ivory's words triggered more questions in my mind. I wondered, Is there a true definition of a Christian beyond someone who loves Jesus Christ? I knew that the whole basis of New Thought religion stemmed from Jesus Christ's teachings in the New Testament. Yet I had to admit that I hadn't studied the Bible *that* carefully. Did this make me less of a Christian? I also wondered about what Ivory had said about a "personal relationship with Jesus."

That night in my Manhattan hotel room, I recalled an incident that occurred when I was 18 years old and spending the summer at my friend Kathy's home near Palm Springs. I'd awakened one night to a vision of three well-lit figures hovering above my bed. The figures were floating toward me very slowly, and I sensed that the middle figure was Jesus and one of the others was Mother Mary. I couldn't see their faces because they shone so brightly, but I just knew who two of the figures were.

I thought death must be near, so I shut my eyes to make the images disappear. When I reopened my eyes, the figures were still there and drawing nearer. I'm too young to die! I thought, alone in the darkened room. I kept closing and opening my eyes, yet the trio continued getting closer. Finally, I decided to surrender to them. I thought, Okay, I'm not afraid to die. Come take me. I'm yours.

With that, the figures enveloped me with light and were gone. I felt relief that the frightening experience was over, yet I was left with a lingering sense that my decision to surrender had somehow shifted my consciousness. For days afterward, I kept thinking, This must be what it means to accept Jesus into your heart and be reborn.

My "700 Club" experiences reawakened my memories of this incident, but I still didn't know what to make of my confusion about Christianity. A part of me was also furious at the judgmental treatment I'd received from the studio crew. And, I was disappointed in my defensive reaction to Ivory's questions. "I should be more secure in my beliefs," I chastised myself.

Wide awake in my Manhattan hotel room, I recalled working with patients who had struggled to overcome negative childhood experiences that they'd had with religion and church. Often, I had found myself sitting with crying patients who told me of their overwhelming guilt stemming from church teachings. Many clients held harsh self-judgments because, as children, they'd heard sermons about how everybody is a sinner. I also thought about a woman client who once told me that her minister had preached that it was wrong to be angry. Ever since, she'd repressed her accumulated wrath until she eventually collapsed into depression.

I had tried different churches, some traditional and many nontraditional. Each church offered a unique beauty; however, no one church offered everything I sought. I tried to find a church that combined group discussion, Gospel teachings, and high-level metaphysical wisdom, as I had experienced in Christian Science Sunday school. Consequently, I frequently attended more than one church on any given weekend. However, none of the church services I'd attended offered what I was craving to hear and experience.

I thought of Ivory's question about whether I was afraid that God was angry with me. I've never had any conception of what it must be like to see God as vengeful or unloving. I was raised to know that God is 100 percent love and that there is no room in His mind even to see or acknowledge error. Additionally, since God didn't make error, it is not real. So it makes no sense that He would punish anyone for doing what is unreal. All He knows is what is real: love.

I've witnessed many clients struggle to let go of their "angry God" images. One client raised in a fundamental religion told me, "I'm afraid to change my mind about God, although I really want to. What if the New Thought churches are wrong, and God punishes me for seeing him as a loving God?" After many counseling sessions in which I prayed for guidance, combined with her reading of the New Testament, she gradually allowed a loving image of God to grow within her consciousness.

"How ironic," I told myself, "that so many of my friends and clients who attend metaphysical churches feel rejected by their own family members who belong to traditional religions. I, on the other hand, was raised in metaphysics and only feel comfortable discussing my true beliefs with my family. I'm afraid to reveal my beliefs in public completely lest I get the same sort of rejection I experienced at the '700 Club' today."

Finally, I slept. The next day, I scrambled to get ready for the Charles Perez show, so I didn't have a chance to think further about what had happened on the other program. The limousine driver picked me up in the lobby of my midtown hotel and whisked me to the CBS studios. The talk show had booked me as the guest expert on the topic of "Torn Between Two Lovers," in which three couples plus the "other man or woman" would discuss their infidelities. I was to give them advice and suggestions during the show. Twenty minutes before we were set to tape the show, however, a producer called all of us into the green room and announced that they had canceled our episode. "Two of the guests didn't arrive, and we can't do the show without them," she explained.

The producer arranged for limousines to take all of us to our hotels or the airport. They booked me to take an evening flight from JFK airport back to California. As I waited outside the CBS studio for the limousine router to tell me which car to get into, I felt relieved to be going home. It had been a trying journey!

Finally, the router directed me to a silver Lincoln Towncar, and I gratefully plopped into the back seat. I exchanged hellos with the driver, an elegantly suited dark-skinned man with a gentle voice. In broken English, he explained that he regularly drove talk-show guests to the airport, and then asked why I was on Charles Perez's show.

"I'm a psychotherapist," I answered.

"Oh," he replied in broken English, "what do you see in my future?"

He'd obviously thought I'd said "psychic" instead of "psychotherapist." But before I could correct him, I received a flood of mental thoughts and visions. His question, in which he'd had complete faith that I was a full-fledged psychic, must have triggered this reaction within me.

I was suddenly aware of knowing great details about the driver's life. I told him that he had a beautiful girlfriend in India with long, blunt-cut black hair. I said, "Her name is 'Syrena,' or 'Syria,' or something like that." The driver speechlessly handed me a large Valentine's card to open. It was signed "Syrina," from his girlfriend in India.

He asked advice about their relationship, especially how he could convince Syrina to move to America and marry him. The answer was among the information I had received, and I explained that Syrina was unsure of his true intentions and sincerity. "She wants you to commit to the idea of marriage by actually buying an engagement ring and then formally proposing," I explained, still unsure how I knew these personal details about a complete stranger. The driver replied, "That's exactly what I had suspected," and thanked me for confirming his feelings.

My vision continued, and I saw the couple married and living in a nearby New Jersey suburb. I also saw that one of their sons would become an important physician. The driver gasped and said, "I have been praying to one day have a son who would greatly help the world."

I didn't share with the driver my own amazement over this impromptu psychic reading, because I didn't know how it had occurred. I just knew that I had spontaneously been privy to this man's innermost thoughts, and was also seeing his past, present, and future. But how? We spent the rest of the journey to the airport talking. He shared with me that his father was a Christian minister in India, and we discussed how our faith could blend with the psychic reading we'd just experienced.

I arrived in California determined to explore my questions further. I could no longer ignore the powerful earthquake of spiritual experiences trembling within me. I had to find out more, and I had to find out fast.

VISIONS OF THE LIGHTWORKER'S GIFTS

*"Those who have developed 'psychic' powers
have simply let some of the limitations they laid
upon their minds be lifted."*

— A Course in Miracles

The day after my return from New York, I enrolled in a psychic-development course at the Learning Light Foundation in Anaheim. I wanted to discover whether my experience with the limo driver had been a fluke, or whether I really possessed psychic abilities.

The evening of my first class, I sat among 20 students at a large *U*-shaped table in a second-floor room of an old church converted into a school for psychics. Everyone looked nervous, and we made small talk while waiting for the teacher to arrive.

Finally, our instructor, a poised and striking raven-haired woman named Lucretia Scott, came into the classroom. She distributed some papers to us, and one sheet was a self-quiz. "This will help you determine what your primary channels of communication are," Lucretia explained.

The quiz asked questions such as:

1. After returning from a vacation, are you more apt to tell your friends: (a) what you saw, (b) what you felt, (c) what you heard, or (d) what you learned?

2. When you recall your favorite movie, are your first thoughts about: (a) the beautiful scenes, (b) how the movie made you cry or laugh, (c) the movie's music or the sound of the actors' voices, or (d) the message in the movie?

Lucretia explained that the a, b, c, and d answers respectively related to visual, emotional, auditory, and cognitive channels of communication. In other words, "a" answers related to sight, "b" answers to feelings, "c" to hearing, and "d" to thinking.

"Psychics have one or two channels in which they are naturally gifted," our teacher explained. "You will receive psychic impressions as pictures if you are primarily visual. This means you are 'clairvoyant,' or 'clear seeing.'"

Lucretia said that those who are primarily feeling-oriented get their psychic information in the forms of hunches, emotions, smells, or physical sensations. We call this "clairsentient," which means "clear feeling."

Similarly, those who are auditory receive psychic impressions as sounds or voices. We call this "clairaudience," or "clear hearing." Finally, people who are highly cognitive, or thinking-oriented, are called "claircognizant," or "clear thinking." They receive psychic information as complete ideas. They just *know* information, without knowing how they know.

My self-quiz showed I was primarily clairvoyant and claircognizant. In other words, my psychic information would come as mental pictures and a knowingness about a situation or person.

Lucretia then explained how the body's energy centers, or "chakras," related to psychic work. I was quite familiar with chakras, having learned about them in an undergraduate parapsychology class. Chakras resemble colored water whirling down a drain, in that they are circles of energy swirling around vortex-like centers.

Although the body has many chakras, psychics and healers

generally only concern themselves with the seven major ones. These major chakras are each found next to a hormonal gland. The chakras push vital life energy (also called "ki," "chi," or "prana") through the body to ensure vitality, like pinball game paddles pushing balls along their course. This life energy springs from the Divine, and gives us access to all wisdom, or psychic information.

Our chakras radiate and receive energy constantly. If we hold negative thoughts, our chakras become dirtied with dense, dark energy. Clogged chakras can't push through enough energy, and people feel sluggish and out-of-balance. They also lose touch with their natural psychic information resources.

Each chakra corresponds to specific life issues or "thought forms." The first or "root chakra," near the base of the spine, regulates issues of survival, and fulfillment of our physical needs for food and shelter. About five inches below the belly button is the second or "sacral chakra," which corresponds to physical desires and appetites. Directly behind the navel is the third or "solar plexus" chakra, which responds to issues of power and control. The fourth chakra, behind the heart, is logically called the "heart chakra," and deals with matters of love. Next, the "throat chakra" is located by the Adam's apple, and corresponds to our beliefs, thoughts, and actions involving communication. Between the two eyes is the "third eye chakra," which governs spiritual sight and clairvoyance. The seventh, or "crown chakra," is on the inside of the top of our heads. This chakra lets in universal and Divine knowledge, and is our inlet for wisdom, guidance, and understanding.

The lower-body chakras deal with physical issues. As we move up the body, the chakras correspond to increasingly spiritual concerns. Consequently, each chakra's energy vibrates at different rates, depending on whether they govern earthbound or ethereal issues. The lower chakras have slower and denser vibrations, while the higher chakras spin at faster speeds with higher vibrations. The chakras' energy patterns emit colors corresponding to their light-wave frequencies. Thus, the root chakra is red, which is the slowest light-wave frequency, and the sacral is the slightly faster frequency of orange. As you go further up the body, the light-wave colors reflect their increasing vibratory rate. So, the solar plexus is yellow, the heart is green, the throat is light blue, the third eye is dark blue, and the crown is the fastest light-wave frequency, violet.

A person's focus upon a particular issue enlarges the corresponding chakra. For example, someone who thinks about money a lot will have a large root chakra, because this energy center responds to issues of physical survival. There is nothing wrong with having large chakras; in fact, there are advantages to widely radiating one's chakras. However, if the seven chakras vary greatly in size, the body's vital energy flow becomes imbalanced. In other words, it's important that all the chakras be equally large.

Dirty or imbalanced chakras impair psychic communication. So anyone wanting to open their psychic channels needs to clean and balance their chakras through visualization and meditative means. I also learned, years later, about scientific studies confirming that meditation increases one's psychic abilities because it changes the rate of brain waves.[1]

Several months before taking Lucretia's class, I had begun regularly meditating and cleansing and balancing my chakras. (I describe my method in Chapter 17, and on my Hay House audio-cassette, *Chakra Clearing*.) While listening to Lucretia's discussion, I understood that my clean and balanced chakras had triggered my psychic experiences with the limousine driver.

Lucretia asked us to pair up with a student whom we had not yet met. I felt nervous. Did she actually expect us to perform a psychic reading right away? After all, we hadn't heard any instruction about how to do psychic work. We'd only learned *about* it, not how to *do* it.

Reading our thoughts, Lucretia assured us that we were

ready. She explained that psychic work is a natural phenomenon and not an acquired skill. "You learn to trust your psychic impressions by doing psychic readings," she said. To help us relax, she described a reading she'd given as a beginning psychic. "I was with a client, and I was very nervous. I kept getting a mental picture of a merry-go-round horse, and I thought, This can't be right. But the image kept popping up until I finally told the client what I was seeing. The man said he had recently been involved in finding and purchasing a rare merry-go-round horse, and my accuracy impressed him. From then on, I learned to trust whatever psychic impressions I receive." She added that the difference between an average psychic and a great psychic was the level of confidence and trust in their received impressions.

My partner for my first formal psychic reading that night was a pretty Hispanic woman in her 20s named Suzanne. Lucretia instructed class partners to sit facing one another while holding both of the other person's hands. She told us to close our eyes and mentally ask our Divine Source, "What do you want me to know about this person?" Then, Lucretia instructed us to quiet our minds and wait until we received an impression as a picture, feeling, sound, or thought.

Holding my partner's hands with my eyes tightly shut, I worried, What if my psychic impressions are wrong? Then, recalling Lucretia's merry-go-round story, I took a deep breath and decided to enter the experience in a spirit of fun and adventure. That helped me to relax.

I mentally asked, "What do you want me to know about this person?" and took deep breaths until my mind eased. Suddenly, I saw what looked like a fast-moving film of my partner Suzanne's life. I saw a man, who I somehow knew to be her father, violently whipping my partner's bottom when she looked to be about six or seven years old. The father held Suzanne with one of his hands, and a belt in the other. I watched Suzanne struggle futilely to escape his grip and whipping belt. I also saw a small boy.

Again, I knew without a doubt that this was Suzanne's younger brother, hiding to avoid the violence.

The movie lurched ahead to the present, and this time, my psychic impressions came more as thoughts than as pictures. Information about Suzanne flooded into my mind like a disk loading text into a computer. In an instant, I knew that she was considering enrolling in a college-type course involving creative work. This knowledge was accompanied by another bit of information that resembled a combination of advice and a warning I knew I was to convey to her. My reading told me that Suzanne was an extremely intelligent woman. However, the child abuse she'd endured at her father's hands had convinced Suzanne that she was stupid. She had the intellectual capacity to succeed in any college of her choosing. She also had the desire and motivation to pursue a high-level education and career. However, she was settling for an unchallenging and second-rate education due to her fear that she would flunk out of a better college.

I received all this information in less than five minutes. Lucretia asked us to open our eyes and to share our impressions with our partner. When I told Suzanne what I'd seen and learned, tears fell from her eyes. Suzanne said that their father *had* beaten her and her younger brother, and that this definitely had affected her opinions about her intelligence. She then told me she was about to enroll in cosmetology school and that I was correct in saying that this was not her first choice in careers.

I was stunned that I had actually conducted a purposeful and accurate psychic reading, but I was concerned about the message I'd been told to convey to Suzanne. I wondered, Should I emphasize to her the admonition I'd received not to sell herself short by pursuing an unwanted career? I barely knew this woman and didn't want to push unwanted advice upon her. Still, my own experiences with being psychologically abused had taught me the impact it has upon a person's self-image. So, I explained the gist of the warning as I'd received it. I figured that instead of interpreting the psychic impression on my own, I would just convey it verbatim and let her do what she wanted with the information. Later, I would learn that this method of conveying psychic impressions is the best way to give an accurate reading uncontaminated by personal opinions.

During my psychic reading of Suzanne, she had simultaneously been reading me. Now it was her turn to tell me what she received. As with me, Suzanne's psychic impressions primarily came in clairvoyant pictures. She described my co-directing a hospital or clinic, along with two other people. The descriptions she gave of these two people sounded identical to my fiancé, Michael, and my departed grandmother, Pearl. Suzanne's secondary psychic channel was clairsentience, or feelings. She told me she felt this clinic was in South Laguna Beach, California. She also relayed a message that she had received for me: "Don't worry so much, because everything is going to work out perfectly."

With that sentence, I blushed. I *had* been worrying. So much of my world, my thoughts, my beliefs, and my relationships were shifting, and I felt that my foundations were very shaky. The more I reopened my long-neglected spiritual interests, the less interested I was in traditional psychology. Yet, I feared my income depended upon my writing about and conducting "academically correct" psychological work. What would I do for a living if I walked away from traditional psychological methods and beliefs?

Another one of my overriding concerns was my relationship with my fiancé, Michael. Although I deeply loved him, I wondered whether my emerging spirituality would pull us apart. I longed to talk with him about my exciting clairvoyant experiences, but I expected him to scoff at or overanalyze my words. Michael had never given me cause to draw these conclusions; I just didn't feel comfortable discussing my fragile new world with him. In fact, I only felt safe sharing my psychic discoveries with my mother and a few friends.

I was certain that Michael was my soulmate. However, I wondered how I could truly be happy in a relationship where I kept important parts of myself hidden from my partner. I also chastised myself for not putting "spirituality" on my list when I manifested the relationship. At the time, spirituality hadn't been an important characteristic for me in a life mate.

I longed to tell Michael about my new world, but also I dared not risk his rejection. After all, I still carried raw wounds from when I'd discussed my spiritual beliefs as a child. I also still smarted from my experiences at the "700 Club." I didn't want to add to my pain by having my fiancé reject me as well. Besides, I still didn't know where my spiritual path was leading me. I was walking blindfolded with extreme trust that my guides and angels would lead me past my chaotic turmoil and I'd eventually get to experience some peace. I decided to wait until my inner spiritual storm settled down before deciding what to do about my relationship.

Meanwhile, I continued taking psychic development classes, which ultimately convinced me of the authenticity of my psychic impressions. I also devoted time every morning and evening to meditation and reading spiritual books. I bought audiocassettes of the New Testament, which I listened to during my daily exercise workouts. Listening to the Bible was a new experience for me. Before, my Bible readings had been piecemeal. Now, I was appreciating the chronological continuity of the entire story of Jesus and his disciples. I also paid close attention to his advice about how our faith is the "secret" to healing our bodies and lives.

I also read Bible passages, both to savor the comforting words and to answer my questions about how Christianity fit into my mystical experiences and beliefs. A friend of mine who had been born and raised in a New Thought religion, and who later changed to a more traditional Christian faith, was especially helpful to me during this time. When I openly discussed my concerns about my psychic abilities, she immediately told me that Apostle

Paul called this "the gift of prophecy." As I read his words, I felt supported and understood:

> And though I have the gift of prophecy, and understand all mysteries and all knowledge, and though I have all faith, so that I could remove mountains, but have not love, I am nothing. Pursue love, and desire spiritual gifts, but especially that you may prophecy. For you can all prophecy one by one, that all may learn and all may be encouraged. Therefore, brethren, desire earnestly to prophecy...[2]

I was looking for this key! Love. How simple, yet how important to know the distinction between psychic abilities used in loving service and psychic abilities used out of fear or manipulative reasons.

As Apostle Paul said, we all have the gift of prophecy, or psychic abilities. You receive psychic impressions constantly, such as when you know who is calling on the telephone, or you think about an old friend and then see him or her later that day.

Several scientific studies have shown that we all have the capacity for psychic communication. One of the more impressive bodies of research on this topic comes from the extensive study conducted by Daryl Bem and Charles Honorton at Cornell University. The research began when Bem (who practices stage magic as a hobby) sought to prove that "psychic powers" were nothing more than the psychics' ability to read their clients' body language and use ordinary magical tricks. So Bem designed a scientific study using methodology so tightly controlled that no one could possibly employ fakery to pass themselves off as a psychic. Unwittingly, Bem's research program ended up *supporting* the evidence that psychic abilities are real. Even more, practically every person whom Bem tested showed evidence of possessing psychic ability.

Bem and Honorton's research, composed of 11 studies conducted between 1983 and 1989, left scientists around the world groping to explain the findings. The results converted many scientists, including Bem, into believers of psychic communication after analyzing the research data.

The study used 100 male and 140 female volunteers. During the experiment, subjects sat in a sealed room designed to block any chance that they could see or hear information coming from outside the room. For example, subjects wore headphones that had a steady humming noise, and they had ping-pong ball halves firmly taped over their eyes. Researchers told the subjects to state every image that entered their mind during the 30 minutes they sat in the room.

Simultaneously, subjects outside the room successively viewed 160 randomly selected photographs and video clips. Researchers asked these subjects to mentally "send" these images to the person in the sealed room. If the subject in the sealed room stated a thought that matched the image simultaneously being viewed by the sender, it was designated a "hit." The law of chance would expect that one in 4 guesses would be correct. However, the subjects got one in 3 images correctly. Students of art, music, and drama got an even more impressive one in 2 correct. These results show a statistically significant effect, and since the researchers designed the extraneous variables out of the study, one can only draw the conclusion that this study shows the existence of telepathy. The study was replicated 11 separate times, and each time, the researchers received the same astonishing results.[3]

The more you accept psychic abilities as a natural part of life, the more frequently they occur. Some ways to amplify your gift of prophecy include keeping a journal of each day's "coincidences," or driving through a parking lot while allowing your gut feelings to guide you to an empty parking space. Additionally, *trust* your psychic impressions, and you will feel increasingly guided by your higher self and your angels.

I loved meditating and reading about spirituality, but I also worried that it was overtaking my life. For several weeks, all I wanted to do was sit in my meditation room and pray or read. I thought, This is crazy. I have to work and make some money! I can't just sit in this room all day. Still, a strong pull kept guiding me to read and meditate. Many days, I spent two, three, or four hours in meditation. I somehow felt assured that there was a reason for my taking a respite from the world. I wished desperately that someone could pay me to meditate, but part of me retained an old belief that we must suffer for our income. Meditating was fun and seemingly nonproductive; therefore, how could I use it to support myself?

I continued writing magazine articles about relationships topics such as "How to Know If a Break-up Is Coming," and "Is He the Cheating Type?" While I felt these articles made minor contributions to the world, I didn't enjoy writing them and had little satisfaction seeing them in print. I just didn't see myself as a "Love Doctor," but the media seemed to have typecast me in this role. Talk-show producers constantly called to ask me to appear on their programs as a relationship expert, and magazine editors continually gave me relationship-article assignments. I agreed to these requests because I feared turning down the steady income.

I was only remotely aware of the high price I was paying at a soul level for betraying my true self. Deep down, I knew what I wanted to do—write articles and books purely about metaphysics and spiritual healing—but I feared that I could not earn a living by following this gut instinct.

This pull in my consciousness that worried about money, and yet longed for serenity, led me to search for books that could help. I bought and read *The Abundance Book* by John Randolph Price and several of Catherine Ponder's prosperity books. I also studied the Sermon on the Mount in the book of Matthew.

The 40-day prosperity meditation in Price's book helped to heal my worries about money. I also experienced a curiously mysterious experience during that time period. Although I'd written many checks to pay for insurance, utilities, and such, not a single check was cashed for nearly three weeks. My bank account stayed constant as if it were frozen in time, and I dared not question what felt like an affirmation of God's power. I prayed that I would overcome the remaining doubts that kept me from completely surrendering to God's care.

My readings and meditations taught me that my financial concerns were the root cause of any money problems I experienced. That made perfect sense to me. Just as Christian Science teaches that thoughts of disease create physical problems, my fears of lack had manifested into experiences of lack.

While in meditation, I would sometimes pose questions. The answers would come as pictures inside my mind or outside my eyes, like a movie. I asked, "How is that everybody is connected as one, when we all seem so different and separate?" Immediately I saw a tree and received the knowledge that every person is like a leaf on a giant tree. Each leaf has its individual experiences apart from the other leaves. Still, each leaf affects the other leaves. For example, if one leaf becomes distressed, its negativity pours poison into the entire tree's veins.

I asked about the nature of matter, and saw images that looked like miniature colorful soap bubbles clinging to one another in a giant chain. I understood that I was looking at life's tiniest particles. Next, I wondered about life-after-death and was immediately surrounded by the very real image of a blue skyscape with a long, tall crystal building. I felt someone outside of me ask, "Do you want to take a tour of this crystal castle?" I hesitated, unsure if it was safe to go. Then I quickly answered affirmatively, and felt myself being carried around the beautiful blue-white castle spires. Just as quickly, I was returned to my meditation room.

The more I meditated, the more I understood how easily we all could get answers and information *simply by asking*. This was explained to me in meditation when I heard the words, "Your experiences follow your intentions." I saw how we miss out on this great resource because our intentions are focused on human efforts to take care of our needs, instead of intending to reunite with God's love. The light dawned within me as I realized that we don't need to struggle to meet our needs. We simply need to ask for guidance and then follow it. I thought of the times in which I'd pushed against life, straining to achieve goals. Those efforts always resulted in more stress and short-lived manifestations. I also recalled the times in which I had effortlessly manifested my needs using faith, visualization, and affirmations.

As I pondered this, I received a chunk of information as if someone had scanned pages of a book into my mind. The message I got was that lightworkers, like myself, could manifest and heal anything. I saw a vision of a future in which traditional health care and food was artificially limited by a government-type agency that wanted to control the masses. It reminded me of the Revelations prophecy that warns of supplies being controlled by an anti-Christ.

I saw lightworkers helping the sick and the hungry so that they could avoid succumbing to the governmental manipulation. Lightworkers, in this vision, were manifesting food out of thin air. They were also spiritually healing purely with thought and prayer, since no herbs or medicines were available.

My vision also contained the information that all prophecies, such as that in Revelations, could be averted through lightworkers' collective consciousness of love. In other words, we could avoid the whole scenario of diminished food and medical supplies through the united efforts of lightworkers. However, if lightworkers did not unite in time to avert the prophecy, they could still bring peace, healing, and supply to people through their spiritual gifts.

I understood, after I received this vision, that I needed to rekindle the teachings about spiritual healing I had learned as a child. I was to dust them off and eventually write about and teach them to lightworkers who felt guided to read and hear my words. With that vision, I knew it was time to fully commit to my spiritual path.

OPENING THE THIRD EYE

"There is but one man. On the spiritual side of his being, every man in the universe has access to that man, eternally existing in Divine Mind as a perfect-man idea."

— Charles Fillmore, founder of Unity Church, and author of *Christian Mental Healing*

I was looking through a course catalog for The Learning Annex adult education center, when I saw the familiar-looking face of bestselling author Wayne Dyer. As I read the description of his upcoming day-long seminar in San Diego, I felt drawn to attend. It wasn't any one single phrase or word in the catalog copy that attracted me. Instead, an inner prompting urged me to "go and attend this seminar."

A decade earlier, I'd been a "seminar junkie" who attended every workshop on psychology I could find. I went to lectures by Carl Rogers, Rollo May, Irvin Yalom, William Glasser, and other leaders in the psychological field. At some point, though, I became oversaturated with listening to speakers and had no further desire to attend another workshop.

Now, however, I was drawn to attend an eight-hour seminar. I asked Bonnie Krueger, the editor-in-chief of *Complete Woman* magazine, whether she would be interested in an article about Dyer. Bonnie gave me the go-ahead, and I proceeded to find out how to contact Dyer to arrange a photo session to coincide with the article.

Since Dyer wrote books for Hay House, I asked Reid Tracy for help in arranging the interview. He put me in contact with Dyer's publicist, Edna Farley. Edna, I discovered, promotes many metaphysical authors and acts as an intermediary between the media and her authors. She arranged for me to interview Dyer by telephone one week before his lecture, and then to photograph him at the conclusion of his lecture.

The auditorium of The Church of Today in San Diego was packed with hundreds of people who, like me, awaited Dyer's lecture. I had learned to appreciate the value of being in a room filled with spiritually minded people from attending the large services at the Huntington Beach church. There is a spark of energy that collectively gathers in peaceful crowds. Often, I receive ideas that seemed divinely inspired while sitting in packed church services.

Dyer told us that he had spent time with the Indian mystic, Sri Guruji. After reading Dyer's book, *You'll See It When You Believe It,* Guruji wrote to Dyer. The two men later met when Guruji flew from India to Los Angeles. Guruji presented Dyer with an audiocassette of meditative chants specifically designed for manifesting desires into material form. The mystic asked Dyer to teach the chants to people in the Western world, and Dyer was doing so at the lecture and on a Hay House audiocassette called *Meditations for Manifesting.*[1]

Dyer began the meditation by asking us to close our eyes and to put our attention on our third-eye chakra. He then led us in a series of chants where we said "Om" and "Ah" in various pitches. He explained how the sound "Ah" is in virtually every religion's name for the Divine, including God, Allah, Buddha, and Krishna. By chanting "Ah," we synchronize with the vibrations of creation. If we chant while simultaneously holding an idea, that mental picture manifests into physical form rapidly.

Sitting among the hundreds of other audience members, I focused on my third eye and chanted "Om." At first, most people's chants were faint, but we gradually uttered booming "Oms" with great feeling.

As I chanted, I saw an oval-shaped image surfacing in front of me. The oval rested horizontally in the darkened space between my two eyes. The image became progressively clearer and brighter with each chant, like the first glimpse of land as your airplane dives through clouds. Suddenly, I clearly recognized what I was seeing. I gasped with surprise as I recognized an eye—a perfectly detailed female eye—looking at me. It's my third eye! I thought. The eye slowly blinked a couple of times and radiated love in its expression as it looked at me.

I felt I was peering through Alice in Wonderland's looking glass as the eye and I stared at one another. I knew I was seeing myself, yet this self lived in a whole separate world. She was me, but she was in a parallel universe peering at me through a port-hole. Just like some people can instantly determine whether a new acquaintance has had a difficult or an easy life, I saw that she had lived a life filled with peace, security, and love. She radiated these qualities.

The eye looked exactly like my own, with a few important differences. She showed no sign of weathering life's pain, and the skin around her eye was smooth and unwrinkled. The eye's expression beamed with happiness and perfect peace, and I felt it was saying to me, "Welcome home. It's so good that we finally get to meet one another." The eye was as beautiful as any sight I had ever seen—not physical beauty so much as an ethereal aura of love, patience, peace, and goodness that it emitted to me. I swallowed hard, feeling complete love for and from this being.

I suddenly knew, without any doubt, that my true self had never suffered or experienced pain or hardships. Only my unreal self, the ego, had believed she was undergoing tragedies and tri-umphs. My true self, *everyone's true self*, stayed in the eye of the hurricane where peace reigns eternally.

The experience of meeting my true self was knee-buckling,

and the photographs taken of me with Dyer after the lecture captured my awe-struck expression. I drove home with a million questions swirling in my head and found driving on Interstate 5 incongruous with my state of mind. While I was practically floating from the elation of that day's events, I was also aware of driving a two-ton piece of steel. So I forced myself to stop thinking about spirituality so that I could concentrate. Maybe if I turn on a radio talk show, I'll feel more grounded, I thought.

I turned on KFI, an all-talk radio station from Los Angeles that normally focuses on political issues. But that night's topic was the mystical Jewish text, *The Kabbalah*. I listened for a while and felt my consciousness rising far above the freeway again, so I quickly changed the dial. But every station I turned to seemed to focus upon spiritual topics.

I felt the car's interior air pressure thicken, and I sensed Spirit's presence. For a moment, I felt like a drowning person struggling for air. I wanted to get away from spiritual thoughts and spiritual messages so I could concentrate on driving my car. But the palpable and auditory signs of Spirit were everywhere in my car and on my car radio.

With fear-laced fury I asked, "What do you want with me?" The presence conveyed to me mentally: "There is no place that I am not. You cannot avoid Spirit, for you are Spirit. I am all-and-all." I realized that, since I had ignored His earlier command to "quit drinking and get into *Course in Miracles*," God was now taking a more direct route. As much as I wanted to rebel against anything or anyone controlling me, I knew that God's help was also what I desired.

Deep down, I welcomed God's intervention. I wasn't happy and realized that my drinking and attempts to make a living as a Love Doctor didn't reflect my authentic self. I knew that my human attempts at happiness hadn't yielded what I was really after. It was time to surrender to God's loving care and try His way.

The day after Wayne Dyer's seminar, I purchased a paper-back copy of *A Course in Miracles* at a Barnes & Noble book-store. The book had three separate parts to it: a text, a workbook, and a manual for teachers. I felt guided to start reading the work-book and discovered that it consisted of a one-year meditation program, with one meditation given for each day. Each medita-tion was designed to help you loosen limiting beliefs about the world and to learn ways to train your mind to replace negative thoughts with thoughts of love. I eagerly committed to this one-year study program, and although many *Course in Miracles* study groups existed near my home, I decided to study the text on my own. I was pleased to discover that the basic philosophy and overtones of the *Course* dovetailed with the teachings I'd learned as a young girl. In fact, the meditations happily reminded me of my experiences in Sunday school.

Quitting drinking was a simple matter of making the decision to stop, and I haven't craved alcohol since that day. I immediate-ly noticed how much better my sober mind obeyed my will to stay focused upon thoughts of love and happiness. Whenever my thoughts would slip into the ego's territory of guilt and fear, I was better able to catch and correct this mind-wandering. I felt my mental muscle grow stronger and more disciplined through my sobriety and meditation practices.

In the days following Dyer's seminar, psychic impressions flooded into my consciousness at a steadier rate. Nonstop, I would get clairvoyant and claircognizant information. Sometimes, my psychic insights created confusion for myself and others, as when I would meet a new person and would know information that they had not yet shared with me. For instance, I met a woman and as we were talking I addressed her as "Mary." I knew that was her name but didn't notice that we hadn't yet for-mally introduced ourselves to one another. She stared at me and asked, "How did you know my name was Mary?" Uh-oh, I thought. Some people welcome brushes with the unseen universe, while others such as Mary consider such experiences undesirably "paranormal."

Another time, a new acquaintance showed me photographs of her young daughter. As I looked at the little girl's picture, I mentally saw movie images of her twirling like a ballerina. Without thinking, I remarked to the woman that her daughter was so cute to be dancing like a ballerina at such an early age. As with Mary, I received a reaction of, "How did you know that?" in a tone that showed that my new acquaintance found my prescience to be more horrifying than pleasant. After that exchange, I became more cautious in my conversations. Although I would see and know a great deal about the people with whom I was involved, I would only volunteer this information when someone asked.

In meditation, I asked God about the source and nature of this precognition. I summarized the reply I received in my journal:

> *"Time is an illusion, and when our minds are free of earthly 'rules,' time knows no restrictions. It is a meaningless term. When someone tells me a story, I 'know' the story in my being afterward. With 'psychic,' I know the story without the restriction of having to first hear words."*

So that was it! Precognition wasn't a "special power," but an illustration of time as an illusion. We don't need to have someone tell us about themselves in order for us to know this information. That implies that there is a time *before* and a time *after* we receive personal information about a person. In truth, there is no past or present; there is only *now*. Therefore, all conditions are present to us right this moment, including all knowledge about every topic.

I also understood that every one of our thoughts is imprinted on our energy fields in the same way that data is compressed on a compact disk. This information is openly available to others who are sensitive to energy. We all receive and "read" energy every day. For example, you've probably had instances of immediately distrusting a person whom you've just met. This comes from your tuning into his or her energy field, and sensing that the person's thoughtforms are about dishonesty. Full psychic readings take this energy-sensing activity just one or two steps further. If you practice daily chakra cleansing and balancing, as described in Chapter 17, your psychic receptivity will naturally occur. The only other requirement is a willingness to trust the impressions you receive.

I learned, however, that there is a huge difference between *judging* and *receiving* impressions about another person. If you judge the impressions you receive, your psychic readings will come from your ego or your lower mind. Judgments are a major cause of inaccurate psychic readings, and something against which we need to guard.

Let's say a psychic is giving you a reading, and she receives impressions about your spouse or lover. A psychic who guards against giving ego-influenced readings will simply tell you exactly what she is seeing and feeling as she receives the information. She will allow you to draw your own conclusions from her psychic reading. However, a psychic who is unaware of her ego-influences will filter her psychic impressions through her personal judgments about your lover or spouse. Negative experiences she's had in her own love life could influence her judgments, and what she tells you will not be purely about you.

Almost anyone can receive psychic information about another person. What is not so easy is the ability to transmit this information to your client without running it through the filter of your ego. It is best simply to tell your client exactly what you are seeing, feeling, sensing, or knowing during your psychic reading. Trust the information you receive, and then trust your client to be able to interpret the information in her own way.

I had introduced my counseling clients to my spiritual beliefs several months earlier and was overjoyed at their ready acceptance of spiritual mind treatment practices. My fearful fantasies that my patients would run screaming out of the room if I shared my spirituality with them had thankfully not come to pass. Instead, I witnessed my clients rapidly healing from low self-esteem and eating disorders due to our spiritual psychotherapy work.

During my counseling sessions, I would silently ask Jesus and my angels to guide my words and thoughts. I always sense their help and presence in response to this request, and often, I receive their clear directives. For instance, I was working with a new client who had previously seen many other therapists. She complained that therapy hadn't healed deep feelings of unworthiness connected to her childhood sexual abuse. I mentally asked Jesus, "What do you want me to say to this woman?" Immediately, I felt guided to ask her, "What is the secret that you are keeping?"

After I asked this question, the woman was silent for so long that I worried I'd offended her. Finally, she stammered a story that she'd kept hidden from everyone since her adolescence. This hidden story had created much of her shame and low self-worth. As she talked about the story openly, however, she realized that the details weren't as horrible as she'd imagined. She realized that when a secret is hidden in the dungeons of our soul, it feels akin to lodging a hideous monster.

With each new clinical success involving the use of prayer and spiritual affirmations, I felt happier and freer. I began blending psychic readings into my counseling practice and openly told my clients about the psychic impressions I received during our sessions. Every one of my clients expressed gratitude for these impressions because they helped us uncover core issues.

I vowed never to return to the old style of psychotherapy that viewed problems as real. Since I was no longer conducting psychotherapy, I adopted a new title for myself as a "metaphysician."

Meeting my true self, and realizing that we really don't experience any pain in truth, had dramatically changed my thinking. Before, the spiritual aphorism that "pain is an illusion" had been a pleasantry. Now I knew it as a fact. This knowledge made me feel as elated as someone who is newly in love, and I didn't want anything to rob me of this joy. So I avoided the newspaper, television news programs, radio, and all discussions about political or social problems. I knew that these situations required correction at a mental level, and that if I read or talked about them, I would see them as hardened realities.

I also prayed for guidance about some of my friendships that had become unbalanced. Like many lightworkers who are naturally helpful and loving, I attracted people with multiple life problems. I struggled to find how to be a good friend without being pulled into their conversations about worries and fears. I knew that spiritual healing could resolve any relationship challenge, but I also recognized that I wasn't yet to the point of being able to objectively see my friends as perfect, whole, and complete.

I didn't want to talk to people who saw their dilemmas as hopeless. My knowledge about the unreal nature of problems was still in fragile infancy, and I needed to shield it until I could more confidently look these issues in the eye and see through their illusory nature. Until then, I knew I needed to avoid people with negative mindsets. I had to distance myself from them temporarily, in the same way I avoided newspapers, radio, and television. So I told several people that I would be unavailable for one month, and I was surprised by how graciously they accepted this announcement. My ego had blackmailed me into believing that if I followed my inner guidance, the sky would fall on my head. I was slowly discovering, however, that my only source of turmoil came from the ego's so-called advice.

PARTING THE VEIL

"If spirits really exist, and if we all live in One Mind;
and if mentality can communicate with mentality without
the aid of the physical instrument, then spirit
communication must be possible!"

— Ernest Holmes,
founder of The Church of Religious Science,
and author of *The Science of Mind*

Wayne Dyer's publicist, Edna Farley, called me and said, "I'm publicizing a channeler who has written a book. Would you be interested in seeing a copy for a possible interview and article?" Before I could think about it, I said, "Yes." After I hung up the telephone, I thought it odd that I had agreed, since "channeling" was outside my interests and expertise. I didn't even really know what a channeler was, except what I had seen of Kevin Ryerson in Shirley Maclaine's movie, *Out on a Limb*.

When I first opened the advance copy of the book Edna sent me, *The Eagle and the Rose*[1], I instantly sensed that I was holding an important work. The book's author, Rosemary Altea, is a British medium who talks to the living spirits of those who have physically died. As I mentioned before, I hadn't reconciled my beliefs about life-after-death. So, as I read Altea's case studies in which she discerned dramatic details about her client's deceased relatives, I didn't know what to think.

Still, I found the book fascinating and wanted to read more.

Unfortunately, various duties hectically filled my hours, and I was only able to read a few pages each day. Finally, on a Saturday afternoon, when Michael was on a sailboat race and the boys were visiting friends, I had time to curl up with the book completely.

When I was nearly three-quarters of the way through reading about Altea's case studies, a sudden and overwhelming revelation crashed through my consciousness. It hit me that Altea's words were truthful and that her descriptions of communicating with the dead were a fact. At that instant, I felt a presence behind me on my right, and I began to sob. I recognized the presence as my Grandma Pearl, and I also sensed that she had orchestrated many of my recent miracles, including my receiving a copy of *The Eagle and the Rose.*

"Oh my God!" I said aloud through sobbing cries. "There really is life after death!" I felt my grandmother consoling me, telling me that everything was going to be okay.

This realization gave me comfort, and in the following days, I began talking to my grandmother during my meditations. I also discovered that mediumship had been studied by scientists for centuries, and that well-controlled studies within the past two decades presented convincing evidence that mediums actually communicate with the living spirits of dead persons.[2] One of my overriding concerns, though, remained my relationship with Michael. I was now viewing him as a decidedly unspiritual person and feared that a breakup was inevitable. Still, I hesitated because I deeply loved him, and I absolutely detested the process of breaking up.

Three days after I finished reading Altea's book, a woman named Renée Swisko called. She explained that she was a spiritual healer who was seeking someone to write a book about her work. Renée said that she'd gotten my name from Reid Tracy of Hay House several months earlier and had been meaning to call me but kept putting it off. She then asked if I was familiar with

A Course in Miracles, which was the basis of her spiritual practice. I explained that I had just recently begun studying the text, and that if she had called me when she first intended, I would not have been familiar with the work. The timing of her call was an example of divine order, I thought, as I agreed to go to her house to experience a demonstration of her spiritual healing work.

The morning I was to drive to Renée's home, I was outside on my patio exercising on my Stairclimbing machine. On the boat dock attached to the patio, I watched as Michael scraped barnacles off the bottom of his sailboat. I also noticed a boat, slowly motoring in the bay behind Michael, that had unusual writing painted on its side. When the boat got closer to the dock, I saw that its hull read, "John 3:16."

The sight of that Biblical reference added to my mystical feelings about meeting Renée. She'd told me enough about her work over the telephone to intrigue me sufficiently, yet I also was aware that something bigger than I had arranged for us to meet. This feeling was confirmed when, as I stepped off the elevator to her apartment building floor, I heard an inner voice distinctly say, "After tonight, your life will never be the same."

Renée and I talked for a while before beginning my healing session. She asked whether I had a specific problem or question I wanted to address, and I decided to focus upon my relationship with Michael. Specifically, I wanted to know what to do about our seeming gap in spiritual beliefs.

Renée had me lay upon a futon as she began a hypnotic induction. She asked me to open myself up to Jesus, whom she called "Emmanuel," and to be willing to forgive Michael. I closed my eyes and felt my body pulsate with shivers. This pulsation reminded me of seeing Michael scraping barnacles from his boat, because that's exactly what I felt occurring inside me.

Suddenly, I saw a man's face in front of me. Although he had died before I was born and I hadn't seen his photograph since I was a small child, I instantly recognized the man as my maternal grandfather. The recognition was on a soul level, in the same manner that I'd recognized the identities of the spiritual presences who had come to me.

Wordlessly, my grandfather conveyed essential information to me about my relationship with Michael:

"Your fears about being authentic with Michael and others come partially from me. When your mother was young, I was very frustrated because of a lack of money, and I'd frequently argue with your Grandmother Ada in front of your mother. This frightened your mother so much that she isn't comfortable talking openly about her feelings, especially with men—and this includes your Dad. You learned this pattern of behavior from your mother, who actually learned it because she feared me so much. So please forgive me, and don't break up with Michael, because you aren't seeing him accurately."

I was reeling from this message, but he continued to give me even more shocking news. He told me that I was originally going to be born as his and my Grandmother Ada's second child, as a son. However, he convinced my grandmother to abort her pregnancy because of their financial problems. I would have been my mother's second-oldest brother, had I been born. After the abortion, my soul hung around my mother when she was growing up, and then years later, I incarnated as her daughter. His message rang true, and I immediately believed him. My grandfather again asked me to forgive him for the pain he'd inflicted, and then he vanished.

The morning after my session with Renée, I finally opened up to Michael. I told him about my psychic episode with the New York limousine driver and about my frequent experiences with clairvoyance. I told him about seeing my grandfather, Ben, after his car accident, and about seeing my other grandfather during my session with Renée. Michael was wonderfully accepting of my words and never caused me to feel belittled or judged. In turn, he shared some remarkable psychic experiences he'd had. We then discussed some of our deepest spiritual beliefs and happily discovered we shared many similar viewpoints.

I realized how mistaken I'd been to view Michael as "unspiritual," especially since my own spiritual consciousness had been dormant for so many years. *Everybody* is inherently spiritual, even the most ardent atheist, since we are all children of the same God. In fact, if I judge someone as being unspiritual, that judgment is from my ego. And the ego is the only thing unspiritual about any person. However, since the ego is just an old airbag without any substance, there is nothing unspiritual about any of us. I think that if we focus upon the spark of divinity in other people, we inspire the spark to grow like the pilot light of a furnace.

Later that day, I told my mother about my encounter with her father's spirit. When I explained about being nearly born as her elder brother, my mother gasped. "I always felt I had an invisible male friend next to me as a child," she shared with me. She also confirmed that, because my grandfather had just lost his job, my grandmother had indeed had an abortion two years before my mother's birth.

If my third eye had been opened up widely before, it was now open wider than ever. Many spiritual texts claim that our spiritual vision naturally becomes sharper as we lose our judgments, unforgiveness, and limiting beliefs. My encounter with my grandfather, and my recent revelation about the certainty of life-after-death, had stripped away many of my ego's barriers. As a result, I could see and communicate with both spirits and angels.

Whenever anyone would call me, I would see not only the caller in front of me, but also their spirit guides and angels around them. My clairsentience also told me the family relationship of the spirit to my caller. Somehow, I could *feel* the relationship of one soul to another, as if they had different vibratory rates. For example, I would see a female spirit and know whether she was an aunt, sister, or mother of the person with whom I was speaking. I only had trouble determining whether a spirit was a grandparent or a great-grandparent, as all levels of grandparenting share similar vibratory feelings.

The spirits were simultaneously aware of my mediumistic abilities. Once I was at a church meeting seated next to an elderly woman whom I knew. I noticed her deceased husband, and he saw me notice him. Right away, the man began pestering me to tell his wife that he was with her. "No way!" I mentally told the man, knowing that his wife was staunchly opposed to the idea of life-after-death. I was a clairvoyant medium, but I wasn't a crusader for a cause.

Everywhere I went, I saw crowds of spirits and angels around people. Many spirits begged me to tell their living hosts about their presence, and occasionally, I felt guided to do so. But such situations were always awkward, and I treaded carefully in talking to people about their spiritual companions. For example, when I attended Michael's high school reunion, he introduced me to an old friend who had recently lost his mother. The friend was grief-stricken, as he and his mother had been extremely close.

The situation conflicted me, because I clearly saw his mother with him. She showed me that her son had been crying nonstop since her death, and she asked me to console him somehow. So I took the man aside and gingerly broached the topic of life-after-death with him. First, I mentioned my interest in spiritual books, since I knew that he was a book lover. But he said he only read novels. Next, I talked about some counseling work I'd been doing in the spiritual realm, carefully choosing my words so that he'd know I had a pragmatic take on the topic. Again, he met my words with a blank stare. I tried a couple other ways to begin a conversation with him that would lead to a discussion about his mother's spiritual presence. But he wouldn't talk beyond one- or two-syllable replies. Finally, I gave him my telephone number and said he could call me. He probably thought I was trying to ask him for a date. As we shook hands and parted, his mother continued to beg me to tell her son about her presence.

Another time, I was in a Manhattan book store purchasing a book about life-after-death studies. As I approached the cash register, I saw an elderly female spirit next to the cashier, and I knew this spirit was either her grandmother or her great-grandmother. The spirit had a huge smile and the personality of one with a generous nature.

As I handed the book to the cashier, she noticed its title and said, "Oh! Life-after-death! I definitely believe in that, don't you?" Before I could say a word about her grandmother's presence, the cashier said, "You know, sometimes I'd swear that my grandmother is with me. But I'm really terrified of spirits and ghosts and such, so I'd be really afraid if I ever found out she was actually with me." I smiled at her and her grandmother, and then left the store without saying a word.

I began feeling overwhelmed by my new spiritual sight, and longed to regain a sense of normalcy. Although I believed my mediumistic ability was a gift that I could use for healing clients, I didn't want the spirits overrunning my life. During my meditations on this issue, I discovered that through my intentions, I could adjust my clairvoyance to a more comfortable level.

Soon enough, the day arrived for my interview with medium Rosemary Altea for *Complete Woman* magazine. Michael, the assigned photographer for the story, and I arrived at the Four Seasons Hotel suite in Los Angeles where Rosemary was staying, hoping that she would shed some light on my new spiritual vision.

Rosemary told me that she, too, saw spirits wherever she went. She told me that in the beginning of her mediumship, she would openly tell people about the spirits she saw beside them. Then one day, Rosemary told a woman she'd just met at a dance hall that her father was beside her. The woman reacted with shock and ran away in obvious distress. From that day, she adopted a firm resolution never to talk to a person about their spiritual companions unless they first requested.

Then Rosemary began speaking to my Grandmother Pearl, who was beside me, and to Michael's late father, who was next to him. I was happy to watch Rosemary at work, and found that her style of communicating with spirits was similar to my own. However, when I asked her about "the spirits," she sharply corrected my vocabulary. "You call them 'spirits,'" she said, "but I call them 'people.'" Of course she was correct. Just because a person has shed their physical shell, their soul is still human. The word *spirit* implies that they are less than human.

Meeting Rosemary helped me to relax with respect to my changing spiritual perspective. I decided that I needed to seek out other mediums to further compare notes. Fortunately, The Learning Light Foundation, where I had taken psychic-development classes, was offering a one-day course on mediumship. The course description said the class was only open to "Advanced Mediums." At first, I decided that this meant long-time mediums, meaning I wouldn't qualify. But then I felt Grandma Pearl's loving energy urging me to enroll in the class.

The "Advanced Mediums Only" class requirement must have intimidated many people, because there was only one other student enrolled. Our teacher, Rose, was an Englishwoman who conducted mediumship sessions in Great Britain and America.

Immediately, Rose asked us to perform mediumship work. I gulped as she asked me to be the first one to do a mediumship reading aloud. On top of that, I was to conduct my reading on *her!* I felt intimidated, wondering why in the world I had signed up for this course when my teacher and classmate were much more experienced than myself. Nonetheless, Rose firmly told me to begin, so I took a deep breath.

I closed my eyes, and Rose said, "No, no! You must learn to do your readings with your eyes open!" So I unfocused my eyes to give my inner senses my fullest attention. I let go of my mind and allowed it to become blank. I immediately felt a small presence at Rose's left side. When my awareness bumped into the presence, I began seeing it take the shape and form of a person.

"I see a young boy next to you," I said.

Rose's face grew pale, but she obviously tried to remain deadpan, so as not to influence my work. "Tell me more," she said. "How old is he?"

"I can't tell, because he seems small for his age. He looks to be about eight years old." I went on to describe his appearance, and I noticed Rose's eyes redden and fill with tears.

"He's my son," she explained. "He was killed in a soccer accident many years ago."

At first I felt awful about bringing up a topic of grief for her. But Rose assured me that my mediumistic reading was very appropriate and even appreciated. After the other student conducted a reading on Rose, our teacher told us our next assignment. "There's a class going on upstairs right now that is expecting you," she explained. "You are going to do mediumship readings for the class members."

Again, I felt intimidated and unprepared, but Rose wouldn't let me skip this assignment. She marched us upstairs and, as before, I was to go first. As Rose had instructed us to do, I stood in front of the class with my eyes open, and one by one, gave each student a "psychic and mediumship reading." Each reading was different; sometimes I would receive and deliver information about the person's career, and sometimes the reading would concern the person's love life. Each time, the students would smile and confirm the accuracy and relevancy of my readings.

When Rose, the other student, and I returned to our classroom, she congratulated us on successful readings. I understood that Grandma Pearl had urged me to take this class because my confidence in my psychic abilities needed boosting. The class helped me feel comfortable publicly giving psychic and mediumship readings.

In the days that followed, it seemed that members of the spirit world were spreading the word about my mediumistic abilities. New people would call and specifically ask for psychic counseling appointments with me, saying things such as, "I don't know how I found out about you. However, I came across your name and *something* just made me call and make an appointment with you."

Many of these callers were adult survivors of child abuse with whom their deceased abuser wanted to make amends. During the counseling session, I would facilitate conversations between my client and her abusive father, uncle, brother, or grandfather. If my client was willing to forgive her abuser, his spirit would leave her side, often escorted by angels or evolved loved ones from the other side. As the spirit left, my client would feel intense physical sensations, like a vacuum around her body, accompanied by strong feelings of relief. Usually, she would discover that parting company with her deceased abuser would alleviate depression, anxiety, insomnia, and compulsions such as overeating.

I found that whenever new clients would come to me complaining of depression or addictions, they almost always had an "earthbound" spirit next to them. In other words, a deceased person other than their assigned spirit guide accompanied them. I learned that deceased people can choose to stay close to earth. Many of them hang around because they are afraid of "God's wrath," and others stay here because they don't want to leave their loved ones, their home, or their business. Some deceased people are kept earthbound because their surviving kin are extremely grief-stricken, and the deceased person chooses to stay near them. With many of my abuse survivor clients, their deceased loved ones were around due to remorse over their abusive behavior.

Although these contrite spirits had good intentions in wanting to undo their harm, their presence had unhealthful effects upon their living hosts. Remorseful people are usually depressed people. If you hang around a depressed person, you eventually find that some depression rubs off on you. It doesn't matter whether the depressed person has a physical body or not; you've probably talked to a depressed person on the telephone and felt awful when you hung up. It's the same effect when you have a depressed spirit living next to you.

As a result, much of my counseling work involves "spirit-releasement therapy." This means I facilitate a resolution between my client and the remorseful spirits around her. After we sufficiently convince the spirit that my client forgives her, I call upon the Archangel Michael or an evolved spirit to escort the deceased person to the afterlife.

I always watch each spirit being guided away, as I'm curious about where they go. I have found that there are different levels of the afterlife, and each level has a different-colored backdrop. We naturally gravitate toward the afterlife level corresponding to our own level of spiritual understanding. Those people who vibrate at higher levels of love, compassion, and understanding go to higher levels in the afterlife plane. Just as it is with chakras, the lowest level of the afterlife has a red hue, and the highest level is colored in blue, violet, and white lights.

Most of the spirits whom I help in my releasement work are taken to a yellow place. This makes sense if we consider that the orange sacral chakra is focused on earthly desires. Most abusers are hooked on desires of the flesh, such as sex, alcohol, and drugs. Once people move past their human appetites, they ascend to the next level, which is signified by the yellow solar plexus chakra.

I received an understanding that different levels of the afterlife don't signify a punishment or a reward. They are simply appropriate places where we are assured of fitting in. On earth, we find a similar experience when we naturally gravitate toward people who hold similar views to our own. It's important that we recognize that attractions to other people are simply a matter of having energy rhythms that synchronize with one another. It's not that people we like are "more spiritually evolved" or "better people," than others. If we indulge in such judgments, our egos enlarge, and this impairs our abilities to give psychic readings and spiritual healings. No one is "good" or "bad"; they're just vibrating at a level different from our own.

I also learned from talking with deceased people that just because people die, they are not radically different from the people they were on earth. Yes, they have a richer understanding about the importance of love and the irrelevance of material gain. However, death doesn't automatically lift the ego-self, and people's personalities pretty much remain the same. Often when I describe what their deceased loved ones are saying, my clients will exclaim something like, "That sounds just like the Aunt Edna I knew and loved!"

For example, my client Sandra's cousin, Marcus, had molested her when she was a small child and he was a teenager. The memory of the sexual abuse she had experienced had preyed upon Sandra's self-esteem over the years, and at the age of 40, she came to see me to try to resolve the residual effects. Marcus had died of a drug overdose several years before, and I wasn't too surprised when he suddenly appeared during the beginning of the session. Appearing high above Sandra's head, Marcus relayed his regrets for inflicting such intense emotional pain upon her.

"I was just a damn grease monkey, and I didn't know what the hell I was doing," was Marcus's crude apology. "It *really is* Marcus!" exclaimed Sandra. "He was a grease monkey who worked at an old gas station!" She was suddenly glad to speak with the man whom she had so long despised. The two talked at length about the abuse incidents, and Sandra released much of her unforgiveness toward Marcus during that first session. By the end of the session, Marcus was considerably relieved by the opportunity to make amends. He expressed regret to both of us (he apologized for frightening me because his sudden appearance at our session had startled me). Several more sessions were necessary before Sandra could completely forgive Marcus, but we never saw or heard from Marcus after that first session.

Sometimes my clients are unwilling to forgive their deceased relatives. Amy came to me after reading *Losing your Pounds of Pain*, and she connected her overweight body to the years of rage she carried toward her father. As Amy talked, I knew that her father was deceased, as I could feel his presence in the room. I learned more about her tragic story from the conversation I facilitated between Amy and her father.

As a child, Amy had witnessed her father stab her twin brother, Andy, to death. When her pet dog, Ronnie, tried to intervene, her father fatally stabbed him, too. During our session, Amy's father begged for her forgiveness. Amy refused, although she acknowledged that forgiveness would help her own mental health considerably.

Then I felt another presence show up who felt, from his vibratory pattern, like Amy's brother. After I described how he looked, Amy confirmed that I was seeing her deceased brother, Andy. Andy asked Amy to please let go of her anger. After all, Andy explained, he was the one who'd been killed, and *he* had forgiven their murderous father. However, Amy said she would rather die than forgive this unforgivable act. So I asked Amy, on a scale of one to 10, how much she was willing to forgive her father if "one" represented "not at all" and "10" represented "completely." Amy told me "2." I asked that small part of Amy to open up to Holy Spirit's intervention, to release the rest of herself from her anger.

Amy agreed to open up that little part of herself, and that was all it took! I watched her body shudder and then relax as she released much of her hostility. When I spoke with her later, she reported feeling much lighter and happier after the session. She also told me that when she got home, something made her look into her dog's eyes. Instantly, she recognized her childhood dog Ronnie's eyes staring back at her. Amy's dog had returned from the afterlife to complete his mission of being by her side.

Another client, Anthony, was the eldest of six boys. Growing up, he suffered severe physical beatings and verbal abuse from his father. This abuse made Anthony insecure and nervous, and he came to me with a general complaint of unhappiness with life. During our session, I felt a male presence enter the session. I knew from its vibratory pattern and because it was next to Anthony's right side—which signifies the male or father side of the family in right-handed clients—that this was a paternal grandfather. However, I couldn't tell if it was Anthony's grandfather, great-grandfather, or even great-great grandfather. So I began describing his physical characteristics, and Anthony quickly identified the man as his paternal grandfather.

The grandfather said that he had abused Anthony's father, and that the abuse cycle had continued into the next generation. "I am so, so sorry," said the grandfather. "It's all my fault." Anthony was sobbing as he explained to me that his grandfather, while living, had been a Mafia leader who had created a great deal of pain for many people. The session was highly emotional, as Anthony and his grandfather reconciled generations of anger, resentment, fear, and unforgiveness.

I also communicated with deceased relatives who acted as my clients' "spirit guides." These spirits, who receive afterlife training before taking on their role, serve protective and guiding functions in the lives of living people. We all have one or more spirit guides with us at any time. Unlike earthbound spirits, though, spirit guides lend energy and joy to their living companions. While earthbound spirits try to control their living hosts' thoughts with fear, spirit guides give loving suggestions that don't usurp the person's free will. Spirit guides are similar to guardian angels, except spirit guides have lived an earthly life.

Much of my work with spirit guides involves relaying messages to my clients. Almost always, the client has previously "heard" these messages from the guide but has ignored them. So when I deliver spirit guide messages, my client usually says, "I had a strong feeling that was what my spirit guide wanted me to hear."

For instance, a woman named Maureen came to see me because she had been to my seminar about "Divine Life Purpose," and she wanted a psychic reading about her life path. Since my seminar had been held at a church, I inquired if she frequently attended the church's services or spiritual seminars. Maureen said that she did and then casually mentioned that her mother had been a minister. Right away, I heard a voice say, "A Methodist minister," but I shook it off. I thought I must be making the phrase up, since at the time I attended a Methodist church myself. Then Maureen said, "My mother was a Methodist minister, but she died in 1985."

I asked Maureen if she ever felt her mother's presence, and she confirmed that her mother frequently visited her. Since Maureen's mother enunciated beautifully from her years of pulpit preaching, I let her do all the talking through me during the session. Maureen and I were enthralled with her mother's poetic and powerful sermon from heaven, which was laden with much practical and profound advice about Maureen's life. As with my other clients, Maureen reacted to her mother's words by nodding and saying, "Yes, that sounds just like Mama," and "Yep, I know she's right. She's absolutely right. I'm gonna follow her advice, because I know it's the right thing to do."

MAKING PEACE WITH GOD

"Never the Spirit was born,
the Spirit shall Cease to be never;
Never was time it was not;
End and Beginning are dreams!"

— The *Bhagavad-Gita,* spiritual text

Hay House had just published *Constant Craving,* and for the first time, I felt very happy about one of my books. Except for *Losing Your Pounds of Pain,* my previous books had always stopped short of expressing the deepest truth about which I knew I was capable of writing. This time, however, my book reflected the dictate to "teach about the links between mind and body" I had heard during my childhood out-of-body experience.

Kristina Reece, the publicity director of Hay House, arranged for me to appear on several television talk shows to discuss *Constant Craving.* From my experiences in discussing food cravings, I expected that the talk-show hosts would ask me to perform "food cravings interpretations" on call-in and studio audience members. This was easy enough for me to do, as I had interpreted people's food cravings for nearly ten years. I had memorized the psychoactive ingredients in hundreds of food products. So if people told me they craved peanut butter ice cream, I knew that this meant they were craving choline and pyrazine, which act as antidepressants and brain pleasure-center stimulators. Therefore,

I knew that they were feeling depressed because they weren't having enough fun.

I was unprepared, however, for the difference my wide-open chakras would make in performing food-craving interpretations on talk shows. I found myself giving interpretations that included specific details about the audience member's career, love life, and health. My psychic abilities had combined with my knowledge about food-craving meanings, and as a result I was giving on-air psychic readings. The telephone lines jammed with callers on each talk show, and afterwards, many talk-show staff members requested private psychic readings.

When I returned to California, I decided to visit Rose, my mediumship class instructor, so I made an appointment to see her on July 15, 1995, a Saturday afternoon. As I was getting dressed for my appointment, I heard a voice outside and to the right of me clearly say, "Doreen, you better put the top up on your car or it's going to get stolen."

I recognized the voice as being the same one I had heard just twice before in my life. It was the male voice that had spoken during my childhood out-of-body experience, and then again when I was directed to stop drinking and study *A Course in Miracles*. The voice had made reference to my convertible car, which is an average-looking car when its black cloth top is up. But when the top is down, the white upholstery combines with the white exterior in a very beautiful way. At that moment, my car was in the garage with its top down.

I ignored the voice, thinking, I don't have time to put the top up because I'm already running late. Still coming from outside my body, the voice said to me, "Then have Grant put the top up." Now I felt irritated, as if someone was pestering me. I replied mentally, "That would still take an extra five minutes to do, and I don't have that much extra time!" The voice told me again to put the car top up, but I stubbornly ignored its warning.

I never doubted the validity of the voice's warning, and I

believed that someone probably would attempt to steal my car while I was with Rose. I didn't let this thought bother me, however. I figured that if someone did try to steal my car, my Grandmother Pearl would warn me. I pictured that her warning would give me enough time to run outside and chase away any would-be thieves. Besides, I thought, the car has a good alarm system, and the horn will honk if anyone touches it.

At the time, I only carried liability insurance on my car since it was fully paid for. So if someone had stolen my car, I would not have been insured to receive a replacement car. Still, I had a certain knowingness that I was spiritually safe and protected. While driving to meet with Rose, I listened to *A Course in Miracles* on audiocassette. One particular phrase grabbed my attention: "*God does not help because He knows no need. But He creates all Helpers of His Son while he believes his fantasies are true.*"

In other words, since God is all-love, He does not see anything but love. He does not know of our nightmares and ego illusions. He therefore sees no need to intervene in our lives, because there is nothing wrong with our lives. Our help comes from God's creations—the angels, Holy Spirit, ascended masters, and our brothers and sisters—who see the illusions of problems, just as we do.

A moment later, I turned onto Lincoln Boulevard in Anaheim and suddenly felt a thick paintlike energy pour over my car. The energy felt dense, angry, and fearful. I sensed that someone with dishonorable intentions had "spotted" my car, and I was extra alert to my surroundings. I pulled into a parking spot next to the building where I was to meet Rose. Before getting out of my car, I visualized it surrounded in the white light of God's love. Next, I took the six or seven spirituality books I had in my car and spread them on the dashboard. I felt an inevitability about what was to come, but I felt assured in my heart that everything would turn out all right.

As I got out of the car and stood up, I heard a man's voice

behind me shout, "Don't move! Turn around and give me your car keys now!" I spun around and saw a short, leanly muscled young man angrily facing me. The moment felt surreal, and time slowed as I struggled inside for a solution. Then I mentally called for spiritual support and intervention. Meanwhile, something told me not to surrender my car keys to this man. Instead, my instincts told me to scream at the top of my lungs, and so I did!

Just like my dream years before in which I confronted a burglar with shouts, the would-be carjacker's eyes grew large with surprise and fright at my assertiveness. As I continued screaming, I saw his determination to steal my car dissolve into fear. I also saw his partner waiting in a idling car nearby, nervously looking around for witnesses to their crime. The man turned his attention from my car toward my purse, and he yanked on its handles. I felt extremely empowered, as if a thousand angels thronged my sides. I screamed at him that he would not get my purse, either.

At this point, a human angel intervened. A woman in the parking lot, sitting in her car, realized what was occurring. She pressed against her horn, which in turn caught the attention of the people inside the nearby building. As they came outside to investigate the commotion, the two would-be car thieves drove away. Shaken, I thanked my human and spiritual angels for protecting me. I then put the top up on my car and drove away.

When I got home, I called two prayer ministries, my parents, and some of my spiritually minded friends. I asked for prayerful support in helping me to forgive my two assailants. My concern was that I would hold resentment and fear about the incident, which would rob me of my peace of mind—a far more valuable possession than any car or purse. I had spent so much time and effort freeing myself from unforgiveness, and I wasn't about to return to a life of harbored resentments. To do so would have destroyed my newfound psychic abilities, since resentment covers the third eye and crown chakras like heavy curtains. With prayerful support, though, I knew I could release unforgiveness toward the two men fully.

I also spent time uncovering why I had attracted the situation to myself. I realized I hadn't been listening to my highest wisdom. I was completely ignoring much of its loving guidance, including its warning to put the top up on my car. I asked myself, "Why did I repeatedly rebel against the voice's guidance?" He was always correct, yet each of the three times I'd heard his voice, I had to learn his wisdom the hard way.

This dramatic episode instilled a new respect in me for spiritual guidance. The voice had *known* what my future held and had intervened with a direct warning. I prayed for help in surrendering that part of myself that still rebelled against following God's will. I knew that I was acting like a teenager who defied her parents' loving wisdom, but I wasn't yet ready to trust that what God wanted for me was in line with what I thought I wanted.

Now I realize that God always spoke to me loudly, even when I wasn't listening. In hindsight, I see that God arranged for me to interview metaphysical authors to awaken my spiritual awareness. Bonnie Krueger and *Complete Woman's* associate editor, Martha Carlson, continually assigned me interviews. From each one, I learned valuable insights that would guide me further along my spiritual path.

For instance, I learned from Dannion Brinkley, the author of *Saved by the Light,* about the after-death life review.[1] This is the process immediately following death in which we see the effect we have had upon every person we have ever met or influenced. During our life review, we become the other person and feel their emotions as if they were our own. Thus, if we have triggered another's pain, we experience that pain as our own. If we, however, have brought someone joy, then we experience that joy as our own. Dannion inspired me to redouble my efforts to extend kindness to everyone I met. He also taught me the importance of taking deep breaths. "This is how the spirit world transmits information to us," he explained. I also delighted in speaking with his deceased mother, who functions as Dannion's spirit guide. The woman has a very powerful sense of humor, a gift that her son definitely inherited.

Another time, *Complete Woman* assigned me to interview Denise Brown, the sister of the late Nicole Brown Simpson. Although I avoid reading, watching, and listening to news reports, I had watched the closing arguments in the Simpson criminal case. "Look, there's Nicole!" I exclaimed to Michael as I watched the last phase of the trial. I clearly saw Nicole in the courtroom. Her face was red, and her cheeks were puffed up with fury as she pointed to O.J. and screamed that he was guilty. Nicole desperately tried to get the attention of those in the court-room, and she was overwrought with frustration and anger at their inability to hear her screams.

Several months later, when I interviewed Denise Brown, Nicole was in the room with us. Her presence felt as if she'd made peace with the situation, as there was a strength that only comes from someone who has released unforgiveness. I asked Denise whether she was aware of Nicole's presence, and she talked about several instances where Nicole had come to her and given advice. Denise discussed how she definitely believed in life-after-death and that she fully expected an afterlife reunion with her sister.

Another one of my magazine article assignments didn't seem very spiritual at first. Martha Carlson asked me to interview the authors of a new book about Doris Duke, heir to the American Tobacco and Duke University fortune. Doris was one of the world's wealthiest women, and she was also tall, blonde, and attractive. In addition, Doris was a tireless philanthropist who gave millions of dollars to charitable causes. Although Doris seemed to have everything a person could want, she was terribly lonely and miserable throughout her life. During my interviews, I discovered the reason why: her father had taught Doris at an early age never to trust anyone. When we don't trust other people, we automatically don't trust ourselves!

The interviews about Doris Duke underscored what I was learning in my psychic and spiritual work about the importance of watching my thoughts about other people. Every spiritual text I read emphasized that the way we think about others instantly affects the way we think about our own selves. During this period, as I was finishing writing an article one evening, the telephone rang. When I picked it up and found that an MCI telephone solicitor was on the line, I was furious at being interrupted. I made some rude remarks and practically slammed down the receiver. A few moments later, I was aware that I felt absolutely terrible. So I stopped, closed my eyes, and asked, "What is this all about?"

The answer I received stunned me. "You and that phone solicitor are one. How you treat and think of her is how you think of yourself." After that, I began consciously working to look and treat others with the same sort of respect I wanted to feel toward myself. This lesson brought to life for me the true essence of the second commandment to "love your neighbor as yourself." The word *commandment* had always bothered me, because it felt like some authority was trying to control me. I began to understand, though, that a more accurate description than "commandment" was "rule for happy living."

I was slowly realizing how deeply afraid I was of trusting God. I feared that His will for me might involve an impoverished life where I would live in misery. I also found that my clients and friends wrestled with the same mistrust.

According to *A Course in Miracles* and other esoteric texts, humans were incarnated and Earth was formed the moment we decided to separate from God because we didn't trust His wisdom. We each decided, essentially, to run away from home and build our own place where we could be completely in charge. However, we cannot destroy the memory or awareness of God's love. We continually seek, on our earthplane, to recapture the experience of being totally loved. So we look for people who seem to be happy, thinking they have the key that we know exists somewhere. Always, though, these chases result in disappointment because every earthly experience pales in comparison with our memories of union with God.

Deep down we may even feel afraid or guilty for leaving our Creator. Sometimes we feel abandoned by Him, or worry that He will catch up with us and punish us for running away. We also fear His judgments, since a part of our consciousness is aware that something greater than our ego-self exists.

Fortunately, it is impossible to leave God, so our separation from Him is nothing but an extremely realistic nightmare. The ego and its perceptions of the world are also dreams, and our true self is back home with God. Our true self and God don't even know about the ego, since true consciousness is only filled with love.

The ego is vaguely aware that something greater than itself exists. The ego believes the reason this "something" doesn't acknowledge it is that God and the true self think they are better than the ego. We continually replay this projected rejection throughout life. I certainly created many scenarios where I imagined people were judging, ridiculing, and rejecting me. I then adjusted my behaviors in response to my perceptions of rejection and created self-fulfilling prophecies. Practically all human drama stems from the continual recreation of the ego's initial separation from the Godhead.

Thank goodness it's just a nightmare from which we can awaken at any moment! I realized this fact during a dark night of the soul that helped me to understand that God, I, and you are all eternally linked as one.

It happened when I was at a bookstore with a friend. I was looking at the "New Arrivals" bookshelf and felt upset that none of my recent books were on display. Intellectually, I realized that publishers pay to have their books displayed on the front shelves and that my publisher chose to spend promotional money in other ways. But emotionally, I felt like a child who was jealous because her siblings got better gifts.

I began complaining to my friend that my books were largely unheard of. It didn't seem fair that other authors, writing about topics similar to my own, were receiving much more publicity. To console me, my friend innocently said, "Maybe it's God's will."

Her words struck a sore nerve, and I silently fumed. Later that evening when I was alone in my bedroom, I sobbed hot tears of anger. If God was blocking the success of my books, then I decided I didn't want to have anything to do with Him. I was furious that He would be such a mean and unsupportive Father. "I'm going to another universe where God isn't in charge!" I defiantly cried. I meant it, too. I fully intended to leave God's side so that I could solely control my own life.

The only trouble was, I couldn't figure out where I could go where God wasn't. For hours, I thought about how to escape God and His will. Finally, I had to face the realization that God was *everywhere*. There was no place where I could go in which God didn't exist. Not only that, God's will was everywhere. I could die or become unconscious, and God would still be where I was, because there was no way to escape Him. At first, this realization infuriated me and I felt trapped, like a person living in too-crowded quarters.

I cried until I was exhausted. Feeling calmer, I thought about my dilemma with a more objective outlook. If God's will was everywhere, that implied an overlap between my own will and God's. The logical conclusion came to me like thunder: "God's will and my will are inseparable. Our wills are united!" I laughed with relief, and a great weight lifted as I realized I needn't fear God's will for me. After all, my will and God's will were one. With that, I slept soundly, knowing that my wrestling and straining against God were finally over.

A month later, I interviewed Betty Eadie while she was touring with her new book, *The Awakening Heart*. So much had happened since the first time I'd spoken with Betty! I was so much happier, more alive, and freer than I had been before. Betty said she recalled our first interview and thanked me for the article I had written about her book.

"I understand that your article about *Embraced by the Light* had quite a positive ripple effect," Betty said, as she explained that everything we think, say, or do is the equivalent of throwing stones in a pond. Our actions generate ripples that have far-reaching effects on many people, and we must take care to only throw loving stones into life's pond.

Betty talked about how she, too, had experienced a dark night of the soul in which she confronted God. Like me, her confrontation had helped her realize that God loves us and is always with us. Apparently, this sort of wrestling is a universal experience that most of us must have to make peace with God and our higher self. When we admit our deep-seated anger or mistrust of God, we can fully release these feelings. By doing so, we are better able to stay centered in true self-awareness.

Toward the end of our interview, Betty talked about her deep faith in God's guidance. I said, "You've written that you 'keep an eye open for doors.' How can we notice and recognize the doors that are opening for us?"

Betty replied, "Those doors appear anytime, anyplace. It's one reason why I wake up every day excited, because I know God has things for me to do, and the doors are there. I just have to recognize them. When opportunities pop up, there are no accidents. Those are the doors opening for us. It's a matter of having the confidence in yourself and in God to trust in it and go forward."

I then asked her for clarification to a question I'd had lately. "Sometimes things come up in our lives that are actually detours taking us away from our path. How can we know whether it's a door or a detour?"

Betty answered, "When it's a detour, it's usually something

you *want* to do rather than *desire* to do. You have to find out whether your motive is ego or love. If the ego is motivating you, then chances are this is not the right door for you, and it will dead-end."

MIRACLES OF ONENESS

*"Like the bee, gathering honey from different flowers,
the wise man accepts the essence of different scriptures and
sees only the good in all religions."*

— *Srimad Bhagavatam,*
spiritual text of Hinduism

Before ending my interview with Betty Eadie, I brought up another topic that was still on my mind: Christianity and its relationship to mystical experience and studies. Through my study of *A Course in Miracles* and the Bible, and in my meditations and metaphysical healing work, I had developed a very deep and close bond with Jesus Christ. I continued attending different traditional and nontraditional churches, finding that each offered me something of value, but that alone none of the churches echoed my deepest beliefs. I had developed my own personalized faith that blended Christianity, Eastern philosophy, metaphysics, and my own life experiences. As a personal symbol of my beliefs, I frequently wore crystal cross necklaces. The crystal stood for pure oneness and mysticism, and the cross stood for my gratitude for Jesus's teachings.

Like me, Betty defines Christianity as a deep love and respect for Jesus Christ as a person and teacher. Using that definition, she sees herself as a Christian. However, following the publication of her book, *Embraced by the Light*, some fundamental Christian organizations picketed her workshops. They taunted her with shouts and signs that said, "Which Jesus did you actually meet, Betty?"

The protesters were referring to Biblical prophecies about imposters posing as Christ at the beginning of the apocalypse. They feared that during her near-death experience in which she met and spent time with Jesus, Betty had actually encountered the false Jesus, or the Antichrist. They persecuted her with angry words and signs.

Betty shared that she'd come to peace with her persecutors and neither feared nor judged them. We discussed how we'd both concluded that there is no one "correct" religion, but that all faiths had similar threads connecting them. That thread, we both agreed, was a deep desire for our Divine Creator's love.

Betty told me that instead of responding to her protestors with fear or anger, she would send them loving thoughts. She believes that we can heal the seeming religious divides through such conscious thoughts of love. Her words are important reminders for lightworkers, as we are apt to encounter resistance from people who fear or misunderstand our motives. We must not react to their fears with anything but love, or else we give reality and power to fear.

The Antichrist is the ego within each of us. So often the ego pretends to be the true self or the "I Am Christ" presence. I really believe this is what Jesus was talking about when he warned his disciples to beware of imposters. The ego poses as our higher self to avoid getting evicted. It goes through all the motions of meditation, and it mouths beautiful words of oneness. Yet we know it's the ego when we feel unhappy, resentful, jealous, fearful, competitive, tense, or believe we are superior to others. If we're not at peace, we are in an ego state.

Soon after I interviewed Betty, I had an experience that brought the importance of our discussions about oneness home to me. I was walking on the beach near my Newport Beach home, following a long day of giving metaphysical treatments to clients.

As I neared a long row of rocks known as "The Wedge," I saw a small brown animal. I recognized it as a baby sea lion, and I saw that something was wrong with it.

I sat on the sand next to the sea lion. With his flippers, he pulled himself closer to my side. The little guy's breathing seemed terribly labored, and I sensed his exhaustion and fear. I remembered that a large group of sea lions lived on a floating platform off the end of the Wedge. The baby must have separated from his mother and then washed ashore. Intuitively, I placed my hands above the sea lion and visualized Christ energy coming in through my crown chakra, out my fingertips, and into its tiny body. I prayed for assistance from Jesus and the angels.

Just then, a lifeguard rushed to my side. With a loud voice and abrupt movements, he told me that he'd just telephoned an animal shelter to take the sea lion to a marine life preserve in another seaside town. As he spoke, the sea lion rushed under the shelter of a nearby rock formation. The lifeguard's intense and fearful energy obviously frightened the little animal. The lifeguard took out a stethoscope and attempted to place it upon the sea lion's chest. However, the animal hissed and barked as if about to bite. Embarrassed, the lifeguard walked away and mumbled that he would go watch for the animal shelter truck to arrive.

I realized that something needed to be done. If the animal shelter took the sea lion away, he had little chance of ever reuniting with his mother. I fervently prayed for Jesus to deliver help to the situation, and quickly! As I prayed, the sea lion rejoined my side, and I continued to send him healing light through my fingertips.

I opened my eyes as a young man gently approached the sea lion and me. The man smiled at me as he carefully sat next to us. The sea lion peacefully remained lying on its side. I explained the situation to the young man, and he immediately understood that we needed a miracle to have the sea lion reunited with his mother before the rescue truck arrived. A man of faith, he agreed to join me in prayer.

The young man noticed the positions of my hands as I prayed. I was still sending healing energy through my fingertips to the sea lion, and he asked, "Are you doing some sort of spiritual treatment?" When I replied, "Yes," he explained that his mother was involved in nontraditional healing, and so he recognized that I was conducting "pranic healing" on the sea lion.

When we went back to praying to Jesus for help, the young man suddenly said, "Are you sure that you are praying to the real Jesus?" He looked at me with a combination of fearful judgment and compassionate concern.

I fingered the crystal cross around my neck and smiled at him reassuringly. "Oh, I'm very sure that I'm talking to the real Jesus."

The young man smiled genuinely back at me, and said, "I guess it's true what they say that whenever two or more are gathered in his name, that miracles can happen."

I agreed, and we went back to our joint prayers. Time was running out, we realized, as the animal rescue truck was surely on its way to retrieve the little sea lion. Then a sound to our left suddenly made us look up. There, on the top of the Wedge, stood a man with wildly long gray hair. A blinding white light glowed around him, which made it difficult to see his facial features. The man climbed down the Wedge rocks surefootedly. The man didn't look at me or the young man, and he didn't say a word. We silently watched as the man knowingly took charge of the situation. He grabbed a long piece of seaweed and tickled the sea lion's belly. The sea lion protested, but he also moved toward the shoreline a few inches.

My young male companion put up his hand as if to question the older man's actions, but I stopped him and said, "This is good. This is the miracle we prayed for."

The old man continued tickling the baby sea lion, who responded by inching toward the water. Within minutes, the man had coaxed the little animal back into the sea. His task finished, the man walked away without looking at us or speaking. The young man and I sighed as we watched the sea lion swim in the direction of the floating platform. Five minutes later, the animal shelter truck pulled onto the beach sand, but the sea lion was gone from sight. We both agreed that we'd witnessed a miracle. I then hurried to catch up to the old man and thank him for his kindness, but he shrugged off my attempts to compliment his actions. Instead, he waved me along with a smile that conveyed, "Go in peace."

My life *was* becoming more peaceful, as I was learning how to stay centered in my true self more often. I was no longer afraid to discuss or write about my spiritual beliefs and experiences, and this authenticity added to my peace of mind. I also continued twice-daily meditations and found that they were especially powerful when conducted out in nature.

The day before my birthday, Michael and I took an afternoon beach walk. Usually, we fill our walks with lively discussions. This day, however, Michael and I walked in silence. We were together physically, holding hands. Yet we were both individually in our own worlds, each peacefully absorbed with our thoughts.

About a mile into the walk, we reached the Wedge. I loved sitting on its crystalline quartz stones while meditating, lulled by the sound of pounding surf and the warm embrace of the afternoon sun. But recently, extra-high surf at the Wedge had marred my meditations. I hadn't been able to "let go," and I focused a part of my consciousness on my physical surroundings, making sure I was safe from the 15-foot waves that could suddenly change course and wash me off the rocks.

This day, Michael sweetly offered to watch the surfline while I meditated, freeing me to lose all awareness of my surroundings. We walked next to the Wedge's jetty, looking for two comfortable rocks to sit on. We carefully inspected our seating options, seeking a location near enough to the water to hear the pounding surf, yet far enough away to afford us safety. Finally, we selected two flat quartz stones.

Eyes closed, I deeply inhaled the misty salt air as the spray cooled my warm skin. Trusting Michael to watch for high surf, I rapidly let myself go into a deep meditation. I visualized my chakras and pictured pure white energy cleansing and balancing each one. As I did this, my heart swelled with bliss. I felt so much love right then, a deep love for all of life. I was conscious of the connection of every being, and felt as one with everyone and everything in a powerful state of love. I came out of this glorious meditation stretching my arms with gratitude for the beautiful truth of life. Opening my eyes, I saw Michael peacefully sitting next to me cross-legged. He smiled as he noticed my stirring and asked, "Are you ready to head back now?"

I nodded and started to push myself off the rock. As I turned to climb down, a bright pink object against the gray rock caught my eye. I gasped as I realized what I was looking at. There, next to me was a bouquet of lilac orchids and deep pink rosebuds, tied with a bright pink satin ribbon. The bouquet hadn't been there when we'd sat down—I would have noticed it! We'd inspected the rocks too carefully to have missed seeing such a colorful object. Michael hadn't brought the bouquet—all he was wearing was shorts and a tank top, with no place to hide a bouquet. Besides, these flowers were fresh, not crumpled as they would have been had they been squirreled away under his thin cotton shirt.

There was no other explanation: I had just experienced a miracle. I held the bouquet and excitedly showed the flowers to Michael. Just then, my inner voice loudly said, "Happy birthday, Doreen!" My miracle bouquet was a gift from the universe, celebrating my realization of oneness. Today, I keep the dried bouquet petals in my office as a reminder that a consciousness of oneness and love calls forth beautiful miracles in the most surprising ways.

THE ILLUMINATED PATH

"So in life, some enter the services of fame and others of money, but the best choice is that of these few who spend their time in the contemplation of nature, and as lovers of wisdom."

— Pythagoras (570–490 B.C.),
"The Father of Philosophy"

People often ask me, "If you had such a good childhood, why did you have such a painful adolescence and early adulthood?" My answer is that although I had a wonderful source of love within my family, I sought an "even better" happiness from outside sources.

Unwittingly, I was also repeating the painful moment that gave birth to my ego-self and the seeming separation from God. The separation occurred when my ego wondered whether it could enjoy an even better source of love than God. However, there was no possible way to leave the Creator to investigate the possibility of greater happiness. So, it fell asleep and dreamed of a separate existence. The dream was extremely realistic, and my ego soon forgot that it was just a dream.

However, the ego retained a dim awareness of the presence of God and the true self. It knew that God and the true self were happier than it was, and it figured, "Hey, those guys are snubbing me! They must think they're better than I am. Well, fine. I don't need them, anyway." The ego then set out to prove her independence by gathering things to make her happy. She'd amass awards, applause, money, houses, and prestige. But these gifts were never enough to give her the happiness she knew that God and her true self were presently enjoying. She began to feel jealous and resentful of their happy life, and vowed to redouble her efforts at accumulating happiness. So she wandered farther and farther away from home, searching for the key to contentment.

When she'd see someone who seemed happier than she was, she'd feel the old jealous twinges. Then, she'd indulge in whatever those people were doing to see if she could experience their happiness. But soon enough, she'd get to know those people and would discover that they weren't really as happy as they seemed. She met people who blamed their unhappiness on various sources, and for a while, she joined in this pastime. She occasionally wondered, "What's wrong with me that I can't be happy?"

The ego in all of us suffers from deep feelings of emptiness and undeservingness. It feels rejected by the true self, although in truth, the ego is actually the one who does the rejecting. This leads the ego to continually believe that people are judging and rejecting her, which creates self-fulfilling prophecies. All along, our true self enjoys a peaceful parallel life within us that we can join with anytime we think a loving thought.

The lightworker's way isn't always easy. Often, our caring and curious dispositions lead us into emotionally charged situations. Our search for happiness and meaning takes us on many detours that eventually dead-end, until we finally grasp that what we are looking for is right within us.

Yet, I fully believe that everything we experience can help the world. Every instance in which you have experienced pain can serve as our teacher, helping us learn, grow, and find ways to live in peaceful happiness. Our hard-won lessons while here on Earth are also valuable in our roles as lightworkers. Because we have experienced pain, we feel compassion for those who become our students or clients.

Through trial and error, we eventually understand that ego-based thoughts and actions always create pain. Happiness, we realize, requires centering our thoughts on God and our true self within. At times, though, this feels like a difficult balancing act. We often get pulled into our egos by outside sources such as news reports, complaining co-workers, or unhappy family members. However, with practice, we realize the ability to recognize our ego thoughts soon after they arise. We then consciously choose to change our minds about the situation to restore our higher self's peaceful awareness. Usually, this requires the willingness to relinquish judgments, unforgiveness, and attachments to outcome or material goods. When we have trouble relinquishing the ego, we learn to call for spiritual support from our friends in the visible and invisible universe.

When I was verbally abused as a young adult, I completely forgot my true identity. I began to believe that I was a worthless and defective person. I think that the whole human race has suffered from similar forms of abuse that has caused a mass amnesia about our God-given perfection. When my mother taught me that "nothing is lost in the mind of God," I didn't realize the broad meaning of the word *nothing*. My true self seemed hopelessly lost, to the point where I could barely recall what she was like. But God knew where the true me was. Just as my faith had led me to find everything else I'd ever lost, I was led to find my true self.

We who are lightworkers are among the first to awaken from the sleepwalking dreams that led us to believe the reality of disease, destruction, and depression. The holy masters and angels will continue to help us awaken, and we'll receive their instructions through our intuition and gut feelings. It's vital that we pay attention and then obey these inner nudges.

During my years of counseling abuse survivors, I witnessed many domestic abuse survivors continually returning to their abusive spouses. They would tell me, "He's changed, and this time the relationship will be different." Yet, each reunion would result in more abuse and pain.

In reviewing my own life, I find a similar pattern. Whenever I let go of my spiritual foundation of daily prayers and meditation, I felt empty and afraid. So I tried to fill this emptiness and quell my fears by seeking the external world's prizes, such as popularity, money, accolades, food, or intoxicants. The lure from my lower ego-self was always, "If you achieve this prize, you will feel wonderful!" So I put time into achieving the prize. Always, though, my ego activities resulted in pain and suffering.

Still, I kept going back into this abusive relationship with my ego, saying, "This time will be different. I'll seek a different prize, and that will be the key to my happiness." Eventually, I realized that every prize the ego offered was identically painful.

In the story of Pinocchio, the lure of fun and frolic tempts the little wooden boy off his path. Jimminy Cricket warns Pinocchio to avoid temptation, but the boy succumbs anyway. I now keep a statue of Pinocchio and Jimminy Cricket in my office to remind me to listen to my higher self's wisdom whenever some new ego prize tempts me to go off the path.

Our relationships with our lower ego selves are like the cycles of domestic violence. We keep thinking that the world of materiality and external conditions will make us happy. Yet each time we pursue happiness through worldly affairs, we end up feeling disappointed, dissatisfied, or worse. Of course there's nothing inherently wrong with material possessions, because such a belief is another way of giving reality to matter. In truth, all matter is a neutral part of the great illusion.

In the Sermon on the Mount, Jesus taught that if we keep our focus on the kingdom of God, the Creator automatically supplies all our material needs. Not only that, but we are freed from the stress of worrying about money. With this freedom, we are better able to hear the loving guidance that God and His angels continually give us.

For so long, I tried to ignore God's guidance because I feared He was trying to control me or thwart my happiness. Although I recognized the wisdom and sanity of His advice, I rebelled and chose destructive paths to prove my independence. I kept believing that I could make the world of illusions give me the happiness, peace, and security I craved. Fortunately, every time I buried myself in a self-destructive mess while searching for external forms of happiness, God and my true self dug me out of it.

Our higher self, spirit guides, and angels give us help and good information as we go along the lightworker's path. This help comes as unmistakable and loving messages in a hunch, voice, vision, or knowingness. You may get messages asking you to change the foods you eat, the people you hang out with, or even your job or living situation. When this guidance comes to you, you *know* when it is the right thing for you to do. Your spiritual helpers will never ask you to do anything that would hurt you or your loved ones. They help you so that you can help the world. The more you listen to and trust this spiritual assistance, the easier it is to receive further help.

God wants to guide us to a life of happiness, fulfillment, and beautiful ways to serve our brothers and sisters. Our work first begins with our own consciousness, when we train our minds to stay away from an outward focus. Much of our work involves editing the vocabulary we use in our thoughts and spoken words so that we no longer affirm problems as realities.

As lightworkers, our mission depends upon our learning how to stay centered in our higher self's love. Our promise to help the world obliges us to give our ego a restraining order and to choose thoughts of love instead of thoughts about guilt. We must be willing to let go of our petty ego-based concerns so that we can focus our entire mind on the task.

When I met my true self, I knew without a doubt that all the earthly pain "I" had endured had never really touched me. My true self, who is one with God, has never had any reason to venture out into the world of painful illusions. She knows no need for an outside source of love or comfort. Therefore, she's never experienced anything other than love. It's the same with your true self, and everyone else's as well.

For this reason, lightworkers don't need to be too concerned about what they are doing. *Doing* is a bodily term and implies that you are only valuable as a body. Yogi masters have proven to us that we can accomplish much in the physical world while sitting in a lotus position. This doesn't mean that we should become passive observers of the world, because again, that would signal an outer focus. Instead, lightworkers must concentrate on inner work. We must learn how to train our minds to stay centered in the higher self's love and allow our actions to be guided by that love.

Each lightworker receives his or her own unique assignments about how to help in healing the world. Since so many lightworkers will be healing on a spiritual realm, Part Two of this book is a guidebook of several psychic healing methods. These are my personal guidelines, and you will want to tailor them as needed to fit your own needs and liking. Just as there are countless ways to walk along the spiritual path, so are there many ways to open your psychic and healing channels.

Our sacred mission as lightworkers is to first awaken ourselves from the ego's nightmare of disease, depression, and destruction. As we stir from this deep sleep, we must in turn nudge our sleeping brothers and sisters from their nightmares. *A Course in Miracles* best summarizes the lightworker's way:

> The ego is afraid of the spirit's joy, because once you have experienced it you will withdraw all protection from the ego and become totally without investment in fear. Your investment is great now because fear is a witness to the separation, and your ego rejoices when you witness to it. Leave it behind! Do not listen to it and do not preserve it. Listen only to God,

Who is as incapable of deception as is the spirit He created. Release yourself and release others. Do not present a false and unworthy picture of yourself to others, and do not accept such a picture of them yourself....Of your ego you can do nothing to save yourself or others, but of your spirit you can do everything for the salvation of both.

The earth needs you, lightworker, and heaven calls for you to hear the news that you have nothing to fear. The angels surround you with love and reassurances of your perfect qualifications for your lightworker function. Know this about yourself: you are perfect, and you are very loved. There is no one more perfect than you in God's mind. You don't need to change, fix, or alter anything about yourself because you're already perfect. Be willing to accept and feel the all-powerful love that resides within you right now, lightworker. Your sacred mission depends upon it.

Note to reader: My story continues in my books *Healing with the Fairies* and *Angel Medicine.*

PART II

A GUIDE TO PSYCHIC COMMUNICATION AND SPIRITUAL HEALING

THE PARALLEL WORLDS OF ENERGY AND SPIRIT

> *"Lost energy, lost Love, lost power, lost anything is
> the result of denial, of holding it away from you by not
> accepting it. What was lost returns when you forgive
> yourself for denying it and accept it."*
>
> — *Right Use of Will*, spiritual text
> received by Ceanne DeRohan

Your true self and your ego self live separate but parallel lives. One has a life of peace, health, harmony, and complete fulfillment, while the other suffers a life of worry, illness, and lack.The idea of parallel realities is a favorite subject of research in quantum physics. For example, scientists have discovered that a radioactive atom can exist in both a decayed and a nondecayed state simultaneously. When the decay is observed by a human, however, the decayed state of existence is brought forth.[1] In other words, whatever you focus upon enlarges.

After I met my true self during Wayne Dyer's meditative seminar, I positively knew that another "me" existed in a separate dimension. This other "me" radiated the bliss that can only come from living in the amniotic sac of God's love. So if a "decayed" or ego-me coexists with a "nondecayed" or true-self me, my act of observing the nondecayed self amplifies its existence.

To illustrate this point, Kenneth Wapnick, Ph.D., author of books about *A Course in Miracles*, uses the metaphor of two VCR tapes.[2] If we push the "on" button for our true-self videotape, we experience a happy movie. But if we switch to the ego's videotape, we watch an entirely different movie. We choose our movie with our thoughts of fear or love. A loving thought is the "on" switch for our true-self movie, while a fearful thought is the "on" button for the ego's movie. Most of us go through life continually channel-surfing between the ego and true-self movies. The result is chaos and confusion.

The ego's world seems as real and solid as any of the dreams we have while we're sleeping. Of course, nothing is really solid, as all matter is composed of energy. Thoughts and emotions influence energy, which is the basis of all matter, including our bodies. Kirlian photography shows how the body's moisture level and energy or "auric field" dramatically responds to the emotions of anger, fear, and love. When a person feels love or loved, Kirlian photographs show a white and wispy auric field. When that same person experiences anger or fear, the aura turns dark and dense.

As a lightworker, God may call you to do healing work on either the ego plane of energy and matter or the true self's spiritual plane. In energy healing work, you use your natural psychic attunement abilities to see and feel your client's energy centers. Your energy work may also incorporate psychic healing, in which you tune into your client's emotions and thoughts that are creating her distress and symptoms. Energy work also includes mediumship, which involves working with the energy fields of deceased people who may be affecting your client. If these deceased people are interfering with your client's happiness, then your energy work will include "spirit releasement."

The ego world believes that matter is solid and that it has a mind or life of its own. By understanding that matter is actually energy, and that thought directs energy, humans begin to see how they are the authors of their own reality. They are the dreamers of the dream, in other words.

The true-self world involves working with conscious awareness instead of focusing on matter or energy. The ego world defines "life" as bodies and other matter, so it is continually focused on "doing" or "getting." Energy radiates inwardly and outwardly as a reflection of the material belief in action. This also demands a belief in time, as something to measure what has happened before and after.

"Life" in the true-self world is defined as spirit, and so its focus is on "being." There is nothing to do or get in the true-self world, as all needs are here in the "now." Lightworkers who are called to do spiritual healing will be working in the true-self world. Therefore, their focus is not so much on actions or doing treatments on their clients. Their job will be to help their clients switch from the ego videotape to the true-self videotape. We can accomplish this in many ways, such as talking with the client, praying for the client, or holding an affirmative thought about the truth of the situation. In the true-self world, there is only one mind, and we are all part of that one mind. So a lightworker can use her mindset of truth to heal her client's mindset. The lightworker can also call upon angels and holy masters and "borrow" their mindsets to evoke healing.

Part II describes methods of energy work, followed by spiritual healing guidelines. As you read these descriptions of healing work, notice how your inner guide responds. It's important to honor your true self's guidance as to which forms of healing you are drawn to. Your inner guide will lead you to the path where you can best serve God. Upon this path, God takes care of all your human needs while you joyously work with those who need you most.

PREPARING FOR PSYCHIC AND
SPIRITUAL HEALING

*"The eyes are not prevented from seeing by a hedge;
God has nothing hid from him."*

— African Ovambo proverb

As a lightworker, you were born to perform healing functions. God and His angels know which specific healing role will bring the most joy, so they guide you through intuitive impulses to certain facets of healing. Some lightworkers will be attracted to and involved in physical healing, while others will be involved in emotional healing, teaching, the arts, research, counseling, writing, media, and hundreds of other important roles.

Your inner guide will lead you to the place and healing role where you belong. You will know, through your inner nudges, whether you are supposed to get training or educational preparation. If you are, then your inner guide will lead you to, and help you afford, the school or teacher that you need. Simultaneously, the people who will be your clients and students will be led to you through their own inner guides.

Sometimes lightworkers look too far down the road and wonder, "How could I possibly become a healer?" or "Where will my clients come from?" They then become afraid and abandon their goal. The important point is: Don't worry about how you will learn to do your lightworker functions. The *how* is up to God, and you will receive His guidance step-by-step. Besides, scientific research shows that worrying is detrimental to psychic and spiritual healing abilities.[1] Your inner guidance will come one or two steps at a time. Listen for and complete that one step. Then, you will receive the next set of instructions. A step at a time, you will become completely prepared for your healing function.

You can fully open your intuitive channels through meditation, chakra healing, and other methods I have outlined for you. As you adopt these methods into your daily routines, you will immediately find yourself receiving psychic information about your relationships, job, health, and future. I recommend that you keep a journal of all the transmissions you receive. This journal will help you develop a trust in the validity of your psychic impressions. You will also be able to notice any recurrent themes within your incoming transmissions.

If you ever feel overwhelmed by all the psychic data streaming into your consciousness, you can turn down its volume anytime you want. To do so, simply decide that you choose to be less aware of the psychic frequencies. Use the power of your intentions to adjust the psychic volume to a comfortable level.

Step 1: Meditation

Studies show a definite relationship between meditating and psychic abilities.[2] Scientists have observed that meditation synchronizes the wave patterns of the left- and right-brain hemispheres. This synchronization apparently allows a free flow of information from the "psychic" right brain into the left brain's verbal centers. Research also shows that a synchronization occurs between the brain patterns of a meditator and the person she is thinking about.[3]

You don't need to spend a great deal of time meditating to

achieve benefits from its practice. A mere ten minutes devoted to meditating first thing in the morning and then ten minutes before going to sleep can greatly influence your intuitive, psychic, and healing capabilities. Remember that time is an earthly idea, and there is no authority figure in the heavens clocking us to make sure we have completed our meditation exercises.

Meditation has two purposes. First, it centers your mind upon spirit within. In that way, meditation helps you to stay calm, creative, and loving during the day. You are more apt to see the true perfection in all situations, instead of reacting to the illusion of problems. Meditation is a method that helps you exist in the eye of the hurricane during your daily affairs.

Second, meditation gives you access to the infinite universal wisdom so you'll receive whatever information or guidance you seek. We are often so busy that we don't hear the answers to our prayers. Meditation is a quiet period in which you have a private tutoring session with Spirit. You get to ask anything you want, with full assurance of receiving an answer.

Sometimes you'll receive ongoing guidance during successive meditation sessions. For example, when I once asked the question in meditation: "How can I increase the quality of my clairvoyance?" I got continual answers for weeks. Like a skillful coach, my spiritual guide gradually helped me to reach my objective. First, I was told to cut back on my coffee consumption, because the stimulation of caffeine was interfering with my receptivity. After I followed this suggestion, I was told to give up chocolate, for the same reason as coffee. Next, my guide advised that if I really wanted to increase my clairvoyance, I would benefit from eating a largely vegetarian diet. The explanation I received was that when I eat the flesh of an animal, I absorb residuals of that animal's dying pain. This ingested pain was blocking my sensitivity to psychic transmissions.

Meditative guidance always comes as loving suggestions in response to your questions. So please don't worry that a spirit is going to take over your life. When I received my dietary guidance, I had the full choice whether or not to follow it. I chose to follow the advice because it felt right for me. It's important that you, too, only take suggestions that resonate with your highest truth.

One of the pleasantly surprising benefits from meditating was how relaxed I became after discovering my inner guide. This discovery helped me to let go of the false belief that I had to control everything to maintain peace and harmony. I realized that there is a divine order to life. This trust in life's process, in turn, gave me a deep peace and serenity that I'd never experienced before.

Today, I wouldn't dream of skipping my twice-daily meditations. I am fully committed to this practice because it makes me feel so good. If you want to know more about meditation, you may want to enroll in a class on the topic at a metaphysical bookstore, church, or adult education center. There are many different ways to meditate, and you will know which method is right for you. Here is a guide to the basics of meditation.

Basic Meditation Steps

1. Commit to meditating upon awakening and right before bedtime.

2. Select a quiet and comfortable place where you won't be interrupted. It doesn't need to be an entire room. A corner of a bedroom or a bathroom will do.

3. Get comfortable. Lying down is fine if you know you won't fall asleep. Keep your arms uncrossed so that energy can flow freely through your body. Loosen or take off any binding clothing.

4. Close your eyes.

5. Inhale deeply and slowly through your nose. Allow

yourself to enjoy the feeling of taking in fresh air until it completely fills your lungs. Hold the breath for four seconds or longer.

6. Slowly exhale through your mouth. Feel the release of all worries, concerns, or tension as you let the air out.

As you continue to breathe in and out, there are many ways to enjoy meditating. You can use a guided meditation in which you hold a specific image, question, or prayer in mind. Or, you can allow your mind to go blank and then notice what thoughts come to you. Here are some examples of guided meditations.

A Morning Meditation for Lightworkers

Begin with the basic meditation steps, then:

Visualize the top of your head opening up like a sky dome or the petals of a flower. Picture a beautiful cloud above your head. See it brightly illuminated in your favorite color. This cloud is the infinite wisdom and the all-encompassing love of the Divine Creator. Ask the cloud to enter the top of your head. Continue to take deep breaths, and see the cloud being drawn into your entire body with each breath you take. See yourself filled with and surrounded by this beautifully colored cloud.

Know that during the hours that follow, you only need to think of this color, and you will instantly have access to any answers or information you need. Your thought of this color will remind you that you are completely loved and cared for. Allow yourself to relax and enjoy the moment, knowing that during the day, the infinite intelligence and love within will always guide you. You can let go of any concerns about your upcoming day because you trust this wisdom to guide you in every way.

Ask your inner guide to help you stay centered in thoughts of divine love and intelligence throughout the day. Release this request in full faith, reassured that you are truly loved and fully supported.

Finish with the Chakra Healing, as described in Step 2.

An Evening Meditation for Lightworkers

Begin with the basic meditation steps, then:

Concentrate on the region of your heart. As you center your attention in this area, notice that with each deep breath that you take, a feeling of warmth radiates from your heart. Know that this warmth intimately connects you to the Source of all love.

As you inhale, feel love, warmth, and goodness drawing into your heart. As you exhale, feel yourself giving love back to the Source. Continue to breathe in and out, and feel yourself receive and give love until your chest expands with great feelings of warmth and joy.

Spend a moment thinking about some people and experiences you encountered during the day. Mentally say, "I am willing to forgive you," to the people who irritated you, including yourself. Although you may not be willing to forgive their deeds, your willingness to forgive them as a person releases you from your ego bindings.

Then, mentally list the gifts you received during the day in the forms of situations, love, and insights. Give thanks to the Source for these gifts. Breathe in and out deeply until you feel filled with gratitude. Ask your angels to enter your dreams to give you guidance and any information that you may need to know. Visualize your home surrounded and protected by white light and angels as you drift off to sleep.

Step 2: Chakra Cleansing and Balancing

After you have attuned yourself with your morning meditation, the next step in opening your channels of psychic and spiritual healing is to do a meditation specifically designed to cleanse and balance your chakra energy centers. This step will immediately increase your psychic communication abilities and boost your energy.

It's a good idea to do this meditation daily. I also recommend that you practice this meditation before doing a psychic reading. The more you work with your chakras, the more detailed your psychic communications will become. Once, I was at a weekend workshop where we devoted much of our time to various chakra-cleansing activities. At the end of the weekend, I did several psychic readings and found that I accessed minute details that I wouldn't normally receive.

In one reading, for instance, I saw a mental image of my client's pale yellow stucco house with a wood shake roof. I intuitively knew that my client had recently sold that house and had just moved. Now, that sort of information is easily accessible during an average psychic reading. However, on this day, because of the extra chakra work I'd done, I received particularly detailed psychic information, including the fact that the home my client had sold was in the Southern California city of Downey. I had no way to know that specific detail since I had just met my client, knew nothing about him, and we were nowhere near Downey.

(I have tape-recorded an expanded version of my chakra balancing and cleansing guided meditation method on an audiocassette called *Chakra Clearing*, available through Hay House.)

<u>Meditation to Cleanse and Balance Your Chakras</u>

Begin with the basic meditation method, then:

Visualize or feel a round and transparent ball, colored in a beautiful shade of ruby red, floating inside your body near the base of your spine. This is your "root chakra," the center of your strength and individuality. Mentally look at or sense the ball. Notice if it has any areas of darkness. These are energy imbalances, and you can immediately wash them away by simply intending the ball to be perfectly clean. Hold the image of your beautifully transparent ruby red ball in your mind, and see it illuminated from the inside with powerful, pure white light. This is the universal light of God, of all power, love, and knowing.

Inhale deeply through your nose, and watch or feel how your breath increases the intensity of the white light inside the red sphere. Continue breathing in and out deeply to fan the intensity of the white light inside the red ball, until it is perfectly clean and transparent.

Next, move your attention upward about three inches until you see or feel a beautiful orange glass ball floating within you. This is your "sacral chakra," the regulator of your physical desires. Scan the ball for any areas of darkness. Breathe in deeply to fan the white light within the chakra's core to wash away all darkness instantly until the ball is perfectly transparent, like orange glass.

Now, concentrate on the area immediately behind your navel. See or sense a beautiful clear yellow ball within you, shining like a little sun. This is your "solar plexus chakra," the area affected by your beliefs concerning power and control. Check to see if there are any opaque or dark areas on your solar plexus. If there are, breathe in deeply until the chakra becomes a brilliant light yellow color and is perfectly transparent, like a sparkling ball of yellow glass.

Then, move your attention to your heart region. Visualize or feel a gorgeous green glass ball in your chest. This is your "heart chakra," the center of your loving energy. Scan the heart chakra for any shades of darkness, and then deeply breathe them away with white light. Fully illuminate the heart chakra from within and feel it expand in your chest with warmth and good energy. Keep breathing until the green ball is perfectly transparent and spotless.

Next, concentrate on your throat in the Adam's apple area. See or feel a ball in a beautiful shade of light blue. This is your "throat chakra," the center regulating the clarity of all your communications. Mentally scan the throat chakra, looking for or feeling for dark areas. Take a deep breath and watch it ignite into a white ball of light in the chakra's center. Illuminate the chakra from the inside, making the light grow brighter and brighter until the white rays completely cleanse the blue ball. See and feel the ball as perfectly transparent, with no spots or dark areas.

Then, move your attention to the area between your two eyes. Without forcing yourself in any way, gently notice a round or oval ball between your two eyes. This is your "third eye chakra." Allow the image of the chakra to become clearer and clearer. Notice its coloring as shades of dark blue mixed with some purple and white. As the image becomes clearer, you may notice that you are looking at an eyelid. If you don't see an oval or an eye-shaped object, then breathe deeply and keep cleaning the chakra with white light until the image becomes clear. Once you get a glimpse of the third eye, notice whether it is open or shut. If it is shut, ask it to open and make eye contact with you. Allow the third eye to communicate any loving messages it may have for you.

When you are ready, place your attention on the inside of the top of your head. This is your "crown chakra," the area that gives you access to universal wisdom. Feel or see this chakra as a deep violet or purple glass ball. Using your deepest breathing, clean the crown chakra with white light until it is pristine.

Continue to breathe in and out deeply and give thanks to your Divine Creator for filling you with love and wisdom. Surround yourself with a layer of white light, followed by a second layer of green light, and followed by a third layer of violet light. This triple seal of light will help you to stay centered during your psychic readings.

Mini Chakra Cleansing Method

If you don't have time for a full cleansing and balancing, this method will certainly work. It just takes two minutes and is a good way to prepare for a last-minute psychic reading session. While the chakra-cleansing method described above is the equivalent of deep-cleaning your house, this one is more like a surface cleaning. It will be "good enough" in a pinch, but you wouldn't want to rely upon this method on a daily basis.

Picture seven glass balls stacked on top of one another in the colors of the rainbow. The order of the balls from bottom to top is red, orange, yellow, green, light blue, dark blue, and purple. Visualize this stack of balls as inside the center of your body. Imagine a beam of pure white light going through the center of the stack of balls. See the white light cleansing each ball. Mentally inspect the red ball and see it glowing with light. See the red ball as perfectly cleansed. Do the same inspection with each ball in the stack, one by one.

Make sure the balls are all the same size. If one ball is much larger or smaller than the others, mentally ask it to change size until it matches the others.

Your chakras are now clean and balanced enough for psychic readings.

Step 3: Mental Attunement

Meditation and chakra cleansing are two important steps to opening your channels of psychic and spiritual communication.

The third step, mental attunement, is equally important. Mental attunement involves centering your awareness upon your higher self's connection to the Source of knowledge and love. If we allow our mind to slip into the ego-self, our psychic readings become inconsistent and unreliable. Even worse, we become unhappy and afraid. We certainly have every reason to want to live in our higher self. Here are some ways that are helpful.

1. *Identify yourself with God's love.* See yourself and everyone you meet as one with God, and your thoughts and actions will automatically align with love. You won't even have to think about what to do or say, because the wisdom will spring naturally from the well within you.

2. *Avoid identifying with others' egos.* If you view other people as needy, sick, afraid, angry, unenlightened, impoverished, and the like, you are seeing their ego-selves as real. Anytime we declare the ego as a real state of being, we give power and life to the illusion.

    A more loving and helpful way to react to other people's seeming problems is to react as if they were describing a frightening movie. You sincerely give them your attention and loving compassion, but always know that what they are discussing is just a movie. Know that there is nothing to fear, and like all movies, your friends' situations will end well. Remember that if you worry on their behalf, you are pouring gasoline upon their fire.

    However, by seeing the truth about your friends, you amplify the strength and power of their true self's qualities. The true self and its heavenly life—which includes perfect health, right relationships, and right livelihood—manifests into fruition.

    Always guard your thoughts about other people, including public figures such as movie stars, high-profile criminals, and politicians. Anytime you indulge in seeing someone in the light of jealousy, pity, or scorn, your judgment of them automatically triggers you to judge yourself. As we see others, so we see ourselves.

On the other hand, we can gain valuable growth and insights about ourselves whenever another person irritates us. Do you have a friend who grates on your nerves? We've all been in such a situation, and there's a reason for it. That friend acts as a mirror for some part of ourselves that we need to let go of. Whenever this happens to me, I use this phrase: "I am willing to release that part of me that irritates me when I look at you."

Train your mind to view everyone as one with God, and you will tap into so much power and love that it will amaze you.

3. *Adopt a "zero tolerance for pain" policy.* Anytime you feel emotional or physical pain, it is a sure sign that you have slipped into your ego. Do not give this pain a habitat within you, or you will have a lodger who is difficult to evict. Conversely, it's not a good idea to try and ignore the pain in the hopes that it will go away. To deny pain is to cut off a part of you. You also miss the lessons and growth that are valuable gifts awaiting you.

4. *When you are aware of pain, release it.* Face the pain without fear, since it is not real. Do not judge the pain, but simply notice it. Say to your higher self, angels, ascended master, Holy Spirit, or God, "I notice that my ego is engaged right now, and I don't like it. I fully release this pain to you, and ask to see this situation in another way so that I may feel peace instead of pain. I send this pain away and know that only the lesson within it remains behind to help me to grow in love." Be will-

ing to release any attachments to the outcome of the situation, and your reward is peace. Keep saying this affirmative prayer until you feel the pain lift away.

5. *Honor your true self.* God within you will direct your actions during the day. If you spend too much time doing something that is not part of your sacred mission, your inner guide will nudge you. It's important to honor this nudging.

   Lightworkers often attract relationships that become unbalanced. For example, a friend who seems to need your help may telephone you constantly. Or an organization may ask you to lead different projects or committees. Perhaps a client will continually be on the verge of a crisis, claiming that only you can help. Beware of these traps of the ego that come disguised as divine helpfulness. As *A Course in Miracles* says, "Preoccupations with problems set up to be incapable of solution are favorite ego devices for impeding learning progress."

   Try to notice whenever your ego asks you to delay your lightworker function by taking a meaningless detour. If your inner self tells you that you are spending too much time and energy working with one person or cause, then honor and heed that voice. The world needs you to be available to help in ways that truly make a difference.

   If you are afraid to trim how much time and energy you are giving to a friend, organization, or client, remind yourself of this truth:

   "If I judge someone as 'needing' me, then I am seeing their lack as real. That judgment triggers my own ego-self into action. If I focus upon their 'problems,' then I am a co-conspirator in

> *making those problems get larger. I am most*
> *helpful to the world when I stay centered in my*
> *higher self. I now choose to see everyone as they*
> *truly are: completely healed and loved. I refuse*
> *to dance with ego illusions any longer."*

A good rule of thumb for how to spend your time is to never do anything you don't want to do. If you must force yourself to do something, such as taking a phone call from a friend, there is a reason for your resistance. Spend time meditating upon your true feelings. Honor them. Release any pain. During your meditation, you will either decide to say no to requests for your time, or see the situation differently and become lovingly motivated to say yes. Either way, your actions will stem from love and truth, instead of from anger, guilt, or fear.

6. *Watch out for the "special power" ego trap.* As you begin doing psychic readings and spiritual healings, your clients will gratefully thank you. Be sure to guard your thoughts so that you don't fall into the trap of believing you have "special powers." This sort of belief will trigger your ego-self to take over, because if we view ourselves as "special," it is the same as seeing our self as a separated being. If you view yourself as separated, you cut off awareness of your Source of knowledge, healing love, and happiness. This will cause you to lose both your happiness and your psychic awareness. A good antidote is to graciously receive your client's compliments and then say something like, "It's not by me, but through me," or "Thank you. Of course, it wasn't I who healed you; it was God helping you to realize that you've always been perfect."

In the early stages when you are developing your

psychic abilities, it's customary to feel afraid or intimidated. You might ask yourself, "What if I can't do it?" or "What if I give the wrong answers during my psychic reading?" These fears stem from the ego's belief that psychic powers are "special." To lose this fear, simply remind yourself that the power is coming from God and not from *you. You* can't make a mistake during the psychic reading or spiritual healing, since *you* aren't doing anything. If you trust in the infallibility of your Divine Creator, then you won't ever fear that the information you're receiving is incorrect. Trust in God, and you automatically trust that you are perfectly ready to be a conduit for His healing power.

In my earlier descriptions of the vast scientific research conducted at leading universities, we saw how the studies concluded that everyone is inherently psychic. The point of all this is to assure you that you don't need any special powers or education to begin your psychic healing function. You just need to dive in and try it so you'll know this is a skill you already possess.

7. *Take purification steps.* I found that my psychic abilities dramatically increased after I eliminated alcohol, caffeine, meat, dairy products, and most processed foods from my diet. The difference in my mental image before and after my diet changes was the equivalent of changing from a small antenna-style TV to a big-screen set with cable. I could see psychic images clearer, brighter, and bigger.

My dietary changes were gradual, and my spiritual guides gently but firmly told me, "If you eliminate unhealthful eating, you will be a clearer instrument for spiritual communication." First, the guides told me to cut down on stimulating foods and drinks such as coffee and chocolate. Next, they urged me to stop eating chicken and turkey (I was already abstaining from red meat). The guides said that animals suffer during the slaughtering process, and that I was ingesting their pain when I ate their flesh. This pain interfered with my ability to tune into the invisible universe. A few months after I stopped eating fowl, my guides urged me to give up dairy products. They said, "Milk products clog up your system." So I began using soy milk on my cereal and in my tea. Instead of cheese, I now cook with tofu-based cheese substitutes.

There really is a link between diet and psychic abilities. Just look at this quote from the ancient Buddhist text, *Surangama Sutra*: "If one is trying to practice meditation and is still eating meat, he would be like a man closing his ears and shouting loudly and then asserting that he heard nothing."

I want to emphasize that as I gave up these foods, I did not suffer any withdrawal symptoms such as cravings or feeling deprived. I believe this is because I was divinely guided with each dietary choice. So don't force yourself to eliminate certain food groups. If and when you feel ready, you'll naturally make decisions about the foods you eat.

I also discovered that releasing old unforgiveness was important to my psychic development in two ways. First, it seemed to increase the amount and frequency of information I received. Second, I was better able to stay objective during psychic readings, instead of coloring my impressions with my own emotional baggage.

Anyone can feel more at peace and more energized through the process of forgiveness. Here is a description of the method, inspired by the work of author John Randolph Price, that I used to release my old unforgiveness. It is the same method I use with my clients. This process reminds me of throwing off weights when riding in a hot air balloon so you can go up higher. When you forgive the world—including yourself—you become lighter and much less fearful.

a. *Know the benefits of forgiveness.* Forgiveness is different from saying, "I lose," or "I was wrong and you were right." It is different from letting someone off the hook for a perceived wrong deed. Forgiveness is simply a way of freeing your spirit and realizing your unlimited nature. Peacefulness and increased energy are the prizes, and forgiveness is their price.

b. *Take a "Forgiveness Inventory."* Write the name of *every* person, living or deceased, who has ever irritated you. Most people find that they have a three- or four-page list and are able to suddenly remember names of people they hadn't thought about in years. Some people even put down names of pets who irritated them, and everyone writes their own name somewhere on the list.

c. *Release and forgive.* In a solitary room with the phone ringer turned off and a "Do not disturb" sign on the door, go down the list one name at a time. Hold the image of each person in your mind and tell him or her, "I forgive you and I release you. I hold no unforgiveness back. My forgiveness for you is total. I am free and you are free." Visualize and feel your angels whisking away your old resentment. This process may take 30 minutes or longer. However, it's important to stick to it without interruption until the entire list is complete.

    d. *Do nightly releasements.* Every evening before retiring, do a mental review of the day. Is there anyone you need to forgive? I do this every night. Just as I wash my face every night, so too do I cleanse my soul nightly so resentment won't accumulate.

8. *Create a conducive atmosphere.* Your physical environment can contribute or detract from your psychic abilities. Scientific studies conducted at leading universities find that people give more accurate psychic readings in distraction-free rooms that are dimly lit and have soft background music.[4] I also find that I give better readings when I'm well rested, am dressed comfortably, and have fragrant flowers such as star gazers or tuber roses in the room.

HEIGHTENING YOUR PSYCHIC RECEPTIVITY

"That mind which gives life to all the people in the world:
Such is the very mind which nourishes me!"

— "Moritake Arakida,"
poem of Shinto (Japan)

Although psychic ability is natural, like any skill, we can refine and polish it. Here are some ways to increase the clarity and amount of information you will receive during your psychic readings.

Chakra Scanning

You can heighten your psychic receptivity by scanning the chakras of people you meet throughout the day. You can scan anyone's chakras, including people with whom you're talking on the telephone.

Scanning another person's chakras is identical to the method you used when you were visualizing your own chakras. You were easily able to see which chakras were dirty, and where they were dirty. These images were not your imagination; they were real psychic visions of your inner energy centers.

Allow yourself to relax, take a deep breath, and then hold this thought, "I intend to see the chakras within this person." Then focus your attention inside the person's core, and visualize their root chakra. Notice its size, color, and clarity. Do you see any dark spots? Is the chakra noticeably large or small? Move your attention up through the other chakras.

Finally, look at all the chakras as a group. Are any chakras much bigger or smaller than the others? Are any of the chakras especially dark when compared to the others? An enlarged chakra means that the person has spent a great deal of time thinking about the issue connected to that chakra. A small chakra means that the person has fears connected to that chakra's issues. Dark energy around and inside a chakra means the person is holding on to old emotions concerning that chakra's issues and is afraid to admit these feelings to themselves or other people.

You can clean and balance another person's chakras using the same visualization you used on your own chakras. Many healers believe you must first get a person's permission before administering a chakra treatment. They say that it is a violation of karmic law to work on anyone without their consent.

Some healers psychically ask for permission, asking the person's higher self, "Do you want me to work on your chakras?" They then listen for a reply. However, other healers believe that one must verbally ask for permission to do a chakra healing. Still another group of healers thinks that whenever you see someone in need of spiritual help, you must come to their assistance whether or not they ask for help. Your higher self will guide you to the stance that resonates with you.

As a review, look at the chart on the next page listing the characteristics of each major chakra:

Chakra Name	Body Location	Energy Color	Issue
Root	Base of spine	Red	Security and survival
Sacral	Three inches below the navel	Orange	Physical and material desires
Solar plexus	Behind the navel	Yellow	Power and control
Heart	Heart region	Green	Love
Throat	Adam's apple area	Light blue	Communication
Third eye	Between both eyes	Dark blue	Clairvoyance
Crown	Top of head	Purple	Spiritual wisdom

Psychic Activation

There are two main ways to access psychic information: by asking a question, or by deciding to allow the information to flow spontaneously into your awareness.

In the first method, you allow your mind to become as blank and relaxed as possible. I find it helpful to visualize my mind as an giant, empty, ornate bowl, ready for infinite universal wisdom to fill it. Then I mentally ask a question—for example: "What time will I arrive at my destination?" or "What issue does my client who has the 3:00 appointment today want help with?" You can specifically "address" your question to God, the Holy Spirit, Jesus, Buddha, or another loving guide. Or, you can just put the question in your bowl, and trust that the highest wisdom applicable will come. You will receive the answer in your mind or body as a picture, feeling, knowingness, or audible words.

The second method is similar, but instead of asking to know something, you *decide or give yourself permission to know* some information. So after visualizing your mind as an open bowl, relax and make a mental statement. For instance, if you were driving somewhere and wanted to receive directions intuitively, you would affirmatively state, "I now know exactly which roads to take to get to my destination." You will immediately receive guidance by either hearing the names of the roads to take, or feeling yourself pulled right or left at the crucial intersections.

Here are some examples of specific exercises to increase your confidence in your ability to tap into the Source of all knowledge.

Parking spaces: In a crowded parking lot, allow your mind and body to relax and become as open as possible. Relax with deep breaths. *Feel* your way to an empty parking space, and allow your intuition to guide you. Or, ask your angels or spiritual guides to find an empty parking space, and request that they give you signs or directions to lead you there.

While driving: Ask psychic questions about what moves the driver ahead of you is about to make, which road to turn on to reach your destination, or what time you will arrive. You will either hear the answer, see it in your mind's eye, get a feeling about the answer, or else simply know the answer.

Appointments: If you have an appointment to meet new people, ask to receive psychic impressions about them. Ask about their physical characteristics, their personal likes and dislikes, or about their concerns and interests. You can also ask what time the people will arrive at your appointment, or whether they are running late or ahead of schedule.

The telephone: Whenever the telephone rings, allow the psychic impression of who is calling to enter your mind before you answer the call. Ask, "Is this a man or a woman calling?" and "Who is calling?" With practice, you will become very tuned in to your incoming callers. When you are too busy to take telephone calls, you can "psychically block" unwanted incoming calls by affirming, "My telephone calls are in divine order, and I now see that only calls that are absolutely necessary are coming into my telephone line."

The TV: Turn on a television program with which you are unfamiliar. Turn your back away from the television monitor so you cannot see the screen or its reflection. Listen to the actors and actresses talking, and visualize what they look like. Turn around from time to time to check your accuracy.

Keep a coincidence journal: Write down every instance, minor and major, in which a coincidence plays a role in your life. This list helps you to focus your mind on coincidences. The more you pay attention to coincidences, the more of them will come your way.

The Power of Prayer

A 1995 study by William MacDonald of Ohio State University found that people who regularly pray are more likely to have telepathic experiences than people who don't pray. MacDonald explained these findings by saying, "In one sense, the results aren't surprising. You can think of prayer as a type of mind-to-mind communication between a person and God. So prayer and telepathy are related concepts."[1]

Meditation for Increasing Receptivity

Many people want to gain confidence in their psychic abilities before they begin conducting psychic readings on other people. You can use your alone time during meditation to increase your psychic receptivity and to experience some wondrous insights and revelations.

While in meditation, hold an image of a holy master in your mind such as Jesus, Mother Mary, Buddha, Krishna, or a favorite saint. Ask for the holy master to come to you. Let go of any doubts you may have by remembering that these highly evolved masters live in another dimension that allows them to be in many different locations simultaneously. The holy master can be with you and millions of other people at the same time. By relaxing, you are better able to feel or see their presence. Have a wonderful conversation with the holy master, and you will enjoy an experience that is beyond description.

During meditation, you can also ask to go on a journey. Close your eyes and take several deep breaths. Allow yourself to go to a place such as a beautiful foreign country, or the Hall of Akashic Records, which is a heavenly library filled with accounts of everyone's lives and divine purposes.

All of the methods described in this chapter will help you become accustomed to your spiritual communication channels. At first, you may feel like a new driver behind the wheel of a car. You will feel awkward and unsure of yourself, or even afraid for your safety. Very soon, though, you will become comfortable and familiar with your new psychic senses.

CHAPTER NINETEEN

CONDUCTING PSYCHIC READINGS
AND ENERGY HEALINGS

*"There lies the fire within the Earth,
and in plants, and waters carry it; the fire is in
stone. There is a fire deep within men, a fire in the kine,
and a fire in horses: The same fire that burns
in the heavens . . ."*

— *Atharva Veda,*
Hindu spiritual text

A lightworker's purpose in conducting psychic readings is different from the stereotypical image of a "psychic." Lightworkers are here to fulfill healing functions. It would be a waste of a lightworker's time and talents to engage in parlor-style psychic readings merely for others' amusement or financial gain.

There is only one valid reason for a lightworker to engage in psychic communication, and that is to access the root of the mental and emotional source of the client's psychological or physical distress quickly. The father of the New Thought movement, Phineas Quimby, used this form of psychic communication in his healings. He described his method as a combination of clairvoyance, trance, and telepathy that allowed him to enter his client's mind and discover the set of beliefs triggering the disease.

Your psychic abilities will help you to see, hear, feel, or know the source of your client's emotional or physical distress as well. As a clairvoyant, I usually see a miniature "movie" of an incident in my client's life related to his current life challenge. Together, we go over this incident to see where it may have triggered painful feelings. By discovering and releasing the old pain, and by helping clients understand how to differentiate between their ego-self and true-self, the current symptoms are usually instantly relieved.

Beginning Psychic Method

It is not difficult to give a psychic reading, but you can make it difficult by getting all worked up with performance anxiety. Remember, you aren't doing the work in a psychic reading—God is. Psychic abilities are entirely natural gifts to which each of us have access. Once you begin regularly cleansing and balancing your chakras, nature takes over. You'll then find yourself spontaneously receiving psychic information.

Begin with a chakra-cleansing meditation, with special attention given to the third eye and crown chakras, which are sites of psychic receptivity. Your psychic reading will be more accurate if you attune your body. For that reason, avoid ingesting any mood- or energy-altering substances, including soothing or stimulating herbs, before your session. You'll also have better psychic receptivity if your stomach isn't full.

It's a good idea to start a psychic reading by saying a prayer either silently or aloud. This prayer has a dual function. First, it serves as a "Prayer of Protection." Sometimes, unwanted spirits come along during psychic readings. These spirits have no destructive or evil powers; however, they can unwittingly give you incorrect or even harmful information to pass along to your client. You don't want these uninvited "guests" around, believe me. So, saying a prayer, having a Bible nearby, never drinking alcohol before a session, and inviting the holy masters and archangels to watch over you keeps lower vibrating spirits away from your psychic reading.

Secondly, a prayer helps to center your mind in your higher self. It reminds you that *you* aren't doing the reading but are merely being a conduit for the messages that are coming from on-high. This helps you to release nervousness, which can block your ability to receive psychic information.

Use a prayer that gives you a feeling of spiritual protection and that genuinely reflects your faith and beliefs. Because of my Christian background, my prayers and psychic readings involve Jesus and the Holy Spirit. However, many of my clients come from non-Christian beliefs such as Judaism, Buddhism, and agnosticism. I never push my faith upon anyone, and my non-Christian clients are always grateful for the healings they receive. Consequently (and I have asked them), they absolutely don't mind me using Jesus's name during our sessions. If I were to edit my normal vocabulary due to political-correctness concerns, my inauthentic behavior would trigger my ego, and I could not be a conduit for healing. The same is true with your beliefs and background, so choose a prayer that dovetails with your faith and that empowers you spiritually.

I usually begin my readings by saying "The Lord's Prayer," or the one that follows:

Prayer of Protection

I ask for and invite the holy presence and guidance of the Holy Spirit and Jesus into this room. I ask for and invite the Archangel Michael to watch over us during this reading. I also ask for and invite the love and guidance of both of our angels and spirit guides. I now seal this room in the white light of love. If any spirits enter our sessions who are not here for our highest and best purpose, I ask that Archangel Michael and his band of mercy

escort these spirits to the light for their own progress and prosperity. We ask for and affirm clear guidance for the highest purpose for which [name of client] is here today. I ask that this information be given to me clearly and that I be helped to convey it accurately to [name of client].
Amen.

Many psychics also burn sage weed or incense during their sessions, as sage is reputed to repel unwanted spirits.

Crystals

During your psychic reading, you may find it helpful to hold a clear quartz crystal in your receiving hand (the hand with which you don't normally write). While nothing material contains any power, crystals do have the ability—known as "piezoelectric"—to *amplify* the volume and clarity of spiritual power and communication coming through you. Quartz crystals, after all, are used in communication devices such as radios, watches, and computers.

Crystals absorb psychic energy, so after a while, they become "clogged" with psychic residue. If the crystal sits in a room where people have worried or felt afraid, it becomes saturated with negative thought energy. You can cleanse crystals of their oversaturation by setting them in the sunlight for four or five hours. Don't soak them in any salt water or other solutions, as this may erode the crystal.

Conducting a Psychic Reading

Close your eyes and face your client. It is helpful, but not necessary, to hold both of your client's hands. As an alternative, you can hold a watch, keys, ring, or other item with which your client has frequent contact. The vibrations from your client's hands or intimate possessions contain information-carrying energy about her. When you hold these items, you act like a television set or a record player that decodes the energy into a comprehensible image.

If you or your client seem nervous, begin your session by asking her to take two or three deep breaths while you do the same. Another good way to immediately open up the psychic channels is to ask your client to say this phrase either silently or aloud: "One love, one love, one love." This phrase attunes your client's mind with the universal oneness, and allows Divine wisdom to pour into your session.

Then, ask your client to concentrate on her question silently. Simultaneously, you can silently ask the Holy Spirit, Jesus, or a holy master, "What do you want me to know?" Allow your mind to open up completely to receive their answer. Trust what you get, although the information may make no sense to you.

Give your client the information as if you were reporting a live news event. Just report what you see, hear, know, and feel in the exact order it comes into your awareness. If you get a bit of information that you're unsure of, say so. If you get some information that seems to have a dual meaning, say that. If you receive information that you believe may be muddied by your ego, then say that. Be totally candid with your client about every shred of information, detail, and impression that comes into your consciousness. You never know which item will be important to your client. Trust in her ability to sort out the reading in a meaningful way.

If you decide to give your client a bit of humanly advice, preface your statements by saying, "Now, this advice is coming from me." Otherwise, your client may assume that the advice is coming from on-high through you.

If you or your client are unsure of the meaning of some information you receive, ask your spiritual guide for clarification.

Sometimes we psychics are afraid that if we ask the spirits, "What do you mean by that?" or "Could you please repeat what you said?" or "A little louder, please," that they will get mad at us and run away. Nothing could be further from the truth! The holy masters want us to receive their messages clearly, and they welcome our participation in helping them to get the information to us.

If, while you are in the middle of a reading, your ego kicks in with pesky questions such as: "I wonder if I'm making this all up" or "Is this real information I'm receiving?" then stop for a moment and take a few deep breaths. Say a prayer for assistance, and ask the angels to carry away your doubts.

While you are reading your client, you can tap into information about any person connected to her. For example, if your client wants to know about her boss, father, co-worker, or spouse, ask your holy masters, "What do you want me to know about this person?" Instantly, you will have access to information about the other people as if they were in the room with you.

Once, I was doing a reading on a businesswoman who was about to open a charitable children's organization. She was concerned about the integrity of the charity's board members and asked for a reading about each board member's true motives. I was easily able to see and read each person on the board for her. Then as I was about to read the final board member, I found myself looking at a whole group of people huddled around someone in the middle. It was as if they were hiding this person from my view. I told my client what I was seeing, and she told me that he was a devout Mormon. From my understanding of the Mormon faith, I believe that the church members on the other side were blocking his ability to be read. That man and his spiritual companions had my complete respect for his privacy, and I did not try to do a reading on him.

That episode brings up the issue of ethics when doing a psychic reading. You will find that you have access to every sort of private information imaginable. I once had a client ask me about her finances, and I instantly was given a psychic picture of her checkbook, complete with the dollar amount she had in her account! During another client's reading, I was psychically shown a very embarrassing vision of his sexual habits. Just like a physician, you'll want to use compassion in conveying what you see to your client.

Your motivating question in deciding how to handle your psychic abilities is: "What is this being used for?" Are you using your psychic powers for love and healing, or out of misguided fears or desires for drama and excitement? If you ever become confused about your true motivation, be honest with your spiritual helpers about your dilemma. Say to them, "I don't like how I'm feeling and thinking right now. Please help restore my mind to love and peace."

You will most likely encounter clients who will become "hooked" or dependent upon your readings. This puts you in a tricky situation. At first, you may feel flattered. The lure of making a steady income with regular clients may tempt you. Just keep in mind that you do your client and yourself a disservice if they believe you have "special powers." Your work with all clients must be in the direction of teaching them how to hear God's voice through their own inner guide. This is what ultimately heals your clients and is part of our lightworker's role in awakening others to their divinity.

Relaying Verbatim Messages

Nearly every psychic suffers self-doubts about the messages she receives during a reading. She worries, "Is this my imagination or a genuine psychic message?" You eliminate these fears by simply relaying everything you see, hear, feel, and know to your client. Trust that she will be able to make sense of your messages.

Sometimes, if I'm really unsure of the messages I'm receiving, I'll preface my statements to my clients by saying something like, "Now, I'm not sure if this is coming from spirit or coming from my own unconscious, but here's what I'm hearing..." My goal is to be completely authentic with the spirit world and with my client.

Admittedly, though, sometimes I give the client too much information and it temporarily leads to some confusion. For instance, I gave my client Kim a reading about an upcoming romantic relationship. I could see that she was about to meet someone special; however, I also saw a lot of events surrounding her meeting this man. I told her everything I saw and felt about her new relationship even though I was unsure which bits of information directly related to meeting the man. Here is Kim's account of the reading:

> In March of 1996, I talked to Doreen Virtue about my desire for a meaningful romantic relationship. Doreen mentioned that she was pretty sure that I would soon meet a man whose name began with the letter *J*. Unbeknownst to Doreen, four other people with psychic abilities had previously told me the same thing!
>
> Then in early May, Doreen gave me more extensive information. She said I would probably meet my partner's brother *first*, and that he would write down his brother's telephone number. Doreen said that our first date would be at an outdoor restaurant with umbrellas on the tables, where there'd be pigeons and a body of water nearby. Doreen mentioned that the man had very striking blue eyes, and she thought his name might be Joel. She also thought he was divorced, with two small children.
>
> Around the end of May, my friend Susan (who knew this whole story) and I were at a New Age Expo. A tall, handsome man approached me, and we talked briefly about my work. Within about two minutes, he said, "My brother lives near you, and I think you two should meet. Here's his name and num-

ber." Susan nudged me and whispered excitedly, "This must be the guy with the brother!"

I was pretty convinced that the brother could be my long-awaited partner, except that this man's name started with a *B*. Oh, well, I thought, maybe Doreen was wrong about that one detail. So, over the phone, the *B* man and I arranged to meet for lunch at the restaurant of his choice on Friday, June 14th.

As I walked up to the spot (which I had been unfamiliar with up until that time), I saw that the restaurant was right up the street from the beach, there were tables with beach umbrellas, and there were even pigeons wandering about the patio area. I also noticed that the man sitting there waiting for me did, in fact, have very vivid blue eyes. There was only one problem: I knew immediately upon laying my eyes upon him that...*he wasn't "the one"!* To say that I was disheartened would be an understatement.

The next day, Saturday, June 15th, I was scheduled to compete in a local tennis tournament. The tournament director, a nice guy named Jake, gave me instructions, we had a brief chat, and he sent me off to play. I played two matches, lost the second one, and then went home. Nothing too eventful there. But throughout the afternoon, the name "Jake, Jake, Jake" kept going through my mind.

"Why am I thinking about this guy? This is really weird!" I said to myself. The fact that his name began with a *J* didn't even occur to me!

Later that same day, a man named Joel—whom I had talked to on the phone several months earlier but had never met—left an answering-machine message saying that he thought it was time we got together. *Joel was divorced, with two small children!*

However, that meeting never came to pass, because Jake asked me to play in a consolation match on Sunday, we went to a party Sunday night, had lunch on Tuesday, drinks on Tuesday night...and by Thursday—just five days after we met—I told my friends, "This is the guy I'm going to marry."

I had never said that before about anyone!

And so, Jake, the tennis pro with the incredibly vivid blue eyes (which I didn't get a chance to see until our second meeting because he had been wearing sunglasses the first time) turned out to be the *J* man that Doreen had foreseen. Five months later, Jake and I were happily engaged, planning our future together!

Kim's story is a good example of trusting that your client will be able to use and make sense of all the information you receive. Sometimes, I'll get very detailed psychic information related specifically to my client's questions or concerns. Other times, as with Kim's readings, I receive peripheral information surrounding, but indirectly related to, my client's concerns. However, while giving Kim readings, I definitely felt she would soon enter into a meaningful relationship. I continually relayed that feeling to her, and found that everything else was just window dressing upon this central issue.

If Your Reading Seems Inaccurate

Even the world's top psychics give readings that are seemingly inaccurate. In fact, the leading psychics report that between 10 and 30 percent of the information they relay in a reading is incorrect. Why is this?

The most common reason, as I've mentioned, is that the information is coming from the psychic's ego and not the higher self. Everyone occasionally slips into the ego for various reasons—fear, fatigue, and judgments, for example.

Additionally, some of the information we give our clients is based upon their current thought patterns. Let's say you give a reading in which you see your client getting a new job. This reading is accurate at the time. But later, your client changes her outlook in either a healthier or unhealthier direction. This change in thinking will also alter the course of her future, including her job prospects.

Related to this phenomenon is the fact that your reading may actually change your clients' thoughts sufficiently to negate your reading. For example, if you relate that your client is about to meet a wonderful love partner, your client may become petrified with nervousness. This tension can literally bar her from meeting or attracting her love mate.

Sometimes it seems that a reading is inaccurate just because your predictions don't immediately come to pass. Perhaps your reading will prove accurate after a period of time has gone by, though. I find that it is difficult to pinpoint the exact timing of a future event. For example, my client may ask me, "When will I sell my house?" and I can't tell exactly, but I can see that it's when the weather is warm. I may say something like, "It feels like summertime, and I'm hearing the number "2" in my mind. Since August is two months away, I would say that is a strong likelihood. But since timing isn't my psychic forte, I can't be sure. What I do know is that I have a strong positive sense that your house will sell, and that you will be moderately pleased with the selling price."

I think it's important not to get self-judgmental when you make an occasional "miss" during a reading. If you allow yourself to get uptight because you're not 100 percent accurate, you won't enjoy your psychic work. Your clients are loving and forgiving beings. It's unlikely that—unless your entire reading is based upon your ego and is therefore completely inaccurate—your clients will be dismayed if you get two or three items "wrong" during your sessions.

Focus upon your successes, and ask your guides to help you increase your accuracy. You'll probably find that your incorrect impressions were symbols that you were misreading as a literal prediction. For instance, let's say you are shown a baby clairvoyantly. You assume your client is expecting a child, and you hesitantly say, "Are you thinking of having a child?" Your client sternly says something like, "That's impossible because I've been sterilized." Don't despair or hang up your psychic hat! You've probably got spirit guides who symbolize "new opportunities" with a picture of a baby's birth. To avoid confusion, simply tell your client what you are seeing, and explain that you can't be sure if it is symbolic or an actual representation of your future. Check in with your gut feelings often, and you'll soon be able to sort symbols from true predictions.

Distance Readings

A client doesn't need to be physically with you during a psychic reading. I do most of my work with clients over the telephone. You can also psychically read a person during your meditation periods. You'll want to consult your higher self to establish a personal code of ethics about doing readings on someone who is unaware you're doing a reading or who hasn't given permission.

If you are doing telephone psychic readings, you may find it helpful to have your client mail you a handwritten note before your session. Holding this note during the session can help you tap into your client's energy field. There is no qualitative difference, in my experience, between the readings I give my telephone clients and those of my in-person clients.

Giving Thanks

One very important point I want to make is that it's a good idea to end each session by giving thanks to the spiritual supporters who came to your assistance. Gratitude is their payment, and it also helps you feel heightened joy.

Clairvoyant Scanning

To help your clients, you can psychically scan their chakras to check their size and cleanliness. Another method I use is to ask my client to remove her shoes and lie down. I then take my receiving hand (the hand with which you don't usually write) and place it about one inch from the client's sending (the side of the body with which you usually write) foot. This is a method inspired by magnetic healer Ina Bryant that checks someone's "polarity" or energy flow.[1] If I feel steady and strong energy coming out of my client's foot, then I know her polarity is balanced. If I cannot feel any energy coming from the sending foot, then my client's chakras are probably dirty or unbalanced.

I've also discovered that if I stand over my reclining client and run my hand about two feet over her body, that I can feel "bumps" and energy differences where the chakra is shrunken or enlarged. My client has unexpressed issues corresponding to the chakra where the bumps or dense energy exists.

Anytime you discover your client's chakras being extremely disproportionate in size or in cleanliness, you have come across valuable information. Help your client to discover why she is harboring so much energy in that chakra. Usually, fear is at the root of the distress. By talking openly, your client will probably see a different viewpoint that will help assuage her fear. Once the fear is released, the chakras may return to their natural clean and balanced state without further assistance. You can scan your client's chakras after your session to ensure that they are clean and balanced.

There are many ways to clean and balance your client's chakras. You could play an audiocassette such as my *Chakra Clearing* recording, or you could lead a guided meditation that inspires your client to visualize each chakra being cleansed and balanced. At times, I also scan my clients' bodies with my inner vision, checking for areas that look or feel dark. My inner guide then tells me the reason for this darkness. Sometimes the darkness relates to a hardened thoughtform residing in that area of the body. For example, I scanned one client, noticed a thickness in her chest, and intuited that this was congestion. As soon as I received this information, I saw an image of her mother and grandmother standing behind her. These two women were holding my client so tightly that she was suffocating for air. She explained that after her grandmother's recent death, her mother had become very clingy. My client said she'd had a chest cold and agreed that it was connected to feeling trapped by her mother. We worked on releasing unforgiveness and judgments toward her mother, and her breathing immediately improved.

Another time, I scanned a client and found black spots around her ovaries. I intuited that these spots were connected to unhealed grief from abortions. My client said that she'd had two abortions about which she harbored deep guilt. Our work then focused on her releasing unforgiveness toward herself and the baby's father.

Cutting Etheric Cords

Every person with whom we've had an emotional experience stays continually connected with us through an etheric cord. You can do a great service to your clients by psychically scanning them for cords during your sessions. These cords look and feel like rubber tubes or arteries, and they usually extend from the chakras. Intense relationships create thicker cords than casual relationships.

Look for and sense these cords on your clients, and then psychically discern to whom the cord is attached. I usually find huge cords attached to my clients' siblings and former lovers. If these relationships are healthy and built upon love, the cords can be a source of healing energy sent back and forth between the two people. However, usually you'll find that your client is receiving toxic anger and fear through the cord (also known as "psychic attack"), or the person is draining your client's energy on the other end of the cord.

Psychically find and identify the source of each cord on your client. Then ask for permission to detach each problematic cord. You can verbally ask your client for permission and also mentally ask the person at the other end of the cord. If the absent person doesn't give permission (which you receive psychically by hearing or feeling a "yes" response), then just cut it from your client and drop it without cutting the other end.

To cut a cord, visualize a sharp pair of scissors slicing it; mentally dissolve the cord; or picture yourself pulling the cord out of both people. I once had a client who had dozens of cords attached to former lovers. She had so many "old boyfriend" cords that I psychically used a lawn mower to remove them.

The sensation of cord-cutting is powerfully palpable, and your client may wince as you release these connections. You'll probably feel an accompanying change in air pressure. The person on the other end will sense the change as well. That person will think of your client without knowing why, which may result in your client getting some, "Hey, I was just thinking about you" telephone calls.

Sending Healing Energy

Another effective healing method is to visualize pure white light from God coming in through your crown chakra and going out through your fingertips. Point your fingers toward your client to direct the flow of light rays.

Payment

The best source of guidance about receiving payment for your services is your higher self. I recommend that you meditate upon this topic and ask for spiritual assistance in deciding what feels comfortable to you. When I was beginning my psychic counseling work, my spiritual guide told me a specific dollar amount to charge. I balked at the figure and said, "That's too much money. I wouldn't dare ask for that amount!" So, I began charging a considerably smaller fee than the figure I was advised. Soon, though, my caseload of clients became so large that I required a waiting list. I was so overloaded with clients that I wasn't enjoying my work. I thought, If only I had listened to my guide's advice and charged the figure I was told, then my practice would be more balanced and harmonious.

I prayed for guidance about the matter and finally arrived at a comfortable arrangement. Many healers find great value in charitably giving away their services to, for example, one or two clients a month. Other healers—including Edgar Cayce and Phineas Quimby—didn't accept money for their services. Usually, their clients brought gifts of food or other supplies as a way to show their gratitude. Gerry Jampolsky is a present-day healer who also functions in this way.

Follow whatever path feels right to you in setting your fee schedule. Just remember that if you overburden yourself with too many clients, you may not fulfill your sacred mission as a lightworker. Also, if you only give, and refuse to receive, you deny the other person the gift of giving. Honor and balance yourself, and you'll enjoy years of fruitful service.

MEDIUMSHIP AND SPIRIT RELEASEMENT

*"The more I observe and study things, the more convinced
I become that sorrow over separation and death is
perhaps the greatest delusion. To realize that it is
a delusion is to become free. There is no death,
no separation of the substance."*

— Mahatma Gandhi,
Indian nationalist and spiritual leader

Just as you can easily give a psychic reading to your clients' friends and associates, so too can you give a reading of your clients' deceased loved ones. Mediumship is no more difficult or simple than giving a psychic reading. So please don't let the word intimidate you in any way.

As with your psychic readings, you'll want to be clear about your motives for contacting the deceased. Practically every major religion warns of the hazards of soliciting and accepting advice from those who have passed on—and for good reason. A person's physical death does not automatically eradicate her ego. Physical death doesn't give a spirit instant access to high-level wisdom. Wisdom only comes to people, living or dead, through awareness of their true self within God. Sometimes people become so impressed by the fact that they have contacted a dead person that they take his or her every word as gospel. However, a person in the afterlife is not necessarily any closer to God or ultimate truth than a person in this life. So why take advice from the equivalent of a third-grader when you could just as easily talk to God, the ultimate professor, or one of His ascended-master graduate students?

Nonetheless, there are also legitimate and healthy reasons to contact the deceased. One primary reason why you may be called into mediumship work is to help your client resolve longstanding resentments between her and her deceased relatives. This is especially true if you are working with an abuse survivor whose abuser is deceased.

As I mentioned earlier in the book, deceased abusers frequently become earthbound. They often attach to the aura of their living abuse survivor, out of remorse, desires to make amends, or because of unhealthy cravings to be near the living person. In a section later in this chapter entitled "Spirit Releasement Therapy," I detail ways for dealing with this sort of situation.

Another valid purpose for mediumship is to help grief-stricken clients conduct conversations with their deceased loved ones. These sorts of sessions are among my favorites, as they are extremely moving experiences. The dead frequently tell their survivors, "I'm doing fine. Don't worry about me. Please go on with your own life." If the survivors' grief is quite strong, it thwarts the dead person's spiritual progress in the afterlife. We can keep our deceased loved ones earthbound with our grief. This isn't healthy for anyone, and as a medium, part of your work will involve counseling your clients to let their loved ones move on.

Another healthy reason to conduct mediumship is to help you and your client lose the fear of physical death. This fear prevents many of us from fully enjoying life, because half the time we're looking over our shoulders to ensure our physical safety. Once you become convinced that your soul is immortal, you automatically release a great deal of anxiety and depression. When I interviewed James Redfield, author of *The Celestine Prophecy,* for *Complete Woman* magazine, I asked him about the 11th and 12th insights in his forthcoming books. Redfield said he was certain they would involve an increasing amount of teamwork between people on both sides of the veil. Redfield shares my view that the curtain separating both worlds is thinning rapidly.

Controls or Spirit Guides

Many mediums receive their information through a "control." This is usually a highly evolved spirit guide who acts as a gatekeeper in deciding which spirits come through during the session. Very often, the control acts as a conduit for spirit communication. The spirits talk to the control, who in turn passes along the communication to the medium, who then gives it to her clients.

Most mediums don't ask for a control; rather, the control chooses them. However, people could also request that they be assigned a control. If you're not certain whether you have a control with you or not, ask during your meditation or right before going to sleep. As with all questions, you will be answered. I don't use a control since I find it easy to discern spirits and talk directly to them.

Trance Mediumship

Spirit communication is usually conducted while the medium is in a slightly altered state of consciousness, often called a trance. There are three levels of trance mediumship: light, semi, and full. A full-trance medium goes into a sleeplike state, and a "control" takes over her body. The control talks through the medium and is the actual being who delivers messages from the other side. After the session, the full-trance medium won't know what was said or done. She may feel drained or dazed after her session.

A semi-trance medium retains some awareness of what is said during her sessions. Like the full-trance medium, she usually allows her control or her clients' deceased loved ones speak through her. Other semi-trance mediums and all light-trance mediums act as intermediaries, relaying what the deceased loved one says. This type of mediumship doesn't involve any form of "channeling."

The primary difference between a "channeler" and a medium is that channelers normally limit their transmissions to one distinct entity. Mediums, in contrast, talk to many different spirits.

The Mediumship Experience

If you feel drawn to mediumship work, then you are most likely heeding a calling. Healers seem to either enjoy this form of work, or they avoid it altogether because the thought of talking to deceased people frightens them. Please keep in mind that, just like psychic work, mediumship requires no special powers. Everyone can communicate with those on the other side. All that it requires is a little patience and practice. You will probably benefit from reading a description of the experience of mediumship so you'll know what to expect when conducting your sessions.

Imagine walking into a very dimly lit room. At first, you can barely sense the presence of other people in the room. It's that "I'm not alone" feeling. Then, you begin to see the outlines, shapes, and forms of people in the room. You find one person in the room who seems friendly and you begin talking with her. The more you speak with her, the more adjusted your eyes become to the room's lighting. Slowly, you begin to see more details about your companion, including the way she looks. You also get impressions about her personality—whether she's boisterous, quiet, good-humored, intellectual, or emotional. The more you talk to her, the easier it is to focus, just as if you were standing in a fully illuminated room. The experience of talking to a deceased person is not much different from talking to a living person.

Most deceased people will help you during your communications. Very often, the dead are aware of an upcoming mediumship session (or they arranged it to happen), and they prepare ahead of time for it. Most of them are quite anxious to reach their living relatives. The only exceptions I've found to this are remorseful and shame-filled abusers and criminals who fear being judged for their actions. However, for most of your mediumship sessions, the deceased will assist you.

Most deceased persons make themselves easy to identify by appearing dressed and coiffed just as they normally did when they were living. For example, when my client wanted to contact her deceased grandmother, the woman appeared to me wearing a frilly apron. This helped my client know that she was really talking to her grandmother, who had worn such an apron virtually every day of her life. Or, the deceased may carry a symbol to help themselves be identified. For instance, one of my client's deceased aunts showed up carrying an orchid in a glass. My client explained that her aunt always put orchids in glass vases on top of her living room piano.

So, again, let go of any worries about whether you'll be successful at mediumship or not. Between the help you get from God, the angels, and the deceased people, you'll definitely be working with a powerful team of assistants.

Beginning Mediumship

Precede your session with an extra-good chakra-cleansing meditation. Be certain that your third-eye chakra is spotless, because you'll want to access clairvoyant channels to see the deceased people. Begin with a prayer of protection, as described in Chapter 19.

During mediumship, you'll probably want your client to be seated about three or four feet from you. You probably won't want to hold hands during this session unless you feel guided to do so. Help your client relax quietly, and explain that you'll begin talking after a short while.

Close your eyes, and take three very deep and slow breaths. If you begin to feel afraid or anxious, ask for spiritual support from your angels or holy master. Allow your mind to relax and open as in the ornate bowl method described in Chapter 18.

Then, without judging or forcing your thoughts in any way, mentally notice the area around your client's shoulders. Notice whether you sense any differences in the air mass around either shoulder. Try to discern if there is a form or a sense of heaviness around either one. When you get any feeling that one shoulder has "something" different around it, focus on the energy around that one.

Usually, if the spirit is next to the right shoulder of a right-handed person, this is a relative from their father's side of the family. If the spirit is next to their left shoulder, it is a maternal relative. The opposite sides apply in left-handed people.

Go within and sense whether the spirit next to your client's shoulder feels like a feminine or a masculine energy. This is the same set of skills you would use to sense whether you were in the presence of a male or a female in a darkened room. A feminine energy feels softer and higher in frequency than does a masculine energy.

At this point, you have established whether you are talking to a male or female spirit, and the side of your client's family from which the spirit comes. You can next discern the spirit's specific relationship to your client. Each relationship—brother, sister, aunt, uncle, father, mother, and such—has a completely different feel to its energy pattern. Even in the beginning of your mediumship career, you can distinguish the energy patterns of one relationship from another. To me, the older relatives feel like a slower vibration, the parents' vibration is slightly faster, followed by aunts and uncles, then siblings and cousins. Children's spirits vibrate the fastest. The spirit's form also occupies roughly the same amount of space as a living human body, so you can deduce that a small spirit is either a petite woman or a child.

If you are clairaudient, you might hear the spirit's name being spoken. If you don't, you can ask the spirit to identify him- or herself. I've usually found that spirits are happy to answer any of our questions.

After you have initiated contact, the deceased person will begin conveying as much information as you are willing to receive. So, you may suddenly see a "miniature movie," or a symbol, in your mind's eye. You may hear something like a voice or music. Or you may even smell cigar smoke or perfume. These are all signals from the spirit to help you identify him or her.

Don't let these messages distract or pull you out of your semi-trance. Instead, begin to tell your client what you are receiving. Allow your client to help you in interpreting these impressions.

As I brought up earlier, the purpose of your session is to help your client heal from grief, guilt, or other distress. Lightworkers who solicit stock tips, lottery numbers, or even advice from deceased spirits are playing with fire. Be true to yourself, light-worker, and your joy will be unlimited.

Spirit Guides and Earthbound Spirits

Most mediumship sessions end when the spirits tell you that it's time for them to return to the afterlife plane. It takes a great deal of energy and effort for spirits to be able to communicate with the living. They must sometimes obtain "permission" or assistance from their own spirit guides and teachers to be able to communicate with us. The process involves slowing their own vibrations to the dense and slow frequency of the earthplane. Most spirits can only withstand the earth's dense frequency for short bursts of time, in the same way that we'd be uncomfortable at a significantly different elevation.

However, you will also come across spirits who are very comfortable on the earthplane. These are the "earthbound" spirits who don't want to go to the afterlife plane. The reasons for their decision to stay near earth vary. Some spirits are afraid of judgment or retaliation from God. Other spirits, who were addicted to drugs or alcohol when they died, stay on Earth to experience vicarious highs from intoxicated living persons. Still others are so attached to their home or business that they can't bear the thought of leaving. Some spirits are unaware that they are dead. Other spirits stay near their loved ones, usually out of concern for their living relative's intense grief.

Additionally, some spirits stay earthbound because of well-intentioned desires to undo the harm or pain they caused during their lives. This is especially common among child abusers, who, upon their death, realize their mistakes. They then attach to the person whom they abused, hoping to make amends. The trouble is, their presence creates disturbances for the living person. For instance, the deceased abuser is usually a depressed personality. Anytime you have a depressed person around you—living or deceased—the negativity has a contagious effect. The deceased abuser may also whisper misguided advice into the living person's mind, who is unaware where a "sudden idea" came from.

Spirit guides are different from earthbound spirits in that they receive training in the afterlife preparing them for guideship. Although they spend much of their time on the earthplane, they are not earthbound. In fact, spirit guides frequently return to the afterlife plane to attend classes and engage in other activities. They are always within earshot range, so if the living person is ever in trouble, the guide immediately returns to her side.

Many people's spirit guides are deceased relatives. These

guides have learned how to be helpful without interfering in the living person's free will. They also know that we who are living need to learn things on our own. So while a guide is always available to help you, he or she will not agree to make all your decisions for you.

Spirit-Releasement Therapy

Part of your work as a medium will involve communicating with earthbound spirits. If you've ever experienced family therapy sessions, you will find that "spirit-releasement therapy" is similar. Unless you are a trance medium who gives over the session to a control, your role will be as an intermediary who delivers communications between the afterlife and the earth planes.

Let's say your client has an earthbound former-abuser next to her. It is the spirit of her father, who was an alcoholic while he was living. This man abused your client in many ways, and after his death, he truly feels sorry for the pain he inflicted upon his daughter. He sees how this pain affected her self-esteem and ultimately interfered with her ability to fulfill her life purpose. Now he wants to make amends so she can get on with her life, and he won't leave her side until he's certain that she's going to be okay. Usually, this means that he wants her forgiveness.

Your client will probably be wary of forgiving her father, believing this would signal her approval of his abusive behavior. She may also hold fantasies of retaliating against him, and she may even secretly be delighted to discover that he feels pain as a product of his remorse. "Serves him right for what he did to me!" she may tell you upon hearing of her father's situation.

If you have unhealed wounds from your own experiences with abuse, you will need to tread gently to ensure that your own emotions don't color your session. Your role is to explain to your client how her unforgiveness is self-destructive. You'll also want to explain that she needn't forgive her abuser's actions, but merely needs to forgive him as a person. Explain to her that by doing so, her father's spirit will be freed, and she will be relieved of the anguish related to his presence.

Facilitate a conversation between your client and her father. Usually, the abuser will explain that alcoholism, his own abusive upbringing, or some other circumstances influenced his behavior. While this doesn't excuse the responsibility for his actions, your client will most likely listen to these explanations and be willing to forgive.

When your client shows an inkling of forgiveness, call in spiritual assistance. Either aloud or mentally, ask for another deceased relative or the Archangel Michael to escort the deceased abuser to the afterlife. They will immediately respond to your request, and you will see or sense the spirit rising up and away from your client. Your client will feel a physical sensation like a vacuum or air-pressure change.

End your session by giving thanks to those spiritual beings who helped you. Following a spirit-releasement session, your clients will most likely notice a difference in the way they feel and look. Several of my clients have immediately noticed that anxiety, desires to overeat or drink, and depression are lifted. Usually, spirit-releasement therapy creates positive changes in a client's physical appearance, such as a more relaxed facial appearance, and eyes that look happier and brighter. Sometimes skin changes accompany sessions, and a client may either develop or lose a rash. I believe these physical changes are due to the intense nature of releasing strong emotions.

Distance Mediumship and Remote Depossession

Just as you can conduct effective psychic readings on the telephone, so too can you conduct mediumship and spirit-releasement sessions this way. The procedure to communicate with your client's deceased loved ones during a telephone session is identical to the guidelines given for an in-person session. You will see, feel, hear, and sense the spirit exactly as if your client were in the same room with you. Sometimes the spirit *will* actually be with you during the session.

Remote depossession is a related form of healing in which you help to release spirits connected to your client's aura. The only difference is that during a remote depossession session, you work on your client without having any in-person or telephone contact with him or her. There are many variations of remote depossession, and if you feel guided, you can attend training seminars given by one of the "Spirit Releasement" organizations listed in the Self-Help resource section in the back of this book.

One form of remote depossession, which I use, involves mentally scanning your client's body and aura, looking for areas of darkness. Visualize a giant vacuum tube going into the top of your client's crown chakra and vacuuming all of the darkness out of her body. When the client is cleaned, reverse the switch on the vacuum so it pushes out thick white light. Completely fill your client's body with this light and seal her crown with love.

Many remote-depossession therapists work in pairs. One therapist "channels" the spirits attached to the client, while the other therapist works with Archangel Michael to release these spirits to the light. If you choose this type of work, you'll want to use protective prayers, especially if you allow the spirits to channel through you.

Spirit releasement is a powerful way to heal physical and emotional symptoms in your clients. In *The Book of James*, medium Susy Smith channeled the great spiritual psychologist William James as saying that spirit releasement was among the most important work that a psychic could perform. He urged all psychics to become involved in this activity, saying we sorely needed it because of the huge number of earthbound spirits.

James explained that these spirits added to the mass race consciousness of fear on earth. Every time we help a spirit go to the afterlife, we relieve the earth's atmosphere of fear. [1]

C H A P T E R
T W E N T Y - O N E

CALLING UPON ANGELS

"Make yourself familiar with the angels, and
behold them frequently in spirit; for without being seen,
they are present with you."

— Saint Francis de Sales (1567–1622),
author of numerous spiritual texts

Whether you conduct energy work or spiritual healing, you have access to angels. These powerful spiritual helpers are beings of light who have never been in a physical body, and they operate within a different plane than spirit guides. Their purpose is to remind us of God's constant love.

An infinite number of angels are available to help us anytime. Additionally, we each have one or more guardian angels with us from birth and throughout our lives. These angels may offer advice and wisdom but won't ever interfere with our free will. In fact, angels cannot intervene or even help us unless we ask. The only exception to this law of free will is when we are in mortal danger before our time. Only then can an angel intervene without being asked. The angels wish that we would ask for their assistance more often, since they live for the joy of service.

Archangels supervise the angels who flock to the earth. The Archangel Raphael, whose name means "God heals," is closely connected to lightworkers. Raphael helps healers by whispering guidance and wisdom in their ears. Raphael oversees your development as a healer, and you can ask him for specific help and information.

Keeping company with angels will help attune your mind and heart to your higher self. Whenever you feel your ego threatening to pull you down, ask for an angel to pull you back up. You can ask to be surrounded by thousands of angels if you like. It's also a good idea to ask for angels to watch over your children, clients, and other loved ones. You don't need to use a formal invocation to invite angels into your life. You just need to ask sincerely.

Once you invite angels into your life, you will notice a shift in your outward experiences. I see sparkles of white light that tell me whenever an angel is near. Other signs of an angelic presence include miraculous coincidences, a sudden feeling of warm love or peace, hearing a sweet strain of music, or smelling a heavenly floral perfume. The angels' loving presence helps to align your thoughts with God, and this will keep you in the harmonious world of the true self. Angels can also give you guidance and ideas as a healer, so it's a good idea to invite them into your healing sessions.

One main way angels help during sessions is in carrying away released thoughtforms. For example, I'll often work with clients to help them identify the beliefs that are triggering their emotional or physical pain. I use psychic communication to identify the source of distress rapidly. Perhaps an incident in childhood has colored their world view, or maybe they harbor resentment toward themselves or someone else. Whatever the source, it needs to be identified and released to effect a healing.

Often, after identifying the culprit belief, my client will say something like, "Oh, I've been trying to get rid of that pattern in my thoughts for years. I keep going back to that thought, although I recognize it's unhealthful." Sometimes, these clients have sincerely tried releasing their unwanted emotions to God and have felt frustrated by the belief's continuing presence. I've found that when my client visualizes giving her belief thoughtform to the angels, there is an immediate release and lasting healing.

During most of my sessions, I ask Archangel Michael for help. Michael functions as the world's guardian angel, and he is a master at keeping divine order in any situation. If you are involved in any form of energy work, especially mediumship and spirit-releasement therapy, you'll definitely want Archangel Michael's presence during your sessions. As with the other angels, Michael doesn't require a formal invocation or invitation. Simply ask for him, either mentally or aloud, and his presence is instantly assured.

Just like the holy masters, the archangels live in a parallel dimension that operates apart from our physical laws. Therefore, they have the ability to be with many different people all over the world simultaneously. So you needn't worry that Michael, Raphael, or the other archangels are too busy to come to your assistance.

In my book *Angel Therapy* (Hay House, November, 1997), I describe many ways to involve angels in your own or your client's life. The angels are wonderful healers, as they are pure love, and just by thinking about them, healing energy is poured into your sessions. They also view us through the true-self world that only knows perfection. So if you are having difficulty knowing the truth about your client's perfect health, ask angels, holy masters, and the Holy Spirit to help. The angel's mind, continually focused from the experience of love, can substitute for your mindset if you are operating from the ego plane. Since there is only one mind in truth, it only takes one lightworker, angel, or holy master, operating from the perspective of pure love, to effect miraculous healing.

I say a prayer such as this one to God each morning:

Please send Your angels to my side today,
to help keep my mind and heart centered in love.
Help me to live from Your perspective of love,
and to know my oneness with all of life. Amen.

CHAPTER
TWENTY-TWO

SPIRITUAL HEALING

"By detachment from appearances, abide in Real Truth."

— Diamond Sutra,
Buddhist spiritual text

Psychic healing revolves around the world of matter, which in its most finite components is vibrating energy particles. These energy vibrations are encoded with information that the psychic "reads" during her sessions. To understand that energy composes all matter is an important step when conducting healings from the level of the mind.

Beyond the material illusion, though, is the pure awareness and experience of God's love. Your true self is in this experience right now, as is your client's true self. When we give psychic readings, we "read" the ego. If your client or her deceased loved one fully lived in a true-self state, your reading would be, "I see love, I feel love, I hear love, and I know love."

Matter, thought, and energies all intersect on one plane of existence. Spirit is on a different but parallel plane. On the material plane, there is energy and the experience of matter, time, and movement. On the true-self plane, there is only the pure experience of love, oneness, or unity. No thought is necessary because there is nothing to think about and no comparisons to make. There is no *doing*, because doing implies improving or getting something. In the true-self plane, where all is perfect, there is nothing

239

to improve upon and nothing that needs additions or fixing. Those are all functions of the body, which is a material perspective.

Angels, spirit guides, and deceased people function and intervene in our material world. Many spirit guides and most deceased persons who interact with the earthplane operate largely out of an ego perspective that sees the material world as having reality. Angels, Holy Spirit, ascended masters, and evolved spirit guides know the truth of life's divine perfection. However, they also see that we need help while we still believe we are in the material world. Their role is to function in both planes to help us gently awaken to our higher selves in the spirit plane.

The Purpose of Sickness

In this world, no one does anything unless they believe it will help them gain pleasure or avoid punishment. Injury, illness, and self-destructive habits are decisions that the ego makes as a way of serving both these functions.

All physical distress is ultimately a form of mental illness. Injury and illness are symptoms of the insane belief that we can (or would want to) hurt or give pleasure to the body in order to drown out the sound of God's voice. When I was afraid to follow my inner guidance to write books, I tried to silence the gut feelings by pouring food on my gut. The more God urged me to change my life, the more afraid I became. Overeating was my way of protecting myself from the perceived danger of listening to my inner direction. I also believed that eating would give me more pleasure than I could derive from following God's guidance. We all have this inner Voice for God, or Holy Spirit, within us. It is part of our true selves, and if we will let it, the voice will perfectly help us meet every need.

Every illness, injury, and psychiatric condition stems from identical attempts to delay listening to the Voice for God. Mental or physical health conditions are enormously time- and energy-consuming, so they serve the same purpose as continually pressing the snooze button on the alarm clock. God is trying to rouse each of us from our nightmare, but we keep insisting, "I'm not quite ready to awaken yet." So we press the snooze button another day.

Your clients are ill, injured, or seemingly trapped in self-destructive habits because they decided that their bodies had minds of their own. They also receive a "secondary gain" from their distress, such as getting a much-needed rest, disability compensation, revenge, or sympathy. But the primary "benefit" accompanying an ill or injured body is that it allows a person to believe that he or she is a victim of outside circumstances.

In addition, the ego thrives on guilt. It sees the world and God as punitive and so fears retaliation for its imagined crimes and guilt. So the ego decides, "If I punish myself, then God and other people won't punish me." Since the ego believes it is a body, it punishes itself through illness, accidents, and self-destructive behaviors.

The ego sees itself as separated from God and other people, and this is one reason why it intently focuses upon the body. To maintain the illusion of separation, the ego vacillates between feeling superior and inferior to God and others. This wavering outlook makes the ego think one moment, "I'm not worthy of God's company and guidance," and the next minute, "My own guidance is superior to God's."

So the ill or pained body becomes an earplug designed to block the inner voice and the realization of oneness with God and others. Undoing the thoughts causing illness or injury requires your client's willingness to momentarily listen to God's voice. Gently ask your client to discuss what the voice says. Help her heal from the distrust of the voice's guidance. You could ask your client, "What hunches and gut feelings have you been trying to ignore lately?" She may initially protest that she doesn't have any awareness of her gut feelings. However, with your urging, she will soon readily admit that she does hear her inner voice's call. To me, "hearing" and "healing" are synonymous terms, because our willingness to hear the Voice for God is the same as our decision to become well.

You probably have some wonderful stories you could share with your client about your own successes in following your inner voice. As you help your client relax her defensiveness toward her inner voice, she will be more willing to let down her barriers to hearing and heeding the voice. You will also find that the more time you spend in teaching others to trust their inner voices, the easier it will become for you to continually follow your own inner Voice for God. As we teach, so do we learn.

Overcoming Barriers to Healing

The term *spiritual healing* is actually an oxymoron, since to heal from a spiritual level, you must first know that nothing needs healing. Healing does not involve *adding* anything to a client; but rather, helping the client eliminate those beliefs that have caused the experience of illness or injury.

Your power of healing comes from your ability to hold the knowledge that your client is not a body, but a perfect spirit. As healers, we aren't *doing* anything, since again, "doing" implies that we are a body. In addition, perfect health is your client's natural state. You are helping to identify, remove, and release the thoughts that block him or her from enjoying perfect health. Viewing your client as ill, diseased, or injured hampers your effectiveness as a healer, since this viewpoint reinforces or enlarges the illusion that matter has reality.

In the world of time, matter, and bodies, we believe in certain "laws of nature." Among these laws is the belief that illness and injury heal gradually over time. Many people would be terrified of a sudden healing because it seems to defy this basic law. When laws are defied, the person feels confused about his basic understanding of how the world is organized. However, a client who believes in miracles is less likely to be frightened by a sudden healing, and so is more likely to experience one.

Your client may become angry or feel blame as a result of the suggestion that her thoughts caused her condition, or that she has the power to think her way to health. The ego constantly looks for signs that it is being attacked. When it perceives attack, it launches counterstrikes, and you may be its target during healing sessions. Often, your client won't vocalize these attacks because of fears of losing your help. Psychically, you will denote them, and as they arise, you'll want to acknowledge and work through them by helping your client release fears and anger.

The ego believes that when it makes a mistake, it will be punished. So, it becomes defensive instead of admitting mistakes in thinking. Your client may therefore appear defensive or resistant when you pinpoint the core beliefs that trigger illnesses. She may also doubt the validity of your statements, or may fear hoping for a healing to avoid disappointment.

I've also worked with several clients who feared that, once they were healed, life would be dreary, monotonous, and boring. They derived excitement from the highs and lows accompanying their illnesses and compulsions, and so, resisted healing. I find it helpful to share my own experiences with them of feeling excited at being guided to right relationships and right livelihood.

Again, your client may be afraid to overtly tell you of her resistance and may outwardly pretend to agree with you. You will receive much of her resistance on an intuitive level. You can assuage this defensiveness by using extreme gentleness and by teaching your client that mistakes in thinking merely require *correction*, not punishment. Reassure your client that correction simply entails changing her mind about herself, and that she is capable of changing her mind instantly.

During your sessions, though, you needn't worry that your

healing attempts may be unsuccessful because of your client's fears and resistance. Even if your client initially rejects your healing words, your thoughts of truth and love will stay eternally connected to her. They hang from her aura like ornaments on a Christmas tree. When she is ready to hear them, she will receive your loving thoughtforms.

It's also important to remind yourself continually of the unreality of your client's ego. Don't struggle with your client's ego thoughts, because they will enlarge. You will also go into your own ego state of mind if you identify with or judge your client's ego. The same is true if you feel sorry for your client, or see her lacking in any way. Instead, look past her outside ego characteristics and see only her loving true-self state. Remember: as you see her, so you see yourself.

The only thing real in this world is love, and every behavior and word from your client (and everyone else, for that matter) stems from love. If you decide to watch for love's presence in your clients, you'll hear and see love in everything they do and say. You'll understand that when clients speak from fear, they are really saying, "I want to feel safe and loved." When clients speak from anger, they are really saying, "I want to feel safe and loved." And when clients speak from bodily pain, they are really saying, "I want to feel safe and loved."

If you become impatient or irritated with your clients, a wonderful healing affirmation that you can say silently to yourself during sessions is, "I know I am seeing something in you that I don't want to see in myself. I thank you for your gift of serving as my mirror. I lovingly release that part of myself that irritates me about you. I willingly release this in love, asking only that any lessons I need to learn be left behind."

During your sessions, you'll want to continually remind yourself that you are a conduit for God's love. If you continuously check your client's physical condition to see if she has healed, you have not fully released the loving thoughtforms for her to receive. You must completely give your gift of healing for her fully to receive it. You don't want to be like the amateur chef who keeps opening the oven door to check on his creation, and in so doing, makes the cake fall flat. If you are sincerely healing from a place of love, trust that healing *always* works and release it in full faith to your client.

Prayerful Support

Prayer's power to heal has been widely documented by lay persons, theologians, and scientists. Dr. Larry Dossey's book *Healing Words* presents a wonderful overview of the scientific and medical research about prayer's remarkable curative power.

While one person's prayers alone can heal any condition, there is a lot of evidence that group prayers effect remarkable healings. You may recall my describing Betty Eadie's conversation where she said one prayer was like a single light beam going straight to heaven. However, if we join our single prayer with that of like-minded people, it's like a huge rope of bundled light beams shining upon heaven.

For this reason, you may want to supplement your spiritual healing sessions with the prayers of other people. You or your client could put her name on a church prayer ministry list with a single telephone call. One of my clients once asked me for spiritual help with apparent lumps in her breast. Simultaneously, her name was put on the prayer ministry list at several churches. She also had many good friends praying for her. When her biopsy later came back as benign, she told me she believed her original condition was grave and that spiritual intervention had restored her health.

Steps of Spiritual Healing

Spiritual healing can be conducted at a distance or in-person. For an in-person healing, your first consideration is for you and your client to feel relaxed. Your healing setting, whether it's your home or office, can promote relaxation and heighten your psychic abilities with soft lighting, candles, beautiful music, incense, or fragrant flowers. Normally, your client will feel nervous or anxious at the beginning of the session, especially if she is a new client. You may intuit your client's nervousness and mistake it for your own. To help both of you relax, begin the session by taking three or four deep breaths.

I usually say to my client as we are breathing:

"Feel yourself inhaling delicious feelings of relaxation and holding that inhalation for as long as you feel comfortable. When you feel ready, exhale slowly. Blow out all the cares, worries, and stress. Visualize yourself putting any pressing worries on the bookshelf or window ledge, knowing that you can safely retrieve them later if you so choose. But for right now, give yourself permission to set those worries down as you feel more and more relaxed."

Your client's tension is palpable. You'll also feel the moment when she releases this tension. You'll notice the air pressure change from a feeling that the room is holding its breath, to a feeling of the room's air flowing freely. If your client or you continue feeling nervous, state this centering meditation:

"Visualize a white beam of light entering the top of your head and running straight through your body and into the earth. Focus on this light, feeling yourself drawn to your center. Feel this core essence of yourself as perfectly balanced, assured, and totally at peace. Give thanks to this light for reminding you that everything is in perfect and divine order right now."

Your relaxation during the healing session is essential because your client's healing is partially contingent upon her faith in your abilities. When a child is afraid of a thunderstorm, she looks to an adult for comfort. If that adult also shows fear, then the child will feel even more afraid. So be aware of your demeanor's impact upon your client's faith in you. Your mode of speaking and acting will convey harmony through your mental preparation before the session.

As you talk with your client, have your vocabulary reflect your knowingness of her perfection. Use the phrase "seeming illness" or "apparent illness" instead of "your illness." If your client uses words that personify or affirm the illness (such as, "I'm fighting an illness," "I am sick," "I have an ache," or "I'm catching something"), gently explain that these words and phrases enlarge the experience of illness. You don't want to sound as if you are discounting your client's fears; however, you also don't want to fuel the illusion's seeming reality. You can ask your angels or spiritual guides for help in choosing words of love and truth.

Compassionately listen to your clients' complaints, but don't encourage them. Try to keep your focus off of pain—not to artificially cheer them, but to make your intentions (health) grow by a steady focus and awareness of health. It's helpful to listen to your clients' complaints as if someone were describing a nightmare. Nightmares aren't real, yet they contain valuable symbols and metaphors.

I purposely limit the time spent talking about symptoms and complaints with my clients, since such discussions aren't ultimately helpful. I never engage in diagnoses, since labeling affirms the reality of a condition. I only ask my clients enough about their symptoms to get an idea of their general outlook. I also pay close attention to their manner of speaking, looking for phrases that signal their beliefs about themselves and the world in general.

As I listen to my clients, I simultaneously listen to my inner guide's voice, and the voice of my clients' angels or spirit guides.

I also watch my mind's eye for psychic movies of my clients' past experiences connected to their present symptoms.

Your clients' physical health reflects their inner health. Fear, anger, and guilt, when repressed, manifest into all sorts of physical ailments. However, as a healer, you'll regard all forms of problems as identical. Your treatment for a seeming terminal illness will not differ much from your treatments of an apparent cut or bruise. Regardless of form, all problems share identical roots. All are products of the belief that the person is apart, unsafe, attacked, or unloved. None of these characteristics are true about your clients, and as soon as they realize it, their bodies will return to normalcy. If your clients have decided on a soul level to either remain ill or even to depart the earth, however, your healing work is still valuable. Anytime you help someone to identify and release fear, you are a blessing to the world.

Silent Healing

Spiritual healing involves shifting from the perspective of the ego to the awareness of the true self. You are reaching across worlds through the bridge of peaceful awareness. The true self has no need for words, as its complete awareness is of love and fulfillment. It is beyond words, since words are primarily the ego's tools for differentiation and judgments.

Your total awareness—without one shred of doubt—of your client's true perfection and your oneness with your client and God, held for just an instant, is all that is needed to evoke a sudden healing. For this reason, your session may involve silence while you meditate.

During your meditation, know that your client is your beloved, because the essence of God, Holy Spirit, and Christ consciousness is the truth of who your client is. Mentally connect to that core person, within your client, who is your beloved. Feel your heart grow with warm love for your beloved. Know that you and the beloved are one with God.

You may also request spiritual assistance in aligning your thoughts about your client. Your prayers for your client's healing aren't so much petitions for God to intervene in that person's material experience. Instead, your prayers are for intervention into you and your client's *thoughts* about her material experience. This is because only the mind needs healing. If an angel were to swoop in and heal your client's illness without a corresponding change in her belief system, the illness would soon return.

I often turn to Holy Spirit or Jesus and mentally say, "Please enter my mind and heart, and help me see this situation in another way. Please heal my thoughts to harmony and truth." In the true-self world, there is only one mind, and if your mind seems distracted by earthly concerns, borrow the mind of a spiritual master who knows only perfect peace. The awareness of oneness is the instrument of healing, no matter from whose mind this knowledge originates.

You may want to end your meditation with this visualization:

Release your knowledge of oneness to your client and the universe by picturing your thoughtforms as encased in a transparent bubble of light. Launch this bubble from your heart or solar plexus (whichever feels right), and feel or see the bubble carried away to a glowing light of God's love. See God's love purifying every thought and idea within the bubble, so they resonate with truth and love. See the bubble burst in joyous celebration as it merges with this light. See the bubble's contents disperse instantly, raining drops of joy and health everywhere. See your client showered in this gift of love.

Healing with Words

Before and after your meditations, you will of course talk with your clients. The prime value of speaking is to help them shift from a fearful ego perspective to a love-centered state. Your words gently help your clients realize that they aren't victims of their body, germs, or other people. As I mentioned earlier, when your clients realize that their thoughts contributed to their present condition, they may at first become angry with themselves and wonder, "Why did I do this to myself?" This is not a helpful viewpoint for your clients, because it is still a standpoint of victimization—except now they believe that they are victims of their own thoughts.

It takes patience and practice before someone can notice the process of how every thought is consciously chosen. Meditation helps us to notice the little gap in time preceding each thought that enters our mind. However, many of your clients probably won't have much experience with meditation, so they won't understand that they actually choose their thoughts. Most people believe that their thoughts choose *them*.

You won't want to engage in debates with your clients on this topic, however. All debates are from the ego and lead to power struggles instead of healing. Your role as a lightworker is to follow your higher self's guidance in helping your clients to willingly release the thoughts, beliefs, and emotions triggering their symptoms. Many of the methods I describe in the following section were given by my spiritual guides and higher self during sessions, and I can attest to their efficacy. If you feel so guided, you may want to use one or more of these methods with your own clients.

The Role of Forgiveness

Unforgiveness toward another person, toward God, or toward one's self is the most common root of physical illness. *A Course in Miracles* says, "There can be no form of suffering that fails to hide an unforgiving thought. Nor can there be a form of pain forgiveness cannot heal."[1]

To live in the true-self state fully, we've got to be free of ego judgments. The true self is our natural state, and we needn't add anything to ourselves to get there. We must, instead, subtract all ego thoughts about being separate from others and from God. If you believe even one person is "bad" or "sinful," you then see yourself as separated from others. That puts you in your ego, and your true self state of joy and health becomes blocked.

The ego rejoices at seeing "badness" in another person. This judgment makes the ego feel superior or special, which instantly affirms a sense of separation between one's self, others, and God. Usually, what irritates us about another person is a characteristic that we don't want to see in our own selves. In these instances, we are healed when we forgive the other person and forgive ourselves.

Complete forgiveness of one's self and the world is the route to releasing any remaining ego blocks that stand between your clients and the life they truly desire. Spiritual intervention helps us to assist our clients in identifying and releasing stubborn unforgiveness. So your first wave of healing treatments are usually focused on helping your clients release judgments and feelings connected to unforgiveness. When you identify and detach an unforgiving thought from a client, you are literally removing a life-draining vampire.

When your clients release unforgiveness, they regain the peace and health of their true self state. Sickness and injury occur when the ego believes it is separated and feels guilty about the attacks it has made. This guilt leads to the fear of retaliation. The ego believes that by hurting itself first, it avoids punishment from outside sources. Sickness and accidents are the ego's favorite ways of punishing itself, in the insane belief, "If I hurt bad enough, I'll escape further pain."

Your healing sessions *could* focus upon releasing fear, guilt, and unforgiveness separately. However, I have found such a broad focus both time-consuming and unnecessary. By concentrating solely on unforgiveness, you release this core block and simultaneously its residues of fear, guilt, shame, and other ego emotions.

Forgiveness and the release from problems depends on willingness, not on time. Yet, it may take your clients a long time to become *willing* to forgive. They may even stubbornly cling to resentment and say, "Why should I be the one to forgive? After all, the situation wasn't my fault!"

Usually, this sort of protest requires the healer explaining the difference between "approval" and "forgiveness." Your clients needn't condone someone's abusive behavior. They simply need to forgive the person, not the behavior, to release themselves from the imprisonment of the ego. Forgiveness also doesn't mean, "I judge your behavior as unsuitable, but because I'm an enlightened person, I will choose to overlook it." Forgiveness heals when all judgments connected to the entire situation are released and replaced with love. At that point, the true-self state is experienced.

"But it can't be as simple as that!" my client Patricia protested when I explained the link between her unforgiveness and her symptoms. She'd spent years at psychiatrist, psychologist, and hypnotherapist sessions before coming to me for spiritual counseling. All that time and money—how dare I say that her emotional pain hinged upon forgiveness?

A Course in Miracles says, "Complexity is of the ego, and is nothing more than the ego's attempt to obscure the obvious." The ego wants us to believe that we and our "problems" are complex and special, to amplify the belief of separation. The ego wants an exotic diagnosis and then a highly complex treatment program. It wants soap opera drama and endless series of problems, not solutions.

Fortunately, all forgiveness needs is a tiny instant of willingness, and that's enough of an opening to invoke healing. Here are some methods to help your clients release unforgiveness:

— *Metaphoric Healings.* Look for the symbolism within your client's illness. The body usually gives obvious clues as to the origin of its aches and pains. For example, if your client complains of a painful neck, ask, "What or whom in your life is a pain in the neck?" For a client with stomach distress, ask, "What is it that you cannot stomach anymore?" Throat pain may warrant the question, "What are you having difficulty swallowing?" For a client with leg pain, ask, "What is it about your life that you can't stand?" Sometimes leg problems indicate a need to slow down from a hurried lifestyle, so allow your intuition to guide you in the proper direction. Once you have identified the symptom's metaphor, look for an unforgiving thought beneath it. Nine times out of ten, this is the culprit emotion that is triggering your client's illness.

My client Barbara complained of intense pain in her ears, and said that medical treatment had offered no relief. I psychically saw that her pain was connected to her marital conflicts. When I asked her about this, Barbara spewed angry insults about her husband. She told me that he was inconsiderate, rude, and verbally abusive.

Within 30 minutes, Barbara realized that her painful ears were her way of blocking out her husband's voice. She also saw that she used her illness as a weapon against her husband, in a covert "see what you've done to me!" way. We worked on releasing unforgiveness toward her husband.

First, I did a psychic reading on her husband and discovered that his angry behavior was actually anger toward himself. The man saw himself as a failure because his wife was perpetually unhappy, depressed, and ill. Barbara admitted the truth of this. We affirmed that both Barbara and her husband were, in truth, perfect drops of God's love, and were wholly incapable of inflicting or experiencing pain. By releasing unforgiveness, Barbara's ears were virtually pain-free at the end of the session.

Louise L. Hay's book *Heal Your Body* is the quintessential guidebook for deciphering the metaphorical meaning of various illnesses. I keep a copy of the book handy during my sessions, and often find that by consulting its chart, my client is able to make instant breakthroughs that lead to healing rapidly.

For example, my client Suzette complained that her gums were sore, swollen, and bleeding. I read the metaphysical meaning of her symptoms in *Heal Your Body*: "Inability to back up decisions. Wishy-washy about life." I asked Suzette, "What part of you feels like it has no foundation, or can't make a decision?" Suzette responded without any hesitation. She told me of her struggles to change her mind about God from her childhood upbringing of a "jealous, wrathful, and vengeful deity" to one that reflected her desire of seeing God as all-loving. Her spiritual transition had created fears about making the "wrong" decision about God. We spent the rest of the session releasing related unforgiveness that she held toward herself, her childhood minister, and her mother. Suzette later told me that this treatment relieved her gum condition almost immediately.

— The Time Collapse. Sometimes, clients are afraid to forgive because they believe that forgiveness is equivalent to saying, "I was wrong, and you were right." If they admit to being wrong, then retaliation and punishment must follow, they worry. You can use a shift in thought which *A Course in Miracles* calls "collapsing time" to help your client escape the fear of retaliation.

You'll want to first remind yourself that linear time doesn't exist in the true-self world. We have it here on earth because the ego wants to measure and compare its material accomplishments. Since the ego created time, it is a product of an unreal source. Therefore, time is an unreal illusion since only God can create the real and eternal.

We may not be able to slow time down or speed it up, but we can change what we and everyone else remembers within time. After all, the main reason we even worry about our past is because of negative thoughts and feelings connected to something bad that happened. So, if we could remove the memory and any negative effects of those bad things in the past, it would be the equivalent of erasing the past. We would, in effect, be undoing past events.

According to *A Course in Miracles*, when we forgive, we do just that. Our forgiveness of ourselves, and all persons connected to the error in the past, undoes and erases the past. The reason is this: the event in the past was a product of the ego. We know this because it was not centered in love. Therefore, the past error was based on errors in thinking, which in turn led to hurt feelings or anger. Thus, error was the cause of emotional pain.

If you remove the cause, the effect also disappears. Forgiveness removes the cause of painful emotions: ego. And without their cause, painful emotions cannot sustain themselves. Hard feelings then soften and rapidly heal until they fade into distant memory.

The time collapse is being studied in laboratories as well. Scientists in medicine, quantum physics, and parapsychology are discovering how our present thoughts can influence or even erase our past behavior. Several studies on this topic by scientist Helmut Schmidt, for example, used a computer that randomly generates numbers. Previous studies by leading university scientists had already shown that people could mentally influence which number the machine generated.

However, Schmidt took this research a step further. He had the computer randomly generate numbers before his experiments began. No one looked at the resulting numbers picked by the computer. Instead, Schmidt asked subjects to mentally influence the computer's selection of a new set of numbers. The subjects were told to choose whatever target numbers they wanted. At the end of his experiments, Schmidt discovered that a significant percentage of the second set of numbers matched the first set of numbers. Schmidt believes that when he looked at the first set of numbers after the experiment, his thoughts traveled back in time and influenced the experiment's second set.[2]

Experiments such as Schmidt's remind us that time isn't the left-to-right linear movement we normally think of. Lightworkers can help their clients to heal their pasts by changing their thoughts in the present. After all, when we apologize to people, they commonly respond, "Forget about it!" That means, "I've forgiven you and have forgotten the incident."

My studies show that when we forgive ourselves or other people, the people involved in the incident often exhibit a form of mass amnesia. They are often unable to recall a single detail about the forgiven event. I believe that if we truly forgive ourselves for our past unhealthful behaviors such as abusing alcohol, drugs, food, or cigarettes, we can undo their bodily effects as if they had never occurred.

Science backs this theory with evidence, such as a study in which scientist William Braud asked a subject to mentally influence the electrical readings that his skin gave during measurements conducted *in the past* (which were unknown until after the experiment and then compared with the subject's goal readings). Although the results were not statistically significant, Braud found that the subject was able to exert some influence and "will" his skin readings in the past with his present thoughts. [3]

The spiritual mind treatment that I use in evoking a time collapse involves me calling upon Holy Spirit (the Voice for God within us that heals our mind to truth). I verbalize this treatment aloud and alternate between using the first-person "I" with the second-person "we" to signify that my mind needs healing to see my clients' true perfection.

> *"Holy Spirit,* (name of client) *is experiencing pain and needs your help in healing the thoughts behind the pain. We know the pain isn't true, since God did not create it, so we must have chosen an untrue thought. We want to feel peace instead of pain. Please enter our minds now, and help us to see this situation another way. Please correct all our thoughts so they are in alignment with God's truth. We ask that all effects of our mistaken thinking be forgotten in time by everyone involved."*

I voice this, and many of my other evocations in the second-person "we" frame of reference because healing occurs in both the client and the healer. This particular treatment always creates dramatic shifts in the client's relationships, as it simultaneously heals all minds connected to the fearful incident. You may want to ask your client to report these relationship healings to you in order to increase your faith in this treatment's efficacy.

— *The Light Bubble.* This treatment method helps your clients feel oneness with the people toward whom they hold a grudge. Have your client close her eyes and take several deep, relaxing breaths. Then guide her through this meditative treatment:

> *"See or feel* (name of person whom your client is trying to forgive). *Can you see or feel this person? Please nod if you see or feel this person."*

(Keep working with your client until an image or feeling becomes clear; resistance to forgiving keeps her from seeing the other person. When your client sees or feels the other person, this indicates a window of willingness to forgive. That little window is all that's needed for a miracle!)

"Now, I'd like to ask you to look or feel inside that person. Notice a little spark of white light jump in their middle, like a pilot light of a furnace. Let me know as soon as you get a glimmer of a sight or a feeling of that white light, okay?

"Okay, now that you've noticed the white light within that person, I'd like to ask you to make it grow mentally. All you need to do is ask the light to grow. Are you noticing it grow? Good. Now, would you please continue expanding the light until it fills the person completely? If you see any darkness in that person, would you please ask the light to cleanse it away? When you have completely filled the person with light, I'd like to ask you to have the light expand out of the person's body and extend like an aura. Do you see or feel this?

"Now, would you please see if you could get a picture or a feeling of yourself standing next to the other person? Do you see or feel yourself next to the other person? Good. Now, would you mind stepping into the white light emanating from the other person? Can you see yourself bathed in white light with the other person? Notice how the light grows so bright that you can no longer see any division between the two of you. Feel and see the boundaries between both of you blur and disappear. See the white light growing larger and larger like a large and loving cloud. You can ask this cloud of healing love to expand even more, seeing it cover the entire city, then the entire country, and the continent, and the entire world. Feel the love encircling the world, knowing that you and the other person are one with everyone, with the world, and with each other. "

This treatment always evokes miraculous coincidences involving the people we forgive. Since we are all joined as one mind in our true selves, other people can feel you release grudges against them. The taut lines of resentment are snapped at the moment of forgiveness. It's palpable! They may not know why, but the thought of you passes through the mind of the person you are forgiving. First it's a neutral thought. Then, it's a thought softened by love. They have simultaneously just forgiven you, although they have no idea why. Other people automatically treat us differently because we simultaneously release them from resentments during this healing. Their true selves communicate with our true selves across all distance and time, and—regardless of their personality, their geographical location, and whether they are alive or dead—their soul responds to our forgiveness.

You are probably aware that you behave differently when you're with certain people. Everyone is this way. You are responding to the way people think about you. If they are judgmental, you act one way. If they are open and kind, you act another way. These people hold certain expectations about how you will act and behave, and to a large extent, that expectation is self-fulfilled. Also, the other people will only notice the parts of your behavior that conform to their expectations.

Other people respond to your judgments in the same way. Your thoughts are the cause, and their behavior is the effect. If you think about other people from your ego, you evoke negative behavior from them. But if, through the miracle of forgiveness, you view those people with eyes of love, their behavior will shine.

Have you ever spent time with a person who admired or loved you? Didn't you feel more comfortable around this person, compared to being with a critical person? When your client forgives her boss, spouse, co-worker, mother, sister, or children, those people will radiate under her new point of view. They will change, because her viewpoint has changed from the ego's videotape to the true self's videotape. Forgiveness saves us so much time!

— *The Corral Visualization.* After helping your client relax with several slow, deep breaths, have her close her eyes and get into a comfortable position. Gently describe this imagery for your client:

> *"Imagine you are standing in a country field. A road is leading to you, a road that brings all your material, emotional, and spiritual supplies. The road passes through a corral to get to you. The corral has two gates: one facing the road and one facing you. If both gates are open, supplies readily flow to you and your gifts to the world flow from you."*

(Have your client breathe in and out very slowly and deeply three times, or use some other method of deep relaxation, before saying the following to her):

> *"Whenever we hold unforgiveness toward someone, we imprison that person in our mind where we mentally flog them with our pronouncements of guilt and blame. The image of the person we resent is "corralled" in our consciousness, and the gates to the corral slam shut like prison doors. You necessarily go into the corral along with the person you've judged, to monitor their imprisonment. So, both gates are shut, and your locked corral blocks your flow and supply.*
>
> *"Look inside your corral right now and see who's there. See the high price you pay for corralling them. If you are ready to forgive, imagine the gates of your corral automatically opening. Visualize whoever is in the corral walking out, free, happy, and forgiven. Wish them well. If this seems difficult, try forgiving the person, instead of her deeds. As you forgive, feel the release, the relief, and the renewed energy as your resentment lifts.*

*Check to make sure you are not in the corral alone out of
an ego judgment you hold against yourself."*

— *Angelic Releasement.* One of the most powerful and effective methods for helping your clients heal from unforgiveness
involves calling for help from the angels. I have found that when
the above methods don't yield peace for my clients, they usually
are unwilling or afraid to forgive. The angels, who are remarkable at helping during healing sessions, will intervene and sweetly release your client's reservations.

After having your client relax, you can gently guide her to
visualize each unforgiving thought as a piece of paper. Explain
that this paper at one time served a useful purpose. But now, like
an old newspaper, it is no longer needed. Ask your client to see
and feel cherubs circling around her, and to picture handing the
papers of unforgiveness to the angels. See and feel the angels carrying away the unforgiveness to the light, where all thoughts are
purified. The angels return to your client carrying gifts of purified
thoughts of love.

Mental Attunement for Healers

You are an instrument of healing, and so you'll want to take
every step to ensure that your mind stays in harmony with truth.
We all get pulled into our egos at time, and it doesn't mean you
are an unqualified healer if you get pulled into yours. The lightworker's way merely asks you to notice the signs of your ego as
quickly as you can, and then take steps to restore your mind to
peace. Those steps may mean taking a deep breath, saying a
prayer, or meditating.

Mental attunement may also require some lifestyle changes,
such as avoiding discussions and media reports about illnesses,
accidents, or disasters. Your inner guide will help you find a way

of balancing your caring nature (which may draw you to watch television coverage of a tragedy) and your knowledge of the Law of Cause and Effect, which takes your focus and increases it. You will know when it is time to turn off the television news and begin healing the situation through your knowledge of its peaceful truth.

HEALING THE WORLD

*"Everything in the universe, we must realize,
proceeds from the ether, or in the ether."*

— Pierre Teilhard de Chardin,
French scientist, seer, and philosopher

A s with healing a client's body or other matter, healing the world can come from the perspective of matter or spirit. Both energy work and spiritual healing can dramatically alter our experience of the world's health.

Mass Fear Is Self-Fulfilling

Prophecies of world doom have seemingly always existed. History tells us that the belief that "the end is near" was prevalent right before the year 1000. Apparently, every generation that is alive when the year hits a new century mark is convinced that the doomsday prophecies apply to them. The trouble is, if enough people share this negative belief, their collective fears really do create earthly problems.

God is awakening lightworkers to heal right now because the millennium fever of 1990 through 2040 could choke the etheric plane with the dense energy of human panic. Through their consciousness of truth and love, lightworkers can undo the prophecies of end times. If the prophecies do come to pass, however, lightworkers will provide needed services such as healing, manifesting, and ministering.

Weather Changes

So many people are anxiously watching the weather because they believe drastic weather changes are indicative of the end of the world. Within the past two decades, our collective focus has so intently looked for abnormal weather that we have actually created erratic conditions. We must always keep in mind that all matter, including rain, rocks, snow, wind, landmass, and lightning, is a product of our thoughts. God's angels will help us when we create ill weather through our collective fear beliefs. However, this doesn't mean that God created the weather or made it bad.

We are not hapless victims isolated on a planet where weather "happens" to us. We are in total control of the dream. This means that we must remember the Law of Cause and Effect: *Whatever we think about enlarges.* We who are lightworkers must daily meditate upon what we want to see, not upon what we fear may happen.

Intense weather such as windstorms, floods, and earthquakes may be earth's way of releasing oversaturated negative energy. However, lightworkers can assist earth's release of this energy in gentler ways. Scientists are currently documenting evidence that our mental powers can influence the weather.[1] These studies amplify what many lightworkers have known all along. We can visualize the energy dispersing and being carried away by angels to the light of purification. We can also hold mental images of a collective release of unforgiveness. In this way, we help to release the grip of earth's ego which, like our ego, is self-destructive.

As with spiritual healing work involving human bodies,

prayer can evoke miraculous healings of the earth body. We already have well-documented scientific evidence that prayer increases the rate of plant and microbe growth[2] and influences properties in air and water.[3] Why wouldn't prayer also benefit the rest of nature? Your prayers, combined with those of other light-workers, could restore the earth to her natural state of perfect, radiant health.

Energy Work on the World

British scientist James Lovelock proposed a theory that saw the earth as a living organism struggling to maintain homeostasis through its shifts in landmass and weather. Lovelock named his theory "Gaia," after the Greek goddess of the earth.[4] Gaia theory explains earthly disasters as natural effects of human cruelty to nature.

Intuitively, Lovelock's Gaia theory makes sense. We also know from studies using Kirlian photography that the light around matter changes as the emotions of the human holding the matter changes. If someone holds an item while angry, for example, the item will photograph with a shorter or darker aura than if that same item is photographed while its holder expresses happiness.

Kirlian photography has lately come under fire as scientists argue over the source of the aura. Many scientists today believe that Kirlian photography auras are actually a picture of the item's humidity or temperature. However, whether the image surrounding items in Kirlian photographs is actually moisture, heat, or light is not the issue. The fact is that these photographic studies show marked changes in response to emotions. They also show that matter absorbs and reflects the emotions of its holder or owner.

This information wouldn't surprise psychics, as we often hold a client's ring, watch, or keys during sessions. These items strengthen and increase the amount of information we can detect about the person's emotions, thoughtforms, and even their lives. Many times, I've simply held a client's ring and instantly been flooded with psychic information about that person.

The energy that is encoded with information has been called "life force," "ki," "chi," and "prana." In the 1940s, scientists referred to life energy as "orgone energy." Researcher Wilhelm Reich found orgone energy in organic matter, including water, wool, wood, and the atmosphere. Reich eventually developed a pistol-like apparatus that could influence orgone energy, and in several monitored studies, Reich effected weather changes with this tool.[5] Reich believed that the blue sky was actually visible orgone energy, since he surmised that the energy was blue-colored. Satellite photos of earth verify that a blue electrical covering does surround the planet.[6]

We can work on healing the earth as if it's a client's body. Our energy and psychic healing work can involve the same steps we would take with a human client. For example, we would first want to relax and allow our mind to become clear. Then, we would tune into the earth and feel for areas of pain.

You can talk directly to this pain and receive a great deal of information. For instance, ask it, "What are you trying to tell me?" Then listen and you'll find that the pain has a voice of its own. This voice will direct you in the way that it most wants your help. It might ask you to direct some angels or white light to certain geographical locations, for example. You'll want to suspend all doubts and judgments while you follow this wise patient's lead.

You can also psychically scan the earth in the same way you scan a client's chakras. I had a client who lived in a remote area of the country who asked me to psychically scan the acreage around his home during a telephone psychic reading session. I mentally walked around his acreage and was drawn to three separate areas. In each area, I saw a dark shape that looked like a giant wine glass buried in the ground. As I scanned these areas, I felt accompanying chills of intense negative energy. I didn't like connecting with these spots, and immediately informed my client of my discomfort. He explained that the areas I had described were fenced off and had government signs warning of radiation. My client believed that my psychic vision of large wine-glass shapes represented toxic waste wells beneath the ground's surface. I worked on psychically cleaning the areas during the remainder of our sessions.

I frequently conduct spirit-releasement work upon cities that seem to contain high levels of social unrest. A favorite visualization involves seeing a giant etheric vacuum tube, which I point down upon the city. I ask the tube to find any darkness resulting from fear and unforgiveness. I then visualize myself switching the vacuum to a "high" setting so it rapidly inhales all the darkness. I picture this darkness going into the light of God, where it is instantly purified and dispersed. After the darkness is gone, I reverse the switch on the vacuum so that white light comes out like toothpaste from a tube. This blankets the city with love, peace, and complete security. I end the visualization with a prayer of gratitude to God and His angels for the perfect health of that city. I also occasionally use this visualization upon centers of political power. You may feel drawn to use it on prisons, the rain forest, or other areas you feel inspired to heal.

Another effective visualization involves seeing a giant cloud of love colored in your favorite hue. Envelop the earth in this cloud, and watch it send beautiful rain drops of joy into the ground. Feel the earth's joy as it eagerly drinks this loving energy. Watch the plants and animals respond with radiant health as the ecological system circulates your gift of love.

Spiritually Healing the World

Spiritual healing and energy-work healing share identical goals. They only differ in the way they approach the end result. Spiritual healing looks past the illusion of problems and affirms only the underlying perfection as truth, while energy work focuses upon the problem and then tries to heal it. Spiritual healing utilizes thoughts, words, mind, and spirit, while energy work uses light and material or etheric instruments. Your inner guide will help you choose the most appropriate means of healing for each situation.

As with spiritual healing on human clients, spiritual healing the earth primarily involves releasing unforgiveness since it is the mass race consciousness fueling social and environmental problems.

Unforgiveness is a thoughtform that divides the world into good guys and bad guys. The ego-self feels comfortable blaming outside forces for its nightmares. In this way, the ego is assured of its own continuing existence. After all, once a person discovers that the ego and its perceptions are nothing but illusions, the ego is essentially removed from its throne. Like the Wizard of Oz, the ego continually tells us to "pay no attention to that man behind the curtain" while diverting our attention to outside displays of thunder and lightning.

We cannot heal the nightmare of global warming, rain forest destruction, and such by holding on to judgments and anger toward "bad guy" perpetrators. This focus creates a huge petri dish that breeds "bad guy" behavior through the infallible Law of Cause and Effect: Whatever we think about grows.

Lightworkers can, however, spiritually heal the *cause* of the irresponsible behavior of those who are hurting the rain forest, and other perpetrators against nature. However, this may require some courage to trust that the solution—forgiveness—will work.

God has been speaking with those who are hurting the earth. These people know, in their hearts, that they are causing pain. This knowledge has crumbled their self-images, and they see themselves as unworthy of leading happier, more productive lives. Most of them fear that financial ruin would accompany their change of heart. The people who perpetuate criminal behavior are on the verge of healing, and lightworkers' collective mindset of love can provide the little push necessary to awaken their minds.

Lightworkers, you can heal thousands of social ills with your collective decision to forgive and to love these criminals. You needn't forgive their actions, just the person who created the action. This may involve you being willing to forgive some "bad guy" from your own life. Many times, we project old unforgiveness onto new situations that remind us of past hurts.

See the criminals for who they truly are: holy and loving children of God. Visualize them "getting" the insight that their pursuit of security and happiness has created pain for themselves and others. Image them having a revelation that brings them to their knees in awe over God's love. See them, in turn, using their knowledge for good by awakening and healing other criminals.

If you find such visualizations unnatural or difficult, then your spiritual healing efforts can involve you deliberately holding neutral thoughts about crime. In this way, you won't add fuel to the fire through harboring angry or fearful thoughts about criminals. These sorts of thoughts are the landscape that created the frightening illusion of crime in the first place.

Ask for the angels to help you to find love in your heart for criminals. This love will help you to truly experience the wonder of *knowing* that we are all one in God. It may be helpful to reread the quote by Ralph Waldo Trine at the beginning of this book that correctly stated that the knowledge of oneness is the key to healing.

Practicing Conscious Consciousness

When I embarked upon the lightworker's way, my intuition urged me to avoid negative conversations, television shows, and reading material. My intuition didn't have to ask me twice! I readily followed this guidance, as I was anxious to preserve the still-fragile joy of rediscovering my spiritual self.

As I talk with other lightworkers, I find that they too have received and are following this same inner guidance. Yet, some lightworkers' healing activities will place them in "front-line" positions where interaction with the media is unavoidable. Other lightworkers, who have positions in the government or in traditional health-care settings, may find their attentions assaulted with graphic scenes and heated discussions.

Certainly, it is easier to keep one's focus on the loving truth of the world by avoiding news accounts and discussions about "problems." However, this may not always be practical or desirable. One lightworker said that she enjoys watching the evening news because then she knows where to direct her prayers. Her outlook is a wonderful model for those of us who wonder how to balance our desires to keep our minds pure while providing healing services to the world.

We can always ask angels to help us release our fears and anger about worldly situations. Angels *want* to help us heal the world. However, except in cases of dire emergency, we must ask for their intervention due to the Law of Free Will. The angels gladly respond to our calls for help, as they know that they are simultaneously healing the world as they heal the hearts and minds of lightworkers.

Lightworkers' time and energy is best used in healing functions. For that reason, arguments and debates about world problems are counterproductive to the lightworker's way. Conflict stems from the ego and is based in seeing others and ourselves as separated beings. The time and energy spent in a debate could be better used in a session of energy work, spiritual healing, or simple human gestures of kindness toward the earth.

In the same vein, our world healing involves guarding the words we use in our speech and thoughts. This includes avoiding discussions about "how awful" this and that part of the world has become. There is always a way to kindly steer such conversations toward an outlook of hope and healing. I often ask Jesus or the Holy Spirit to help me choose my words, and I'm always amazed at how they instantly give me just the right phrase to say.

World Health and Peace

On a spiritual plane, there is not only nothing *wrong* with the world, *there is no world*. The illusion of solid matter stems from the mind of man, not from the Creator. Nonetheless, the compassionate lightworker can help herself, and her brothers and sisters on earth to enjoy their dreams about earth.

You've undoubtedly had the experience of a lucid dream where you had a split consciousness and were simultaneously dreaming while being aware that you were dreaming. Part of you was doing the dreaming, while the other part of you watched you dream. That part of your consciousness that was watching was able to steer the dream's direction. You can direct the mass dream with your awareness in the same way.

Whenever a lightworker experiences the revelation of being one with God's love and with one another, a contribution is made to the mind of every other being. The effect is similar to the way a wrinkle appears in the brain's cortex whenever something new is learned. The one mind receives this lightworker's sane thoughts about true reality, and the new wrinkle nudges the entire "sonship" and "daughtership" of God to awaken.

Spiritual healing of the planet involves the true-self mind, not the body. Therefore, your treatments will be done within the true-self world. You enter this world through pushing the "on" button to the parallel life with a loving thought. This means you'll need to avoid holding fearful or angry thoughts about the world. You may need to remind yourself of the healing benefits of practicing "nonattachment" to matter, as espoused in Eastern philosophies. Although you, of course, love nature and don't want to see it spoiled or destroyed, you show the most love for it by holding thoughts from the high plane of truth. We can't heal from the level of fear and despair, after all.

The world is healed the instant you decide to see a healed world. I have signs posted in my home that read, "The world is loving, happy, and whole." This reminds me to heal the world by seeing it healed—not as a way of denying ugliness or pain, but to peel away those unwanted outer illusions. The core of our world is beautiful, clean, and peaceful, and we can experience this world with a simple decision to see it.

In this respect, the only requirement of a lightworker who desires to help the world is a decision to stay centered in a perspective of love. As we lightworkers heal individually, the world is simultaneously healed. As *A Course in Miracles* says:

> Thus is your healing everything the world requires, that it may be healed. The resurrection of the world awaits your healing and your happiness, that you may demonstrate the healing of the world.

THE LIGHTWORKER'S PRAYER

*"Heaven-born, the soul a heavenward course
must hold; beyond the world she soars; the wise man,
I affirm, can find no rest in that which perishes,
nor will he lend his heart to aught that
doth on time depend."*

— Michelangelo Buonarotti,
Italian Renaissance artist
and philosopher

Sometimes we say to ourselves, "If only the world were a better place, *then* I would be happy." In truth, such thoughts are backwards, since they reverse the order of cause and effect.

Your happiness is not contingent upon world peace. Instead, world peace is contingent upon your happiness. The entire world and its population are perfect reflections of your inner thoughts. If you view yourself and the world through the lens of your ego, you will see and experience horrible fear, guilt, and unhappiness. The ego will send you on various goose chases, searching for the external condition that promises to give happiness. But the ego and its gifts can never give happiness, because happiness is the pink slip that ends the ego's existence.

If you listen to the Voice for God that speaks to you through hunches and gut feelings, however, you will be guided to view the world through your true self's eyes. The world, through such vision, is instantly healed, because all that your true self sees and knows is love.

The lightworker's way is the path to keeping your awareness centered in your true-self state. It is the path of discovering that the true self offers the only gifts you want. It is the decision to release attachments to the material world, and in so doing, receive the only source of joy available while living in the material world. You heal *in* the world by not being *of* the world.

As we walk along the lightworker's way, let us affirm together:

The Lightworker's Prayer

"*I choose to stay centered in the awareness of love, God, and my true self. In this center, like the eye of a hurricane, all is tranquil, safe, and peaceful. My power, wisdom, and peace comes from staying in this center, and I ask for spiritual support from God and His angels to keep my mind aligned with truth.*

"*I willingly detach from the material world, knowing that by so doing, I can effectively help others. I trust God to provide my every need, and I allow His omnipotent wisdom to direct me in all ways.*

"*I accept a steady diet of love and joy, knowing that I deserve happiness and health. I willingly and lovingly release all ego judgments about myself and other people, knowing that everything I want comes from my decision to experience the oneness of all life.*

"*I know I am meant to be a healer and a teacher for God, and I now accept my mission fully without delay or reservation. I surrender all behaviors that would block me from hearing my inner voice, and I happily trust my inner guide to lead me along the lightworker's way, where I joyfully serve as an instrument of love. I release any doubts or fears I may have about fulfilling my Divine mission, and I now commit to staying aware of my inner Voice for God. I know that this is the only tool I will ever need for my own healing and the healing of the world.*

"Amen."

APPENDIX

(*Editorial Note*: In cases where more than one journal study appears underneath a number, they are arranged in chronological order, with the most recent study appearing first, and the oldest study appearing last.)

Chapter 1: Early Miracles

1. MacDonald, William L. (1995). The effects of religiosity and structural strain on reported paranormal experiences. *Journal for the Scientific Study of Religion*, Vol. 34, pp. 366–376.

2. Nelson, Roger D. (1996). Wishing for Good Weather: A Natural Experiment in Group Consciousness. Paper presented to 15th annual meeting of the Society for Scientific Exploration, based on study conducted at Princeton Engineering Anomalies Research, Princeton University, Princeton, NJ.

    Pyatnitsky, L.N. and Fonkin, V.A. (1995). Human consciousness influence on water structure. *The Journal of Scientific Exploration*, Vol. 9, No. 1, p. 10.

    Robinson, Laurie J. (1995). Cloud Busting: An Experiment in Orgone Energy. Franklin Pierce College (unpublished paper on study of 20 subjects instructed to concentrate on dissipating a randomly selected cloud. Results were analyzed by chi-square and found to be significantly greater than chance expectations).

    Schmeidler, Gertrude R. (1984). Further analyses of PK with continuous temperature recordings. *Journal of the American Society for Psychical Research*, Vol 78, No. 4, pp. 355–362

    Schmeidler, Gertrude R. (1973). PK effects upon continuously recorded temperature. *Journal of the American Society for Psychical Research*, Vol. 67, No. 4, pp. 325–340.

    Barth, L. (1961). The Sectarian Attitude in Orgonomy. *Bulletin of the Intersciences Research Institute*, Vol. 3, No. 2, pp. 125–140.

3. Morse, Melvin (1992) *Transformed by the Light: The Powerful Effect of Near-Death Experiences on People's Lives.* New York: Ballantine Books.

Chapter 2: Family Influences

1. Vreeland, Susan (1996). *What Love Sees: A Biographical Novel.* Thorndike, ME: Thorndike Press.

2. Dresser, Annetta G. *The Philosophy of P.P. Quimby, with Selections from his Manuscripts and a Sketch of his Life* (Third Edition). Boston, MA: Geo. H. Ellis.

3. DeWitt, John and Canham, Erwin D. (1962) *The Christian Science Way of Life.* New York: Prentice-Hall, Inc.

4. Eddy, Mary Baker. *Science and Health with Key to the Scripture.* Boston, MA: The First Church of Christ, Scientist.

Chapter 3: Mind and Matter

1. Foundation for Inner Peace. *A Course in Miracles.* Glen Ellen, CA.

2. Watkins, G. K., Watkins, A. M., & Wells, R. A. (1972). Further studies on the resuscitation of anesthetized mice. *Research in Parapsychology,* pp. 157–159.

   Watkins, G. K. & Watkins, A. M. (1971). Possible PK influence on the resuscitation of anesthetized mice. *Journal of Parapsychology*, Vol. 35, No. 4, pp. 257–272.

3. *The Bible,* New King James Version, Luke 8:50.

4. Haraldsson, Erlendur & Houtkooper, Joop M. (1992). Effects of perceptual defensiveness, personality and belief on extrasensory perception tasks. *Personality and Individual Differences,* Vol. 13, No. 10, pp. 1085–1096.

   Irwin, Harvey J. (1986). Personality and psi performance: Directions of current research. *Parapsychology Review*, Vol. 17, No. 5, pp. 1–4.

Debes, Jeffrey & Morris, Robert L.(1982). Comparison of striving and nonstriving instructional sets in a PK study. *Journal of Parapsychology*, Vol. 46, No. 4, pp. 297–312.

Solfvin, G. F. (1982). Psi expectancy effects in psychic healing studies with malarial mice. *European Journal of Parapsychology*, Vol. 4, No. 2, pp. 160–197.

Benassi, Victor A., Sweeney, Paul D. & Drevno, Gregg E. (1979). Mind over matter: Perceived success at psychokinesis. *Journal of Personality and Social Psychology*, Vol. 37, No. 8, pp. 1377–1386.

Schmeidler, Gertrude R.(1975). Personality differences in the effective use of ESP. *Journal of Communication*, Vol. 25, No. 1, pp. 133–141.

5. Radin, Dean & Nelson, Roger D. (1989). Consciousness-related effects in random physical systems. *Foundations of Physics,* Vol. 19, pp. 1499–1514.

Schmidt (1981). PK tests with pre-recorded and pre-inspected seed numbers. *Journal of Parapsychology*, 45, 87–98.

Schmidt, H. (1978). Can an effect precede its cause? A model of a noncausal world. *Foundations of Physics*, 8, 463–480.

Wigner, E.P. (1962). Remarks on the mind-body problem. In I.J. Good (Ed.), *The Scientist Speculates* (pp. 284-302). New York: Basic Books, Inc.

6. Nelson, R. D., Bradish, G. J., Dobyns, Y. D., Dunne, B. J., Jahn, R.G. (1996). Field REG anomalies in group situations. *Journal of Scientific Exploration,* Vol. 10, No. 1, pp. 111.

Dunne, B. J., Jahn, R. G. (1992). Experiments in remote human/machine interaction. *Journal of Scientific Exploration,* Vol. 6, No. 4, pp. 311–332.

Jahn, Robert G. & Dunne, Brenda J. (1987). *Margins of Reality: The Role of Consciousness in the Physical World*. New York: Harcourt Brace Jovanovich.

7. Dossey, Larry (1993). *Healing Words: The Power of Prayer and the Practice of Medicine*. San Francisco, CA: HarperSanFrancisco.

8. Braud, William G. Consciousness interactions with remote biological systems: Anomalous intentionality effects," *Subtle Energies Journal*, Vol. 2, No. 1, pp. 1–46.

Krieger, Dolores (1981). *Foundations of Holistic Health: Nursing Practices*. Philadelphia, PA: J. P. Lippincott.

Pleass, C. M. & Dey, N. Dean (1990). Conditions that appear to favor extrasensory interactions between homo sapiens and microbes. *The Journal of Scientific Exploration*, Vol. 4, No. 2, p. 213.

Nash, C.B. (1984). Test of psychokinetic control of bacterial mutation. *Journal of the American Society for Psychical Research*, Vol. 78, No. 2., pp. 145–152.

Barry, J. (1968). General and comparative study of the psychokinetic effect on a fungus culture. *Journal of Parapsychology*, Vol. 32, pp. 237–243.

Chapter 4: A Visit from the Other Side

1. Huxley, Laura (1963) *You Are Not the Target*. North Hollywood, CA: Wilshire Book Company.

2. Eddy, Mary Baker. Op. cit.

3. Gillian, R., Mondell, B. & Warbasse, J. R. (1977). Quantitative evaluation of Vitamin E in the treatment of angina pectoris. *American Heart Journal*, Vol. 93, pp. 444–449.

Anderson, T. W. (1974). Vitamin E in angina pectoris. *Canadian Medical Association Journal*, Vol. 110, pp. 401–406.

Uhlenhuth, E.H., et al. (1966). Drug, doctor's verbal attitude and clinical setting in the symptomatic response to pharmacotherapy. *Psychopharmacologia*, Vol. 9, pp. 392–418.

Chapter 5: Trusting Spirit

1. Reeves, Frances R. (1993). *Selected Passages from the Teachings of Sri Sathya Sai Baba.* Tustin, CA: Sathya Sai Baba Society.

2. Peale, Norman Vincent (1982). *Positive Imaging.* New York: Ballantine Books.

Chapter 6: The CareUnit

1. Larsen, Michael (1985) *How to Write a Book Proposal.* Cincinnati, OH: Writers Digest Books.

2. *Writer's Market* (an annually published reference book containing submission information and names and addresses of book and magazine publishers, available at all major bookstores for approximately $25). Cincinnati, OH: Writers Digest Books.

3. Moody, Raymond (1975). *Life After Life.* Covington, GA: Mockingbird Books.

Chapter 7: The Divine Plan

1. *Literary Market Place* (also known as *"L.M.P."*): *The Directory of American Book Publishing*, New York: R.R. Bowker Co., updated annually.

2. Frankl, Viktor E. (1984). *Man's Search for Meaning.* New York: Pocket Books.

Chapter 8: "A New Door Will Open"

1. Foundation for Inner Peace. Op. cit.

Chapter 9: The Presence

1. Head, Joseph and Cranston, S.L., Editors (1981) *Reincarnation: An East-West Anthology.* Wheaton, IL: The Theosophical Publishing House.

2. Eadie, Betty (1992) *Embraced by the Light.* Placerville, CA: Gold Leaf Press. (Re-released in 1994) New York: Bantam Books.

3. Radin, D.I., Taylor, R.D. & Braud, W. (1995). Remote mental influence of human electrodermal activity: A pilot replication. *European Journal of Parapsychology,* Vol. 11, No. 19–34.

4. Hirasawam, Yamamoto M., Kawano, K. & Furukawa, A. (1996). An experiment on extrasensory information transfer with electroencephalogram measurement. Journal of *International Society of Life Information Science,* Vol. 14, pp. 43–48.

　　Radin, Dean I. (1996). Silent shockwaves: Evidence for presentiment of emotional futures. *European Journal of Parapsychology*, Vol. 12.

5. Honorton, C., et al. (1990). Psi-communication in the Ganzfeld: Experiments with an automated testing system and a comparison with a meta-analysis of earlier studies. *Journal of Parapsychology,* Vol. 54.

　　Varvoglis, Mario (1986). Goal-directed and observer-dependent PK: An evaluation of the conformance-behavior model and the observation theories. *The Journal of the American Society for Psychical Research*, Vol. 80.

　　Braud, William & Schlitz, M. (1983). Psychokinetic influence on electrodermal activity. *Journal of Parapsychology*, Vol. 47.

Chapter 10: A Reawakening
1. Robertson, Pat (1972). *Shout it From the Housetops.* Bridge Publishers.

Chapter 11: Visions of the Lightworker's Gifts
1. Alvarado, Carlos S. & Zingrone, Nancy L. (1994). Individual differences in aura vision: Relationships to visual

imagery and imaginative-fantasy experiences. *European Journal of Parapsychology*, Vol. 10, pp. 1–30.

Braud, William G. (1990) Meditation and psychokinesis. *Parapsychology Review*, Vol. 21, No. 1, pp. 9–11.

Rao, P. Krishna & Rao, K. Ramakrishna (1982). Two studies of ESP and subliminal perception. *Journal of Parapsychology*, Vol. 46, No. 3, pp.185–207

Rao, K. Ramakrishna & Puri, Irpinder (1978). Subsensory perception (SSP), extrasensory perception (ESP) and transcendental meditation (TM). *Journal of Indian Psychology*, Vol. 1, No. 1, pp. 69–74.

Rao, K. Ramakrishna, Dukhan, Hamlyn & Rao, P. V. Krishna (1978).Yogic meditation and psi scoring in forced-choice and free-response tests. *Journal of Indian Psychology*, Vol. 1, No. 2, pp.160–175.

2.　*The Bible,* New King James Version, 1 Cor. 13:2, 14:1, 14:31, 14:39.

3.　Bem, Daryl J. and Charles Honorton (1994). Does psi exist? Replicable evidence for an anomalous process of information transfer. *Psychological Bulletin,* Vol. 115, pp. 4–18.

Science News, Jan 29 1994, Vol.145, No. 5, p. 68, Scientists Peer into the Mind's Psi.

Chapter 12: Opening the Third Eye

1.　Dyer, Wayne W. (1995) *Meditations for Manifesting* (audio-cassette). Carlsbad, CA: Hay House, Inc.

Chapter 13: Parting the Veil

1.　Altea, Rosemary (1995). *The Eagle and the Rose: A Remarkable True Story*. New York: Warner Books.

2.　Palmer, John (1975) Some recent trends in survival research. *Parapsychology Review,* Vol. 6, No. 3, pp. 15–17.

Haraldsson, Erlendur & Stevenson, Ian (1974). An experiment with the Icelandic medium Hafsteinn Bjornsson. *Journal of the American Society for Psychical Research*, Vol. 68, No. 2, pp. 192–202.

Chapter 14: Making Peace with God
1. Brinkley, Dannion & Perry, Paul (1994). *Saved by the Light.* New York: Villard Books.

Part II—Introduction: The Parallel Worlds of Energy and Spirit
1. Wigner, E.P. (1962). Op. cit.

2. Wapnick, Kenneth (1985). *Time According to A Course in Miracles.* Roscoe, NY: Foundation for A Course in Miracles Academy.

Chapter 17: Preparing for Psychic and Spiritual Healing
1. Haraldsson, Erlendur & Houtkooper, Joop M. (1992). Op. cit.
   Irwin, Harvey J. (1986). Op. cit.
   Debes, Jeffrey & Morris, Robert L.(1982). Op. cit.
   Solfvin, G. F. (1982). Op. cit.
   Benassi, Victor A., Sweeney, Paul D. & Drevno, Gregg E. (1979). Op. cit.
   Schmeidler, Gertrude R. (1975). Op. cit.

2. Alvarado, Carlos S. & Zingrone, Nancy L.(1994). Op. cit.
   Braud, William G. (1990). Op. cit.
   Rao, P. Krishna & Rao, K. Ramakrishna (1982). Op. cit.
   Rao, K. Ramakrishna & Puri, Irpinder (1978). Op. cit.
   Rao, K. Ramakrishna, Dukhan, Hamlyn & Rao, P. V. Krishna (1978). Op. cit.

3. Honorton, C., et al. (1990). Op. cit.
   Varvoglis, Mario (1986). Op. cit.
   Braud, William & Schlitz, M. (1983). Op. cit.

4.   Bem, Daryl J. and Charles Honorton (1994). Op. cit.

Quider, R.F. (1984). The effect of relaxation/suggestion and music on forced-choice ESP scoring. *Journal of the American Society for Psychical Research*, Vol. 78, pp. 241–262.

Chapter 18: Heightening Your Psychic Receptivity

1.   MacDonald, William L. (1995). Op. cit.

Chapter 19: Conducting Psychic Readings and Energy Healings

1.   Bryant, Ina (1978). *Magnetic Electricity: A Life Saver.* Kingsport, TN: Kingsport Press.

Chapter 20: Mediumship and Spirit Releasement

1.   Smith, Susy (1974). *The Book of James.* New York: G.P. Putnam & Sons.

Chapter 22: Spiritual Healing

1.   Foundation for Inner Peace. Op. cit.

2.   Schmidt, Helmut (1984). Comparison of a teleological model with a quantum collapse model of psi. *Journal of Parapsychology,* Vol. 48, No. 4.

Schmidt, H. (1982). Collapse of the state vector and psychokinetic effect. *Foundations of Physics*, Vol. 12, pp. 565–581.

Schmidt (1981). Op. cit.

Schmidt, H. (1978). Op. cit.

Schmidt, H. (1976). PK effects with prerecorded targets. *Journal of the American Society for Psychical Research*, Vol. 70, pp. 267–291.

3.   Braud, William, et al. (1979). Experiments with Matthew Manning. *Journal of the Society for Psychical Research*, Vol. 50, No. 782, pp. 199–223.

Chapter 23: Healing the World

1. Nelson, Roger D. (1996). Op. cit.
    Robinson, Laurie J. (1995). Op. cit.
    Barth, L. (1961). Op. cit.

2. Braud, William G., Op. cit.
    Krieger, Dolores (1981). Op. cit.
    Pleass, C. M. & Dey, N. Dean (1990). Op. cit.
    Nash, C.B. (1984). Op. cit.
    Barry, J. (1968). Op. cit.

3. Pyatnitsky, L.N. and Fonkin, V.A. (1995). Op. cit.
    Schmeidler, Gertrude R. (1984). Op. cit.
    Schmeidler, Gertrude R. (1973). Op. cit.

4. Lovelock, J.E. (1979). *Gaia: a new look at life on earth.*
    Oxford University Press, Oxford.

5. Starz, K. (1978). The effects of the orgone energy accumulator on air: The creative process. *Bulletin of Interscience Research Institute,* Vol. 2, No. 4, pp. 125–137.

6. Reich, W. (1945). A case history. *International Journal of Sex, Economy, and Orgone Research,* Vol. 4, pp. 59–64.

    Reich, W. (1944). Thermical and electroscopical orgonometry. *International Journal of Sex, Economy, and Orgone Research*, Vol. 3, No. 1.

SELF-HELP RESOURCES

The following list of resources can be used for more information about recovery options for addictions, health problems, or problems related to dysfunctional families. The addresses, telephone numbers and websites listed below are usually for the national headquarters; look in your local Yellow Pages under "Community Services" for resources closer to your area. In addition to the following groups, other self-help organizations may be available in your area to assist your healing and recovery for a particular life crisis not listed here. Consult your telephone directory, call a counseling centre or helpline near you, or contact:

Legal Aid
www.legalservices.gov.uk

Legal Services Online
www.freelawyer.co.uk
www.legal-advice.co.uk

❧ ❧ ❧

AIDS

National AIDS Helpline
Tel: 0845 1221 200

Sexual Health Helpline
Tel: 0800 567 123

Terrence Higgins Trust
Tel: 020 7242 1010
Tel: 0845 1221 200
www.info@tht.org.uk

Positively Women
347-349 City Road
London EC1V 1LR
Tel: 020 7713 0222/0444

Caring for Babies with AIDS
AVERT 4 Brighton Road
Horsham RH13 5BA
www.avert.org.uk

**Children with AIDS Charity
(CWAC)**
Lion House, 3 Plough Yard
London EC2A 3LP
Tel: 020 7247 9115
www.cwac.org

**Holistic Care Programmes for
Men, Women and Children
Living with HIV/AIDS**
Mildmay Mission Hospital
Hackney Road, London E2 7NA
Tel: 020 7613 6300

❧ ❧ ❧

ALCOHOL ABUSE

Alcoholics Anonymous
PO Box 1, Stonebow House
Stonebow, York YO1 7NJ
Tel: 01904 644026
www.alcoholics-
anonymous.org.uk

Al-Anon Family Groups
61 Great Dover Street
London SE1 4YF
Tel: 020 7403 0888
www.al-anonuk.org.uk

Drinkline
Tel: 0800 917 8282

www.dryoutnow.com
Tel: 0845 230 8060

www.addictionnetwork.co.uk

**National Association for
Children of Alcoholics**
PO Box 64, Fishponds
Bristol BS16 2UH
Tel: 0800 358 3456
www.nacoa.org.uk

Alcohol Concern
Waterbridge House
32-36 Loman Street
London SE1 0EE
Tel: 020 7928 7377

**Advice for Alcohol and
Drug Problems**
36 Park Row
Nottingham NG1 6GR
Tel: 0115 948 5570
www.apas.org.uk

**Children and Family
Alcohol and Drugs Service**
CAFADS
Unit 202
Bow House
153-159 Bow Road
London E3 2SE
Tel: 020 8983 4861
www.cafads.org.uk

❧ ❧ ❧

ANOREXIA/BULIMIA

Eating Disorders Association
103 Prince of Wales Road
Norwich NR1 1DW
Tel: 0845 634 1414; Aged 18 and
under: 0845 347 650 or
text: 0797 749 3345
www.edauk.com

NHS Direct
Tel: 0845 4647
www.nhsdirect.nhs.uk

❧ ❧ ❧

CANCER

Cancer BACUP Helpline
Tel: 0808 800 1234
www.cancerbacup.org.uk

**National Cancer
Research Institute**
PO Box 123
61 Lincoln's Inn Fields
London WC2A 3PX
Tel: 020 7061 8460
www.ncri.org.uk

❧ ❧ ❧

CHILDREN'S ISSUES

Child Molestation

www.childline.org.uk
Tel: 0800 1111

**National Association for People
Abused in Childhood (NAPAC)**
42 Curtain Road
London EC2A 3NH
www.napac.org.uk

**National Society for the
Prevention of Cruelty to
Children (NSPCC)**
Weston House
42 Curtain Road
London EC2A 3NH
Tel: 020 7825 2500
www.nspcc.org.uk

**Kidscape (Helping to Prevent
Bullying and Child Abuse)**
2 Grosvenor Gardens
London SW1W 0DH
Tel: 08451 205 204
www.kidscape.org.uk

*Children and Teens' Crisis
Intervention*

**CRISIS (Helping Young People
Overcome Addictions and
Mental Health Problems)**
666 Commercial Street
London E1 6LT
Tel: 0870 011 3335
www.crisis.org

**Centrepoint (Supporting
Homeless Young People)**
Neil House
7 Whitechapel Road
London E1 1DU
Tel: 020 7426 5300

Runaway Helpline
Tel: 0808 800 7070

Message Home Helpline
(for People Who Want to Send
a Message Home without
being Contacted)
Tel: 0800 700 740

Missing Children

**National Missing Persons
Helpline**
0500 700 700
www.missingpersons.com

*Children with Serious Illnesses
(fulfilling wishes)*

Children's Wish
24 Welbeck Way
London W1G 9YR
Tel: 020 7034 1910
www.childrenswish.co.uk

**Starlight Children's
Foundation**
Room PRW1
Macmillan House
Paddington Station
London W2 1HD
Tel: 020 7262 2881
www.starlight.org.uk

CO-DEPENDENCY

Co-dependents Anonymous
Ashburnam Community Centre
Tetcott Road
London SW10 0SH
www.coda-uk.org

❧ ❧ ❧

**DEATH/GRIEVING/
SUICIDE**

CRUSE (Bereavement Care)
Cruse House
126 Sheen Road
Richmond
Surrey TW9 1UR
Tel: 0870 167 1677
www.crusebereavementcare.
org.uk

**National Council for
Palliative Care**
Tel: 020 7520 8299
www.ncpc.org.uk

**Compassionate Friends
(Support for Bereaved
Parents and their Families)**
53 North Street
Bristol BS3 1EN
Tel: 0845 123 2304
www.tcf.org.uk

Help the Hospices
Hospice House
34–44 Britannia Street
London WC1X 9JG
www.helpthehospices.org.uk

**Families of Murdered Children
(FoMC)**
Tel: 01698 336646
Tel: 0777 5626779
www.fomc.org.uk

Child Death Helpline
Great Ormond St Hospital
for Children
London WC1N 2AP
Tel: 0800 282 986
www.childdeathhelpline.org.uk

**Foundation for the
Study of Infant Deaths**
Artillery House
11–19 Artillery Row
London SW1P 1RT
Tel: 0870 787 0885
www.sids.org.uk

**Samaritans
(Suicide Helpline)**
Tel: 0845 790 9090
www.samaritans.org.uk
jo@samaritans.org

❧ ❧ ❧

DEBTS

**Consumer Credit
Counselling Service**
Wode House
Merrion Centre
Leeds LS2 8NG
Tel: 0800 138 1111
www.cccs.co.uk

Debtors Anonymous
Tel: 020 7644 5070
www.debtorsanonymous.info

❧ ❧ ❧

DIABETES

Diabetes UK
10 Parkway
London NW1 7AA
Tel: 020 7424 1000
www.diabetes.org.uk

❧ ❧ ❧

DRUG ABUSE

Cocaine Anonymous
www.ca.org.uk

Narcotics Anonymous
202 City Road
London EC1V 2PH
Tel: 020 7730 0009
www.ukna.org

National Drugs Helpline
Tel: 0800 587 5879
www.knowthescore.info
www.addaction.org.uk

Release
388 Old Street
London EC1V 9LT
www.release.org.uk
Turning Point
New Loom House
101 Blackchurch Lane
London E1 1LU
Tel: 020 7702 2300
www.turning-point.co.uk

≈ ≈ ≈

EATING DISORDERS

Overeaters Anonymous
PO Box 19
Stretford
Manchester M32 9EB
Tel: 0700 078 4985
www.oagb.org.uk

≈ ≈ ≈

GAMBLING

Gamblers Anonymous
PO Box 88
London SW10 0EU
Tel: 0870 050 8880
www.gamblersanonymous.
org.uk

≈ ≈ ≈

HEALTH

Alzheimer's Society
Gordon House
10 Greencoat Place
London SW1P 1PH
Tel: 020 7306 0606
www.alz.co.uk

Pain Relief Foundation
Clinical Sciences Centre
University Hospital Aintree
Lower Lane
Liverpool L9 7AL
Tel: 0151 529 5820
www.painrelieffoundation.
org.uk

British Pain Society
21 Portland Place
London W1B 1PY
www.britishpainsociety.org

**Institute for
Complementary Medicine**
PO Box 194
London SE16 1QZ
Tel: 020 7237 5165
www.i-c-m.org.uk

**Federation of
Holistic Therapists**
3rd Floor, Eastleigh House
Upper Market Street
Eastleigh S050 9FD
Tel: 0870 420 2022
www.fht.org.uk

Help The Hospices
Hospice House
34-44 Britannia Street
London WC1X 9JG
0870 903 3903

Society for Psychical Research
49 Marloes Road
London W8 6LA
Tel: 020 7937 9984
www.spr.ac.uk

Koestler Parapsychology Unit
PPLS
University of Edinburgh
7 George Square
Edinburgh EH8 9LZ
Tel: 0131 650 3348

**National Institute of
Medical Herbalists**
Elm House
54 Mary Arches Street
Exeter EX4 3BA
Tel: 01392 426 022

**Institute for
Optimum Nutrition**
13 Blades Court
Deodar Road
London SW15 2NU
www.ion.ac.uk

**Natural Health
Advisory Service**
PO Box 268
Lewes BN7 1QN
Tel: 09062 556615
www.naturalhealthas.com

**National Council for
Hypnotherapy**
www.hypnotherapists.org.uk

Mind Body Spirit Directory
www.BodyMindSpirit
DIRECTORY.org

❧ ❧ ❧

HOUSING RESOURCES

Shelter
88 Old Street
London EC1V 9HU
Tel: 0845 458 4590
www.england.shelter.org.uk

Housing Associations
www.direct.gov.uk

❧ ❧ ❧

IMPOTENCE

**The Sexual Dysfunction
Association**
Tel: 0870 7743 571

**British Association for Sexual
and Relationship Therapy**
www.basrt.org.uk

❧ ❧ ❧

PET BEREAVEMENT

**Pet Bereavement
Support Service**
Tel: 0800 096 6606
www.bluecross.org.uk

❧ ❧ ❧

STRESS REDUCTION

**Association for Applied
Psychophysiology and
Biofeedback**
www.aapb.org

**Resurgence (Magazine of the
Omega Institute)**
Ford House
Hartland
Bideford EX39 6EE
Tel: 01237 441293
www.resurgence.org

**International Stress
Management Association UK**
www.isma.org.uk
Tel: 0700 078 0430

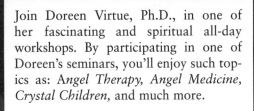

ABOUT THE AUTHOR

Doreen Virtue, Ph.D., holds three university degrees in counseling psychology. She works with the angelic and elemental realms in her writing, healing work, and workshops. Doreen teaches audience members worldwide how to hear, see, feel, and know the messages of the spirit world. She also offers a Hawaiian seminar, in which audience members get to swim with the dolphins.

Doreen has been featured on CNN, *The View, Oprah,* and other radio andtelevision shows where she is frequently referred to as "The Angel Lady." In addition, her work has appeared in *Redbook, Glamour, McCalls, Mademoiselle*, and other publications.

If you have stories of meeting an angel or fairy, Doreen welcomes your submissions by sending them to her in care of Hay House, or to AngelStories@AngelTherapy.com. If you would like information about Doreen's Hawaiian Healing Retreats or her other workshops, please or visit **www.AngelTherapy.com.**